Introduction

What is Europe?

Geographically, 'Europe' is usually regarded as a fairly small peninsula of Asia which extends west of the Ural Mountains, the Caspian and the Bosphorus. If 'Europe' is simply a geographical expression, Siberia and almost all of modern Turkey are not in it. Yet Siberia is the backyard of European Russia, and Turkey has felt itself so European since 1945 that it has enthusiastically joined all the 'European' organizations (see chapters 3 and 9) including one which is essentially concerned with the North Atlantic powers. On the other hand, Britain, although geographically indisputably part of Europe, was for over a hundred years mainly concerned with its non-European empire. Geographical Europe and political Europe are not the same thing.

What, then, of Europe as a cultural entity? The Preamble to the Statute of the Council of Europe, the most 'European' of all the post-war European organizations, affirms the devotion of its member states to: 'the spiritual and moral values which are the common heritage of their peoples and the true source of individual freedom, political liberty and the rule of law, principles which form the basis of all genuine democracy.' And one of the Council's documents speaks of: 'the fundamental cultural unity which exists, in Europe, beneath the diversity of its national traditions'. But the Council of Europe, which up to 1970 was composed only of non-Communist states, was speaking for

3

Western Europe only; was speaking of that great cultural tradition, compounded of the philosophy of the Greeks, the legal ideas of the Romans, and the religious insights of the Jews, which moulded Western Europe for two thousand years, using as its medium the Latin alphabet and language. The cultural tradition of Eastern Europe was very different. It had nothing to do with Greek philosophy, Roman law, or the Latin language. Orthodox Christianity, although derived from Greek-speaking Byzantium, assumed a peculiarly Slavonic, mystical quality, and was expressed in the Kyrilic alphabet, which in 1970 was still the alphabet of the Russian, Bulgarian and Serbian languages. Eastern European culture also absorbed certain Asiatic influences from the Muslim Tartars and Turks.

Anyone writing about 'Europe' is therefore obliged to make some arbitrary choices. For the practical purposes of this book we shall regard Russia, Turkey and Britain as 'European'. The internal affairs of Britain and Eire have, however, been omitted, except in the context of the general discussion of economic and social developements.

The Seminal Ideas of the Twentieth Century

In the four centuries after the Renaissance Western Europe produced the seminal ideas of the global civilization of the modern world: the ideas of science and of humanism. These ideas stemmed from a new attitude: that man should find the truth for himself through his own inductive and deductive reasoning (science), and through his own imagination or vision (enlightenment). He must be 'self-determining', no longer dominated by the external authority of autocratic Church and State, of imposed dogmas and decrees. 'Man is born free, but everywhere he is in chains', was the opening sentence of Rousseau's famous book, *The Social Contract*. This attitude stemmed, in its turn, from a philosophic idea about the nature of man. The Christian Churches had hitherto asserted that he was born in 'original sin', which could be expiated only by serving God in his pre-ordained station in life, however subservient and miserable. Rousseau and his contemporaries affirmed that man

4

is 'naturally good'; that he – and she – has inherent creative capacities *as a person*, and that the purpose of life is to express these capacities. If man therefore were given his freedom, he would spontaneously develop a good society. 'Religion is politics and politics is brotherhood', cried the poet Blake. And Tom Paine, the Englishman who helped the American and French revolutionaries, wrote that, 'Government, like dress, is the badge of lost innocence. The palaces of kings are built on the ruins of the bowers of Paradise.' This fundamental optimism about the nature of man means that the modern world is grounded on the idea of progress, of dynamic change and evolution towards a better society of free, creative persons, united in their freedom by love – fraternity. Marx affirmed, for instance, that the inevitable goal of the dynamic historical process was the classless, communist society, in which the state as an institution which coerces and punishes would 'wither away', and all men would spontaneously live together in freedom and brotherhood.

Humanism in its turn produced liberalism, the philosophy of the 'Rights of Man'. The idea that all men and women, as human beings, possess certain 'natural' and 'inalienable' rights was already embedded in Greek philosophy, in Christian theology and in Roman law. The French revolutionaries proclaimed these rights in their 'Declaration of the Rights of Man'; the Americans wrote them into their Constitution, and since then they have been incorporated into most modern constitutions, including those of Communist countries, and proclaimed as a moral code for all mankind in the United Nations' Universal Declaration of Human Rights of 1948.

These rights – the civil rights to freedom of speech, assembly, writing, worship and travel, to have a fair trial and to own property; the political right to 'self-government' and the social rights to education, food, housing, work, and care in sickness and old age – may be regarded as the practical expression of the ideals of liberty, equality and fraternity. Although these ideals have been proclaimed for at least two thousand years, the determination to put them into practice in all human institutions, and on a global basis, is new in history.

5

It can be no coincidence that humanism developed in partnership with applied science. Scientific ideas had also been discussed in ancient days, notably by the Greeks and the Chinese, but experimental science, leading to the transformation by technology of man's material environment, is also new in history. And since the 'facts' 'discovered' by the scientists are, by their very nature, of universal application, science has joined hands with humanism to create a global culture, a global society. This, again, is new in history.

In two short centuries these seminal ideas, launched in Europe, brought about changes in the whole world of a kind which a European living in 1770, or in 1870, could hardly have conceived. The greatest change of all is perhaps the fact that change itself, change at an ever increasing rate of acceleration, is the basis of modern life.

These changes have been achieved by man's use of his own reason. The establishment of secular societies has seemed to be a necessary pre-requisite, and belief in a spiritual universe has appeared to be irrelevant to the results. Scientific laws, and the technology based on them, work, whether one believes in God or not. The achievements of the scientists thus reinforced the optimism and self-confidence of the humanists.

Nevertheless, the naïve faith in man's natural goodness which ushered in the Age of Reason and of Enlightenment in the eighteenth century, had waned by the second half of the nineteenth century. Darwin's theory of biological evolution through 'natural selection', and the survival of the fittest in the conflict of 'nature red in tooth and claw', profoundly influenced the whole climate of thought. Marx asserted that the exploitation of man by man could only be brought to an end by a bloody revolution in which the exploited toilers and workers would destroy their exploiters, the capitalists.

The crumbling of the old order, in which public religion had assigned to each person his or her secure 'station', left an emotional vacuum. The Rights of Man constitute a secular ethic – for the first time in history a public ethic has been proclaimed which does not stem from a public religion (we shall discuss the implications of this fact in chapter 15). They challenge man to become adult. It is difficult to shoulder the responsibilities of liberty, and harder still to practise fraternity. While the liberals were attempting the rational reconstruction of society, others began to look for a secular religion to fill the emotional vacuum. 'Liberalism' was, therefore, complemented in the nineteenth and twentieth centuries by 'nationalism' – the desire of a group of people to constitute a 'nation', a vague entity whose ingredients may include a common culture, language and religion. Nationalism is not an intellectual theory but an emotional force, which provides the atomized individuals of modern society with a sense of togetherness. Often this force demands uniformity rather than unity; it suppresses rather than stimulates the free expression of individuality. And as liberalism and science dawned first in Western Europe, so did nationalism, producing the bloody conflict of the First World War. As a result of the 'war to end wars', power in most European countries shifted decisively from the traditional upper classes to the semi-literate masses, returning in their millions from the battle fields to find that the homes and jobs 'fit for heroes' to which they felt entitled were not provided. The emotional vacuum yawned wider than ever, and into it rushed something even more sinister than the crude nationalism of the pre-1914 decades – the fanatical ideologies of Marxism and Fascism. Since these ideologies have had a profound effect on post-war Europe, Marxism becoming the public creed of half the continent, we must briefly discuss their basic features.

Marxism is essentially a philosophy of history, formulated by Karl Marx in the nineteenth century, which has been turned by his followers into an ideology. This philosophy is often called 'Dialectic Materialism'. By materialism Marx meant that the cause of all phenomena must be sought in physical matter, for he was an atheist and rejected the idea of a spiritual universe. By dialectic, a concept which he borrowed from the philosopher Hegel, he meant that historical progress takes place through a series of automatic and inevitable conflicts rather than through gradual evolution; and that these conflicts would be finally

resolved in a great consummation, a final synthesis, the establishment of a perfect society (this might be regarded as a secular
version of the Jewish idea of the Apocalypse, the coming of the
Messiah). The materialistic interpretation of history produced
the idea that economic conditions and the social classes which
arise from these conditions determine all other historical
phenomena – political systems, religion, and art – which are
called the 'superstructure'. These economic conditions develop
from feudalism, based on manual labour, via capitalism, based
on industrialization, to communism. In each case the economic
system *inevitably* gives rise to a class conflict. The feudalists are
overthrown by the capitalists – the *bourgeoisie* – as in the French
Revolution; the capitalists will inevitably be overthrown by the
working class – the proletariat – whom they have been impelled
by the profit motive to exploit. The proletariat will then create
the perfect, classless society, the climax and completion of the
dialectic process, because it is based on *Communism*, the only
economic system which does not impel men to exploit their
fellow men.

Marxism is thus based on a variation of the eighteenth century
idea of man's natural goodness. The workers are naturally good,
the capitalists are naturally bad, since they are the products of a
system which forces them to be exploiters. Eliminate the capitalists in a bloody revolution, and *all will be well*. Marxism also
claims to be 'scientific', to offer a hypothesis which fits the facts of
history and of modern events; this means that in principle, if the
facts do not fit, the hypothesis must be discarded. But most
Marxists have turned Marxism into a prophetic revelation, a
dogma which is 'right' and 'true' whatever the facts. Marx
denounced religion as 'the opiate of the masses', a drug invented
by the wicked upper classes to keep the workers quiet. The French
writer Raymond Aron has called Marxism the 'opiate of the intellectuals'. Despite its contradictions, however, it possesses, as a
system of thought, a certain intellectual majesty. Its peculiar
combination of prophetic idealism with 'scientific' materialism
has made it attractive to many fine European minds who could
not accept traditional religion. This was particularly the case in

the inter-war years, when the real facts about the Marxist Utopia in Russia were little known.

Fascism, the name given by the Italian dictator Mussolini to his ideology, came to be applied generally to similar ideologies, and in particular to that of the National Socialists (Nazis) in Germany. The Fascists, like the Marxists, asserted that they were bringing a new and higher kind of man and of society into existence – through violence. Like the Marxists, they provided an enemy to serve as a whipping boy for frustrated emotions; instead of the capitalists, the Jews and the Western democracies. But Fascism was blatantly anti-intellectual. It offered no coherent system of thought. It denied the ultimate goal of freedom and brotherhood. It called on its adherents to surrender their judgment and conscience to a god-like leader – a form of idolatry which, although encouraged by many Marxist leaders, is not an inherent feature of Marxism. It glorified war as a moral good in itself, and asserted the 'right' of the fittest people, in the Darwinian biological sense, to conquer and rule inferior peoples – of the Italians to conquer the Ethiopians, of the Germans to conquer the Slav nations. It exploited the nationalist emotions already endemic in Europe. The Second World War was its logical outcome.

If we accept the simple principles of the Rights of Man as modern man's 'true' creed, we must regard Marxism as an aberration, and Fascism as a complete failure of nerve.

The hideous record of conflict, crime and suffering in Europe in the first half of the twentieth century, much of it perpetrated in the cause of nationalism, Marxism and Fascism, was perhaps inevitable. The idea that man is 'naturally good' is only a half-truth. Freud's work was of crucial importance because he confronted modern man with his irrational nature, not as a religious dogma – 'original sin' – but as a scientific fact. Freud said that man was inspired by two basic urges, the life urge – to be creative – and the death urge – to be destructive. In the first half of the century the irrational forces in the European psyche irrupted like a vast volcano, and the death urge was let loose. The victory of 1945 seemed to be a victory for rationality and creativity. If the optimism of the eighteenth-century thinkers about the nature of man was discredited, so was Darwinian pessimism and its monstrous progeny, Fascism.

Between 1914 and 1945 the old order in Europe was shattered. Between 1945 and 1970 the foundations of a new order were laid – in Eastern Europe on the philosophic basis of Marxism, in Western Europe on a sober revival of the ideals of humanistic liberalism.

1. The Second World War: 1939 to 1945

The Course of the War

The First World War was in a sense the last major traditional war. It was fundamentally fought by foot soldiers as all wars had been fought, and with guns, highly developed versions of the weapons introduced in the Renaissance. Tanks and aircraft, the new kind of weapons spawned by the industrial revolution, were ancillary to the fighting, which was essentially static. After weeks of battle the front would have advanced or receded only a few kilometres. The great majority of civilians were still outside the battle area.

The Second World War was an utterly new kind of war: a mobile war, fought by men enclosed in armoured cars, tanks and aircraft, in which the battle line might move fifty or a hundred kilometres a day. Millions of civilians were involved willy-nilly, as tanks crashed through their towns and screeching dive-bombers dropped bombs containing from half to ten tonnes of TNT equivalent on them.

Only six European countries remained neutral: Ireland, Portugal, Spain, Sweden, Switzerland and Turkey. Britain escaped invasion in 1940 by a hair's breadth. Every other European country, with the partial exception of Russia, was either occupied or controlled by the Germans, and most experienced bitter fighting on their soil.

In Western Europe the Germans invaded Norway, Denmark, Belgium, the Netherlands, Luxembourg and France in 1940, and their ally Italy in 1943. In Central and Eastern Europe, having swallowed up Austria and Czechoslovakia before the War, they conquered Poland in 1939, and Yugoslavia and Greece in the spring of 1941. Hungary, Bulgaria and Rumania allied with them. Their ally the Soviet Union had meanwhile occupied the eastern half of Poland and the small Baltic states of Lithuania, Latvia and Estonia, and had attacked and defeated, but not occupied, Finland. In North Africa the Germans and Italians had the French colonies of Morocco, Algeria and Tunisia in their grip and controlled the shores of the Mediterranean as far as Egypt.

On 22 June 1941 the Germans suddenly turned with immense ferocity on the Soviet Union. For two years a life and death struggle was waged on Russian soil. The German armies penetrated to the Volga and the foothills of the Caucasus, but they never succeeded in taking Moscow or Leningrad, although they besieged the latter city for two and a half years. In 1943, after the epic battle of Stalingrad, they were finally forced to retreat.

The Japanese bombing of the American fleet in Pearl Harbour, Hawaii, on 7 December 1941, brought the United States to the side of the British and Russians in their hard-pressed struggle against the European Fascists, as well as to the aid of China, invaded by Japan in 1937. President Roosevelt's Lease-lend Act of 1941 had already opened the mighty arsenals of American industrial power to the Allies; now the full force of American arms, supplies and men was to be decisive. Even so, it was another three years before the Germans and Japanese were defeated. The military brilliance, technical efficiency and fanatical determination with which they waged war cannot but command a horrified admiration.

The United States' entry into the war led to the development of unprecedented inter-allied co-operation. The British Dominions joined in at Britain's side; and the exiled leaders of the German-occupied countries, established in London, rallied the forces of their escaped countrymen. All the forces of the Western Allies were brought together under an integrated command headed by the American General Eisenhower. The Soviet Red Army fought on its own, but grand strategy was discussed at periodic conferences between the three great leaders, Churchill, Roosevelt and Stalin. They decided that Germany and Italy should be forced to surrender unconditionally, and that Germany, Austria, Berlin and Vienna should then be divided into four zones of military occupation by American, Russian, British and French forces.

In the summer of 1943, after driving the Germans and Italians out of North Africa, the Western Allies moved on to the offensive in Europe. They invaded Italy; the Germans moved in from the north, and for a year the Allies fought them kilometre by kilometre up the peninsula. The Allies invaded Normandy in June 1944, and for nine months fought the Germans back through France, Belgium and the Netherlands. By the summer of 1944 the Red Army had pushed the Germans out of Russia. Hungary, Bulgaria, Rumania and Finland (which had allied with Germany when it invaded Russia) changed sides and allied with the Soviet Union. The Red Army 'liberated' Poland and Czechoslovakia, and, on entering Yugoslavia, linked up with the Communist Marshal Tito's victorious Partisans in a triumphant entry into Belgrade. The Germans withdrew of their own accord from Greece, but British troops had to be called in to suppress a Communist uprising.

The stage was now set for the final scene in this great European drama. In January 1945 the mighty Red Army began to enter eastern Germany; and in March the spearheads of General Eisenhower's four million troops crossed the Rhine. British and American bombers were flattening German cities and communications in round-the-clock raids. In April the Russians fought their way into Berlin, while the Americans raced towards the Nazi redoubts in Bavaria. Hitler and two of his chief henchmen, Goebbels and Himmler, committed suicide. Their successors surrendered unconditionally to the Allies on 7 May 1945.

On 6 and 9 August the Americans, with full British support, dropped their new weapon, the atom bomb, containing 20,000 tonnes of TNT equivalent, on the Japanese cities of Hiroshima and Nagasaki. Stalin, who had been casually informed by President Truman at Potsdam of the existence of the bomb, declared war on Japan on 8 August. On 14 August Japan surrendered unconditionally.

The Second World War was over. It had brought about the death of over 50,000,000 people, including 15,000,000 Russians, 6,000,000 Jews, 3,700,000 Germans, 2,000,000 non-Jewish Poles, 1,600,000 Yugoslavs, 1,200,000 Japanese, nearly 1,000,000 Italians, 600,000 British, 500,000 Rumanians, 300,000 Frenchmen, 292,000 Americans and 22,000,000 Chinese.[1]

Europe under Nazi Rule

The states of German-occupied Europe fell into four categories. First, there were those territories which Germany annexed outright: Austria, the Sudetenland (the former German-speaking province of Czechoslovakia), north-west Poland, Alsace-Lorraine, Luxembourg and north-west Yugoslavia. Second, there were the 'Eastern Lands', which were intended to be a permanent German colonial realm: the Czech part of Czechoslovakia (Bohemia and Moravia), the rest of Poland, the Baltic States and the conquered area of Russia. The inhabitants of these lands were regarded as *Untermenschen* – subhumans – and were to be either enslaved by the *Herrenvolk* – the master race – or exterminated to make *Lebensraum* – living space – for them. Third, there were the 'Occupied Territories', which were allowed a measure of self-government under German control: Norway, Denmark, the Netherlands, Belgium, France, Serbia, Greece, and, after September 1943, Northern Italy. Some of these territories – Denmark after August 1943, the Netherlands, Belgium, and 'Occupied France' (the north and west parts of the country) – were ruled directly by the Germans through local civil servants. Others – 'Vichy France' (the south-east part of the country), Norway, Serbia and Greece, were ruled by local leaders prepared to serve as German puppets. Most of these puppets were loathed by their fellow countrymen, but Marshal Pétain, the aged ruler of Vichy France, enjoyed wide popular support. Germany's satellite allies, Bulgaria, Hungary, Rumania, Croatia, Slovakia and Finland, constituted the fourth group. They retained their internal independence, but were forced to do Germany's bidding on such matters as the rendering up of their Jews.

The whole of occupied Europe was put to work for Germany. All local industries were geared to German needs. The inhabitants of the occupied countries starved because their produce was sent to maintain the German rations. And while the German men were fighting, their places in the factories and fields of Germany were taken by seven million slave labourers from the occupied lands.

In all the occupied countries the Nazis behaved with extreme ruthlessness. Ten, fifty or a hundred innocent hostages would be executed without trial when one German was killed. Mass punishment was meted out in the form of collective fines and the withholding of rations. Torture was employed by the Gestapo (the Secret Police) to extract information. In Western and Central Europe the Nazis made some attempt to control their savagery. The wiping out of all the inhabitants of a French village (Oradeur-sur-Glâne) and a Czech village (Lidiče) aroused international rage because it was a more or less isolated event. In Eastern Europe, however, such episodes were everyday affairs. 'If I wished to order that one should hang up posters about every seven Poles shot, there would not be enough forests in Poland with which to make paper for those posters', remarked Hans Frank, the Nazi Governor of Poland. 'If 10,000 Russian females fall down from exhaustion while digging an anti-tank trench it interests me not at all as long as the trench is finished for Germany', wrote Heinrich Himmler, the head of the Gestapo. Their actions were as good as their words. When German troops entered Lvov, for instance, on 30 June 1941, they massacred hundreds of men and women and turned the children over to the Hitler Youth for target practice.[2]

The 11,000,000 Jews and part-Jews of Europe were regarded by the Nazis not as sub-human but as non-human – 'race-polluting'. In January 1942 the secret decision was taken to adopt for them the 'final solution' – extermination. 'I just couldn't risk merely killing the men and allowing the children to grow up as avengers facing our sons and grandsons', explained Himmler later.[3] In Russia, the land of the *Untermenschen*, the 2,000,000 Jews were killed in the open, the majority by machine-gun fire in mass executions. The Western European Jews were transported to Poland, to be exterminated, together with the 3,000,000 Polish Jews, in gas chambers secreted in remote forests.

There were about 100 Nazi concentration camps in Germany, and others dotted all over occupied Europe. Stalin's forced labour camps were very unpleasant places. But one has only to read two such books as Alexander Solzhenitsyn's *One Day in the Life of Ivan Denisovitch*[4] (see chapter 6), and Eugen Kogan's *The Theory and Practice of Hell: the German Concentration Camps and the System Behind Them*,[5] written by two men who were inmates of Soviet and Nazi camps respectively for several years, to understand the difference between primitive barbarity and sophisticated sadism. Only a tiny proportion of the 8,000,000 inmates of the Nazi camps survived.

Did the German people know what was happening? In 1952 President Heuss of West Germany said at the site of Belsen, one of the most notorious camps: 'We knew about these things'. But in 1965 President Lübke said, also at Belsen: 'What happened did *not* happen with the knowledge of the German people'. In the same year a Social Democratic Member of the West German Parliament said to an audience of young people: 'If your own mother is lying on her death-bed and swears on the Bible ... that she did not know, I tell you that she just cannot bring herself to tell the truth; it simply refuses to pass her lips, because it is too horrible to have known, or to have been able to know but not to have wanted to know'.[6]

The Resistance Movements

The Resistance movements were the people's response to the policies and behaviour of the Germans. In Western and Central Europe a small minority of the population was *actively* involved in organized espionage, sabotage and guerrilla fighting, directed by the exiled leaders in London. The majority co-operated by passive methods, such as listening to the British BBC broadcasts – a 'crime' punishable by death, going on strike, putting sand in German machinery or rotten fruit in food consignments for Germany. The brave Danish Resistance was born out of the nation's rage at the Nazi attempt to deport their 8,000 Jews. The Danes saved almost all of them by smuggling them across the water to neutral Sweden.

In Eastern Europe the Resistance necessarily assumed a different form. When the sight of burning villages and public executions was a daily spectacle, the majority of ordinary people were perforce drawn into active opposition. The Polish Resistance movement, directed by the non-Communist Polish Government in exile in London, developed an immense underground organization – an underground government, parliament, army, law courts, radio service and schools. On 1 August 1944, as the Red Army was approaching Warsaw and the Germans were pulling out of the city, the 40,000 strong Polish Underground Army decided to rise up and liberate the capital themselves. They counted on the arrival of the Russians within a few days. But the Red Army camped on the east bank of the Vistula for two months and allowed the Germans to slaughter 300,000 Poles and to raze Warsaw to the ground without intervening. Stalin was as determined to crush the non-Communist Polish Resistance as he was to crush the Germans. In Yugoslavia and Albania the Resistance assumed the form of a Communist-led guerrilla war, led by Marshal Tito and Enver Hoxha respectively, which liberated large areas from the Germans and Italians before the Red Army arrived on the scene. The non-Communist Resistance movement in Yugoslavia ended up by collaborating with the Germans and being destroyed by the Communists. A million Yugoslavs were killed by fellow Yugoslavs. In Russia the Resistance took the form of partisan activities directed by the Soviet Government as an ancillary to the campaigns of the Red Army.

In Germany itself there was one group of men who could have

stopped the atrocities and even the war: the brilliant corps of generals, one of the most illustrious professional groups in history. Throughout the war they tried to deter Hitler from his acts of aggression; but when he overrode their advice they obeyed orders, and carried out their campaigns with ruthless efficiency. Only in July 1944, when they realized that the military situation was hopeless, did a small group of aristocratic officers attempt to assassinate Hitler and seize power in a military *Putsch*. They failed, and they and their friends, a total of nearly 5,000 men and women, went bravely to horrible deaths. Among those who perished was Dietrich Bonhöffer, a Protestant theologian whose writings from prison inspired a post-war generation of Christian thinkers to develop the 'New Theology', which is reinterpreting Christianity for the modern age.

The Red Army

Even the briefest account of the wartime experiences of Europe would be incomplete without a description of the Red Army, which swept like a tidal wave across Central and Eastern Europe. Here is an eye-witness description by Jan Stransky, a senior official of the Czech Government-in-exile:

> First come 'the tank divisions . . . composed of picked soldiers; the columns of guns and lorries, the parachute divisions, motor cyclists, technical units. . . . But this . . . is only its vanguard. More than anything else the Red Army is a mass . . . columns of marching soldiers, dirty, tired, clad in ragged uniforms. Tens and hundreds of thousands of columns moving on the dusty roads of central and eastern Europe. They march slowly in close rank with a long even step. Sometimes a song bursts from the marching column, usually something slow and poignantly sad. So they march, men young and old, men from Russian towns and villages, from the Ukraine and the Tartar Republics, the Ural Mountains and the Caucasus, the Baltic countries, Siberia and Mongolia. . . . And columns of women and girls in military grey-green uniforms, high boots and tight blouses, with long hair greased with goose fat. . . . And

children, mainly small boys; the *bezprizorni* from burnt-out villages and towns. Soldiers found them in the woods, exhausted and half mad with hunger and fright, without parents, without a home or a name... Behind the spearheads drive the staff.... In German luxury cars.... And lorries laden with furniture; beds ... radios, frigidaires, wardrobes, couches ... cases of china, kilometres of textiles, fur coats, carpets, silver....' and 'lorries with tons of Russian delicacies, caviar, sturgeon, salami, hectolitres of vodka and Crimean wine.... Behind the staffs more marching columns, without a beginning and without an end. And finally the rearguard: miles and miles of small light carts drawn by low Cossack horses. A grey old man sits in front of the cart.... In the back, under the canvas hood, there is a heap of straw and fodder, packages, tins of food, and on top lies a sick soldier, a drunken woman, a pen containing a goose, a leg of smoked pork.... They drive today ... as the Tartars used to drive centuries ago: in crowds and hosts, uncounted and uncountable, infinitely foreign and lost in all these western countries of which they have never heard and which they are utterly unable to understand: a flood from the steppes, spreading across Europe.'[7]

At first the Russian soldiers were welcomed with great goodwill. But, says Stransky, 'a few hours were enough to show the deep chasm between hosts and guests, the chasm which separates civilized people from primitives.... On the one side there arose a feeling of surprise, embarrassment and contempt, and on the other a feeling of inferiority, distrust and hatred'.[8] The Russian soldiers, who had had no leave since the beginning of their war, murdered, raped and looted. Oil paintings were used as shooting targets, and beautiful furniture for firewood. A young Slovakian saw a Russian soldier who had covered his whole arm with looted watches as if they were bracelets. He did not know how to tell the time, or even how to wind them up, and when they stopped, he threw them on the ground.[9] The liberated people, says Stransky, understood and forgave, but 'all illusions were gone, and . . . the terrific moral shock proved to be one of the most important factors in the subsequent development of the liberated countries'. The shock was deepened by the fact that the primitive behaviour of the Red Army had to be covered up by the 'Big Lie'. 'The glorious liberating Red Army' could do no wrong, and anyone who criticized it might find himself in a cattle truck bound for Siberia.[10]

Conclusion

Future historians may regard the Second World War as the turning-point in European history. The mask of centuries was torn off. Millions of men and women touched the very roots of their being; and out of the depths of tragedy and triumph, of suffering and degradation, of heroism and hatred and compassion, out of an unparalleled catharsis, a new Europe was born.

REFERENCES

1. Wood, David, *Conflict in the Twentieth Century*, Institute of Strategic Studies, London, 1966, p. 24.
2. Lord Russell of Liverpool, *The Scourge of the Swastika: A Short History of Nazi War Crimes*, Cassell and Co., London, 1955, pp. 92–4, and 123 *et seq.*
3. Manvell, Roger, and Fraenkl, Heinrich, *Heinrich Himmler*, Heinemann, London, 1965, p. 197.
4. Published by Penguin, London.
5. Published by Farrar, Strauss and Co., New York.
6. Elon, Amos, *Journey Through a Haunted Land*, André Deutsch, London, 1967, p. 23.
7. Stransky, Jan, *East Wind Over Prague*, Hollis and Carter, 1950, pp. 22–5.
8. Stransky, *op. cit.*, p. 28.
9. Told to one of the authors by the Slovakian.
10. Stransky, *op. cit.*, p. 37.

2. The settlement after the Second World War

At the end of the war some 13,000,000 Europeans had been killed in battle, and 17,000,000 civilians had died as a result of the fighting. Houses, factories and communications had been shattered on a huge scale. Nearly all the major German cities, for instance, were in ruins, and 25,000,000 Russians were homeless. Agriculture had been disastrously disrupted; food rationing was general. Allied troops in Germany had to be forbidden to give away their rations, and in the Don region of Russia people were eating cats and dogs and grass. Fuel was scarce, and millions spent the first two post-war winters in unheated homes. American Lend-Lease supplies were stopped by President Truman shortly after the war.

Post-War Relief

Before the end of the war forty-eight states set up the United Nations' Relief and Rehabilitation Administration (UNRRA), the first great international agency to wrestle with the economic problems of peace in a general way. (After 1919 the League of Nations had carried out some special rehabilitation measures). The United States contributed $2,700,000,000 to UNRRA, and Britain $625,000,000. It was the largest import-export agency the world had ever known. The chief European recipients of its aid were Austria, Byelorussia, Ukraine, Czechoslovakia, Italy, Greece, Poland and Yugoslavia. By 1948, when UNRRA ceased operations, 25,000,000 tonnes of goods had been shipped – three

21

times the amount of relief given after the First World War. Requests had been met within half per cent of promises. 'A dozen potential epidemics simmered under the rubble of every bombed city. Millions of refugees were on the march. People everywhere were underfed, cold and dirty. Yet no runaway epidemics surged across Europe'.[1]

Post-War Reconstruction

Reconstruction was initiated by UNRRA, which helped to supply the critical raw materials for the rebuilding of houses, factories and communications and the rehabilitation of agriculture. Rationing was maintained in most countries for two or three years – the British introduced bread rationing for the first time in 1946 so that they could feed their zone of Germany.

The winter of 1946–7 was particularly severe. In many countries food production was still inadequate and foreign exchange reserves for the purchase of imports had been used up. In spite of large loans from the United States and Canada, and the efforts of UNRRA and other bodies, the situation was critical. Each country felt obliged to limit its imports to bare necessities.

At this point the British Government asked the United States to take over its commitment to give economic and military aid to Greece and Turkey. President Truman responded at once, and secured from Congress a grant of $400,000,000 for these countries for the period up to June 1948.

Hitherto the massive American war-time and post-war aid to Europe had been given on an emergency basis. Now the United States' new role as the greatest power in the world impelled it to come to the help of all European countries needing assistance in their long-term recovery. On 5 June 1947 General George Marshall, the American Secretary of State, proposed that the United States should 'help start the European world on its way to recovery'; the offer was made to all European countries, Communist and non-Communist.

General Marshall declared that the initiative for action must come from Europe. The British Foreign Secretary, Ernest Bevin, immediately suggested to the French and Soviet Governments that they should join with Britain in a preliminary conference to make plans for the European response. The Soviet Union was thus confronted with a crucial challenge. Acceptance of the much-needed American help would mean co-operating in the long-term development of Europe with democratic countries, whose capitalist economies it believed to be doomed. So it refused the Western invitation; and when the Czech and Polish Governments applied for 'Marshall Aid', it immediately ordered them to retract. In July 1947 sixteen non-Communist countries (excluding Spain, which was not invited because the Western Allies considered it 'Fascist', and Finland, which dared not join a Western organization for fear of Russian wrath), met in Paris. By September they had prepared details of Europe's immediate import needs for submission to the Americans. In April 1948 the American Congress passed the Foreign Assistance Act, authorizing the immediate allocation of $5,300,000,000; and the sixteen European countries set up the Organization for European Economic Co-operation (OEEC), whose purpose was, broadly to achieve: 'sound European economy through the economic co-operation of its members' – an affirmation that Europe was an economic unit – and, in particular, to ensure the success of the 'European Recovery Programme'. West Germany joined the OEEC in 1949 and Spain in 1959.

Under the Marshall Plan essential supplies began to pour into Europe. The recipient governments paid for them in their own currencies. These 'counterpart funds' were spent on reconstruction programmes planned by the OEEC in consultation with the American Government, or used to balance internal budgets, or kept out of circulation to prevent inflation. When Marshall Aid was wound up at the end of 1951, thirteen billion dollars had been transferred to Europe on these terms; and about a billion dollars had been supplied in loans at low interest rates. The World Bank also made a number of loans to European countries, amounting, by 1960, to $1,350,000,000. This timely generosity – unprecedented in world history – saved Western Europe from the threat of economic collapse and set it on the road to an entirely new level of prosperity. The success of the programme was partly due to the introduction of economic planning, both within the recipient countries and among them. Counterpart funds were used to reconstruct transport systems, develop agriculture, and finance industry and tourism and this in turn made possible a vast movement towards trade liberalization and currency consolidation (see chapter 8).

Refugees

By the end of 1945 over 5,000,000 of the 11,000,000 'displaced persons' or refugees in Europe had found their way home. By 1948 UNRRA and private welfare organizations had resettled most of the rest, but a 'hard core' of about 560,000 remained in camps, mainly in Germany. They included thousands of unaccompanied children, many of whom did not know their own names nor whom their parents were.

The care of these war-time refugees, together with post-war refugees from the Communist regimes of Eastern Europe, such as Jews from Poland, Hungary and Rumania, was entrusted in 1947 to a new United Nations' Agency, the International Refugee Organization (IRO). By the end of 1951 the IRO had assisted the resettlement of over a million refugees, and it was then wound up. In December 1950 the General Assembly of the United Nations appointed a High Commissioner for Refugees, whose task was simply to get governments to accept refugees, to give them a legal status and to provide them with travel papers. He was given no maintenance nor travel funds. Between 1951 and 1970 he helped recurrent waves of refugees, in particular from Hungary in 1956 and Czechoslovakia in 1968. If dictatorships continue to persecute their citizens, more effective international machinery may be necessary to succour innocent refugees.

Germany 1945-7

At the Potsdam Conference of July 1945, Stalin, President Truman of the United States and Clement Attlee, the British Prime Minister, confirmed the decision reached during the war that Germany should be divided into four zones of occupation,

American, British, Russian and French. Berlin, 176 km within the Russian zone, was to be similarly divided. The Russians gave informal guarantees of access by road and rail through their zone to the areas of Berlin occupied by the Western powers. The Occupying Powers were to pursue common policies, supervised by an Allied Control Commission composed of the four Commanders-in-Chief, which would involve demilitarization and denazification. There was to be no central German government, but democratic institutions were to be restored and developed at the local level. There would be common economic policies, involving 'the equitable distribution (by the Control Commission) of essential commodities ... to produce a balanced economy throughout Germany and reduce the need for imports. ... Payments for reparations should leave enough resources to enable the German people to subsist without external assistance'. Subject to this proviso, each Power was to take reparations in the form of capital equipment from its own zone. The Soviet Union, whose zone was mainly agrarian, was to receive some capital equipment from the Ruhr in the British zone.

In the event, the Russians took nearly twice as much equipment from their zone as was provided for under the Potsdam agreement, while the Western Powers gained little. 'The time has passed when a victor in a war can profit from his victory. ... The damages caused by a modern war, won or lost, can never be repaired'.[2]

No time limit was set for the duration of the Occupation, but the understanding was that it would be a temporary affair. In due course the Allies would set up a central democratic German government with which they would make a peace treaty.

The only serious disagreement between the Allied Powers concerned Germany's frontier with Poland. Churchill and Roosevelt had agreed with Stalin in February 1945 that Poland should receive an area of East Germany up to the Oder and Neisse rivers as compensation for surrendering permanently to the Soviet Union the area of Poland seized in 1939, comprising half of pre-war Poland in area, and a third of its population. On balance the change was to Poland's advantage, since the Western lands had better agricultural and industrial resources than those of the East, and the frontier with Germany was reduced from 1,904 to 456 kilometres. There was, however, a misunderstanding. Churchill and Roosevelt had meant the eastern branch of the Neisse, Stalin the western. By the time of the Potsdam Conference Polish occupation of the area up to the western Neisse was a *fait accompli*. Most of the 9,000,000 Germans in the area had fled or been expelled by the Poles, and their lands had been taken over by some 4,500,000 Poles from central and eastern Poland. The Western Powers persuaded Stalin to affirm that the final delimitation of this frontier should await the peace settlement with Germany. This decision to deprive Germany *provisionally* of a fifth of her territory was to be a major cause of tension for the next twenty-five years.

On Germany's western frontier the Saar, with its population of 1,000,000 and its coal, which complemented the iron ore of Lorraine, was given provisionally to France. In a plebiscite held in 1955 the Saarlanders voted against a proposal to 'Europeanize' the Saar, and in favour of its return to Germany. Subject to these changes, Germany's frontiers were restored to those of 1937.

Although it had been agreed that France should have an occupation zone, General de Gaulle, now the French Premier, was not invited to the Potsdam Conference. This was to be one of many episodes fomenting his hostility to the 'Anglo-Saxons'.

The Nuremberg Trials

'The United Nations and the Nuremberg trials were virtually twin offspring of the Allied negotiations and agreements with respect to the peace that would follow victory'[4] – both were decided on in principle by Churchill, Roosevelt and Stalin in 1943. The German 'war criminals' were to be tried and punished by the first international criminal tribunal in modern history. The formal agreement to set up this court, composed of judges and prosecutors appointed by the Governments of the United States, the Soviet Union, Britain and France, was signed in August 1945 by the four Powers and endorsed by nineteen other member states of the United Nations. The court sat at Nuremberg from November 1945 to October 1946 to deal with indictments against twenty-one men who represented the German General Staff, the German Government, and the Nazi Party leadership and organizations. They included Göring and Ribbentrop, Rosenberg, the racial theorist and Minister for Occupied Eastern Europe, Streicher, the Jew-baiter, Frank, the Governor of Occupied Poland, and two generals and two admirals.

These men were tried for two different kinds of crime: for committing 'war crimes' and for waging 'aggressive war'.

The concept of war crimes, such as atrocities perpetrated against prisoners-of-war and civilians, is ancient. It was embodied in international codes of the 'rules of war' in the Hague and Geneva Conventions of 1907 and 1929 respectively. Until 1939 each country was expected to try its own 'war criminals'; the provision in the Treaty of Versailles of 1919 that the German Government should hand over 900 war criminals for international trial was never carried out, for the Allies did not occupy Germany and so could not arrest the men. The Nuremberg trials reaffirmed and extended the principle that, to quote the Court's judgement, 'individuals have international duties which transcend national obligations of obedience imposed by the individual state'.

The concept that the waging of aggressive war is a crime is also ancient. From the time of St Augustine Roman Catholic theologians have asserted that there is a moral or natural law which all nations ought to observe, and have drawn a distinction between a 'just' and an 'unjust' war. During the three centuries before the First World War, when power politics dominated European affairs, this concept was abandoned by secular international lawyers. A commission of the Peace Conference of 1919 asserted that the waging of aggressive war was a moral outrage, but *not* a legal crime. It hesitated to create a precedent. Between the Wars the idea that international affairs should subserve moral principles was revived, this time in a secular form – the interpreter of these principles was the democratically constituted

League of Nations, not the authoritarian Roman Catholic Church; and this led to a revival of the idea of an unjust war, defined rather more specifically as a 'war of aggression'. In the Pact of Paris of 1928 sixty-eight nations, including Germany, Italy and Japan, agreed to 'renounce (war) as an instrument of national policy in their relations with each other'. A unanimous resolution of the League Assembly had already, in 1927, declared that a 'war of aggression' was an 'international crime'. But no means of punishing aggression was proposed. The establishment of an international court to try and punish aggressors was, therefore, a great step forward in the development of international law as the basis for world order and peace. In the late sixties some leading legal authorities in the United States were invoking the 'Nuremberg principle' to condemn the American war in Vietnam.[3]

The court condemned twelve of the defendants to death, acquitted three, and sentenced the remaining six to long terms of imprisonment. The German General Staff was declared to have been a 'disgrace to the honourable profession of arms', having participated or acquiesced in 'crimes of a scale larger and more shocking than the world has ever had the misfortune to know'.

The fairness and dispassion with which the trials were conducted, and the massive weight of the evidence, drawn from 4,000 captured German documents, ensured that the discrediting of the Nazi leaders was complete. The idea of the international accountability for war crimes and waging aggressive war was dramatized and publicized in an entirely new way.

The major weakness of the trials was that the Court was not genuinely international. The prosecuting countries were acting as judges in their own cause. There was no question of arraigning the Italians, for example, for their aggression against Ethiopia, Albania, Greece and Egypt, or the Russians for their invasion of Finland.

Of the four prosecuting nations, only the French identified the Nazis with the Germans. The American Prosecutor specifically stated that: 'We have no purpose to incriminate the whole German people'.[4]

Peace Treaties with Germany's European Allies

The treaties with Italy, Hungary, Bulgaria, Rumania and Finland were drawn up in protracted negotiations between the big five – the United States, the Soviet Union, China, Britain and France, submitted in the summer of 1946 to a conference of twenty-one other nations which had fought the Axis Powers, and signed on 10 February 1947. They represented a diplomatic victory for the Soviet Union. The Finnish treaty confirmed Soviet annexation of the Karelian Peninsula and the ice-free port of Petsamo. In the treaties with Bulgaria, Hungary and Rumania the Western Powers secured the inclusion of guarantees of civil liberties – which meant nothing – and the Soviet Union the right to station troops in Rumania and Hungary – which meant much. On Soviet insistence the treaty with Italy was imposed on the Italians rather than negotiated with them. Italy surrendered its former African colonies. The Greek-inhabited Dodecanese islands it had gained from Turkey in 1912 were ceded to Greece, and the province of Venezia-Giulia to Yugoslavia. Trieste (population 700,000) and its hinterland (population 73,500) were to be a Free Territory administered by the United Nations. In fact, however, the hinterland was subsequently annexed by Yugoslavia, while in 1954 the Soviet Union and Yugoslavia agreed that Trieste could return to Italy. For nine years the city, under temporary Anglo-American administration, was a focal point of tension between the Communist and the Western Powers. Italy's armed forces were reduced to 300,000 men, and most of its ships were divided among the victorious Powers. Reparations were exacted from these countries for the Soviet Union, Greece, Yugoslavia, Czechoslovakia, Albania and Ethiopia.

Austria and Vienna were divided into four zones of occupation, but, in contrast to the treatment of Germany, Austria was allowed to form a national government in 1945 after free elections had produced an anti-Communist parliamentary majority. Although it was decided at Potsdam not to exact reparations, in order to avoid the economic collapse which had occurred after the First World War, the Russians took oil and equipment from their zone. Until 1955 Austria remained an occupied country, because the Russians refused to consider its future apart from that of Germany. Then Khrushchev, who had succeeded Stalin as the Soviet leader, suddenly agreed to a peace treaty, on the understanding that the country should be neutral, joining no political nor military alliances, and having no foreign troops stationed on its soil.[5]

The Communisation of Eastern Europe

It was clear before the end of the war that the Soviet Union would seek to dominate Eastern Europe after Germany's defeat. All the Western Allies could do was to secure from Stalin promises that 'free elections', in which all democratic and non-Nazi parties would have the right to put up candidates, would be held in the countries liberated by the Red Army. Stalin insisted that it was essential to Russia's security that 'friendly' governments should be established in the region between Russia and Germany; and since Germany had attacked Russia with great ferocity twice in fifty years, the concept of a buffer zone in the area was understandable.

By the end of the war self-confident, indigenous Communist régimes were established in Yugoslavia and Albania, under the leadership respectively of Marshal Tito and Enver Hoxha. They enjoyed a wide measure of national support, and no organized opposition parties existed. The pre-war upper classes and intelligentsia had, in the main, been eliminated during the war. In November 1945 Tito held parliamentary elections, at which no opposition candidates were allowed, and ninety per cent of the electors voted for the Communist-controlled National Front. The new parliament immediately proclaimed Yugoslavia a Republic, and in January 1946 a Soviet-type constitution was introduced, establishing Yugoslavia as a Communist state. The Yugoslav Communists looked on the Soviet Union as their natural leader. Red Army troops had liberated Belgrade side by side with the Partisans in October 1944, and Soviet military and economic advisers remained in the country. There was even talk of turning Yugoslavia into a Constituent Republic of the USSR. Albania was also declared a Republic with a constitution modelled on that of the Soviet Union.

The Red Army liberated Poland and Czechoslovakia, invaded Bulgaria, Hungary and Rumania, and 'occupied' East Germany. With the exception of East Germany and Czechoslovakia, these were backward, peasant countries. Before the war they were ruled in the interests of the small middle and upper classes by regimes of a more or less dictatorial nature. But in all of them, and also in Czechoslovakia, the better-off peasants had formed Social Democratic parties, which stood for personal and political freedom, for social and agrarian reform, and for friendship with both the West and the Soviet Union. During the war the local Communist Parties were relatively inactive, and there was no special connection between national feeling and Communism. The post-war Communist Parties emerged from underground (having been banned before the war in all these countries except Czechoslovakia), and took their place side by side with the revived Social Democratic Parties, which in general commanded the support of the majority of the people.

Most of the leaders of these Communist Parties were men of humble origins who had spent long years in underground activity, in prison – often with torture – or in the Soviet Union, where some were given high positions. The latter, dubbed 'Muscovites', were in general men of mediocre stature, self-educated and limited in their outlook, content to be Stalin's stooges – for his pre-war purges had eliminated almost all of them who showed any independence of character. Tito was not a 'Muscovite'; he paid his first visit to the Soviet Union in 1944.

As the Red Army swept across Eastern Europe it brought these 'Muscovites' in its train to lead the reconstituted Communist Parties. Stalin's aim was to bring these parties to power, and thus create an empire of 'satellite' states, sovietized as well as communized. Since the majority of the people wanted social democracy and national independence, not a Communist police state subservient to the Soviet Union, this would not be easy to achieve. Not wanting to provoke the intervention of the Western

Powers, which had atom bombs and were providing UNRRA aid, Stalin and the Muscovites adopted 'salami tactics', destroying the opposition in thin slices, undermining the non-Communist parties from within. Red Army troops withdrew from Czechoslovakia and Bulgaria, but remained in Hungary, Poland, Rumania and East Germany after the signature of the peace treaties of 1947. But they were not called upon directly to intervene in the process of sovietization.

First, coalition governments of Communist and non-Communist parties were formed. Then genuinely free elections were held in Czechoslovakia, Hungary and East Berlin. In Czechoslovakia the Communists won thirty-eight per cent of the votes – an electoral victory; but in the other two states their vote was much lower. The elections held in the other four states were therefore accompanied by intimidation of the voters and purges of the non-Communist leaders. In a number of countries the Communists had managed to gain control of the Ministry of the Interior, and hence of the police. Secret political police forces were recruited from villainous characters who had served in the Gestapo or the local Fascist parties, and who now switched arm bands to save their skins. The torture chambers of the pre-war and wartime regimes were revived under new management. (The face of Janos Kadar, the Communist leader who became ruler of Hungary in 1956 and was still in power in 1970, was pock-marked with the scars made by the cigarettes of his various jailors). Bands of Communist rowdies behaved much like the former Nazi storm-troopers. Non-Communist party leaders were forced by torture to 'confess' at show trials intended to intimidate their leaders and disillusion their electors. Iuliu Maniu, for instance, the leader of the Rumanian Peasant Party, whom many of his countrymen regarded as the greatest living Rumanian, was sentenced to solitary confinement for life. The rank and file were reduced by various forms of bribery and blackmail. ' "Take my case", said the village mayor in a remote Czechoslovakian constituency. "If we [the Social Democrats] lose, I go to prison, as I did during the Occupation. Next door in

Plana there is a Communist mayor. If the Communist Party loses, at worst he will become the mayor's third deputy." [6]

When the Communists had finally eliminated the other parties or swallowed them up into Communist-controlled 'National Fronts', a single list of candidates would be elected by ninety per cent of the votes, and a Soviet-type constitution imposed.

Until February 1948 Czechoslovakia remained a free country, in full contact with the West – no doubt because of the great international prestige of President Beneš and Foreign Minister Jan Masaryk. The threat presented by Marshall Aid, combined with the declining vote of the local Communists, finally impelled the Russians to act. With Soviet troops on the Frontier, and the Soviet ambassador active behind the scenes, the Communists carried out a bloodless *coup d'état*, forcing President Beneš to appoint a majority of Communists to the government. A few days later Masaryk's body was found in the courtyard of the Foreign Ministry, having fallen from a window. He had probably been murdered. Shortly afterwards President Beneš resigned.

The Czech frontier with the Western world was now sealed off. Before the *coup d'état* a person who crossed this frontier illegally might be sent to prison for two weeks. Now he faced execution. The same situation prevailed along the Western frontiers of all the other Eastern European countries, except for East Berlin.

The Establishment of the United Nations

After the First World War the ideal of an international organization embodying the principles of an international moral order, which would resolve conflicts and promote progress, was brought to birth. The League of Nations was founded – but the United States did not join it, and the Soviet Union was not admitted until 1934 and was expelled in 1939 for attacking Finland. During the Second World War Churchill, Roosevelt and Stalin agreed that the League should be revived in a new form. The Charter of the United Nations, adopted at a conference at San Francisco in June 1945, came into force on

24 October. This time the United States and the Soviet Union were founding members. At Soviet suggestion the headquarters were established in New York, instead of Geneva, the seat of the League.

At its foundation the United Nations had fifty-one member states. At first, for reasons connected with the Cold War, a number of European countries were excluded; but as a result of a 'package deal' concluded in 1955 between the Western Powers and the Soviet Union, all the ex-enemy states except Germany were admitted: Bulgaria, Rumania, Austria, Hungary and Italy, together with Albania, Eire, Finland, Portugal and Spain. The League of Nations had been an essentially European body, only ten of its member states being in Africa and Asia. By the end of 1970 European decolonization had raised United Nations' membership to 127. Only eight independent states of any importance were not members: Communist China, East and West Germany, North and South Korea, North and South Vietnam. These were excluded for political reasons, while Switzerland refused to join in order not to prejudice its neutrality.

The concept of collective security – the automatic obligation of all members to defend any victim of aggression – which was the cornerstone of the Covenant of the League of Nations, is not written into the Charter of the United Nations. Its members have merely bound themselves to settle disputes by peaceful means. On the other hand, it has undertaken to promote economic and social development and the establishment of human rights throughout the world – a commitment never assumed by the League; and the colonial powers have also undertaken, for the first time, to establish these rights in their dependencies. Article 2 of the Charter, however, precludes the United Nations from intervening in the domestic affairs of member states.

The main deliberative body of the United Nations is the General Assembly consisting of representatives of all member states with equal voting rights. Resolutions on all important matters require a two-thirds majority. Disputes and threats to the peace are brought in the first instance before the Security Council. In order to counterbalance the 'one state one vote' structure of the Assembly, which expresses the principle of equality but not the reality of power in a world of states which vary enormously in size and strength, the five 'great powers' of 1945 were made permanent members of this Council, with the right of veto. These powers were the United States, Britain, France, the Soviet Union, and China (after the Communist Revolution of 1949 in China, the Chinese seat was taken by Nationalist China, the regime established in Taiwan. In 1971 the seat was resumed by the mainland Chinese government). The other member states of the Council, increased from seven to ten in 1965, are elected by the General Assembly for two years. It can order mandatory economic sanctions, which member states are morally bound to support, and it can call on member states to provide armed forces to enforce its decisions. These powers represent real limitations on the sovereignty of member states, but they cannot become effective unless the five permanent members are in agreement. The Charter therefore relies for the maintenance of world peace on the co-operation of the great powers in the Security Council with each other, and on the co-operation of the Security Council with the General Assembly. Because of the Cold War, however, such co-operation has been fitful and partial. By the end of 1970 the Soviet Union had used its veto over a hundred times, and the other great powers only two or three times each.

The League of Nations was essentially concerned with political matters; its economic activities were subsidiary and were carried out in certain limited fields. (The International Labour Organization was, however, established in 1919 – the first of the 'Specialized Agencies' which have played such an important part in world economic and social development since 1945). One of the main purposes of the United Nations is, according to its Charter (Article 1), 'To achieve international co-operation in solving international problems of an economic, social, cultural, or humanitarian character, and in promoting and encouraging respect for human rights and for fundamental freedoms for all without distinction as to race, sex, language, or religion'. The United Nations' activities in these fields have probably been at least as important as those concerned with political and security matters. They have been carried out under the supervision of the 27-member Economic and Social Council (proposed to be increased to 54 members), which works through five functional commissions – for statistics, population, social development, human rights, status of women and narcotic drugs – and through four regional economic commissions – for Europe (see chapter 11), Asia and the Far East, Latin America and Africa, as well as through certain special bodies, such as the United Nations' Conference on Trade and Development (UNCTAD), and the United Nations' Development Programme (UNDP).

Linked with the Economic and Social Council are a number of independent 'specialized agencies', each with its own membership, constitution and budget, of which the most important are the Food and Agriculture Organization of the United Nations (FAO), the World Health Organization (WHO), the United Nations Educational, Scientific and Cultural Organization (UNESCO) and the International Labour Organization (ILO). Between 1945 and 1970, the United Nations and these bodies carried out surveys and research into almost every aspect of economic and social development on a global basis. They set out standards and recommended practices for governments to follow both as regards their relations between themselves and within their own countries. They promoted co-operation between richer and poorer countries for the development of the latter (see chapter 13). In addition, the General Agreement on Tariffs and Trade (GATT) arranged for collective trade negotiations and established rules of good behaviour in this field, causing many restrictions to be removed and providing the basis for a great expansion in trade. The International Bank for Reconstruction and Development (IBRD, often referred to as the 'World Bank') helped with the post-war reconstruction of Europe and provided funds and know-how for the development of the poorer countries. The International Monetary Fund (IMF) helped to establish parities between various countries and rules for changing them, to minimize the impact of short-term changes between them and to make possible the financing of a great expansion in international payments, both for trade and for other purposes (see chapter 8).

The Universal Declaration of Human Rights, adopted by the United Nations General Assembly in 1948, generalized for all mankind the Rights of Man, some of which had been proclaimed by the American Constitution and the French Revolution towards the end of the eighteenth century.

The third main organ of the United Nations is the International Court of Justice, first set up in 1919, which deals with cases of international law and treaty enforcement submitted to it by member states.

Finally, there is the United Nations' Secretariat, a highly prestigious international civil service. It is headed by the Secretary-General, who is appointed by the General Assembly on the advice of the Security Council. The three Secretary-Generals who held office between 1945 and 1970 (Trygve Lie of Norway, Dag Hammarskjöld of Sweden and U Thant of Burma), acted not merely as civil service heads, but as world statesmen, inculcating a world perspective in policy making and offering world leadership. Their achievements are a portent for the future in a world still dominated by national power-politics.

Conclusion

The developments of the years 1945–7 set the scene for the next quarter century. On one hand was the prospect of solid co-operation between the great powers of Europe and America to solve the problems of peace and to develop a new world order based on the establishment of the Rights of Man. On the other were symptoms of deep distrust and hostility between the war-time allies. How could men who believed sincerely in the Rights of Man create a new world with men who were violating all these Rights in Eastern Europe?

There were three possibilities: that states would work together constructively in the United Nations and other international forums; that they would use these forums as arenas for fighting verbal battles with each other before the audience of world opinion; or that the United Nations would collapse.

REFERENCES

1. UNRRA, *The Story of UNRRA*, New York.
2. Speech by M. Bousquet, French Ambassador, at the closing session of the Inter-Allied Reparations Agency, 20 November 1959.
3. Taylor, Telford, *Nuremberg and Vietnam: An American Tragedy*, A New York Times Book, Quadrangle Books Inc., Chicago, 1970, p. 78.
4. See Jackson, Robert H., *The Nuremberg Case*, Alfred Knopf Inc., New York, 1947, and Davidson, Eugene, *The Trial of the Germans*, Macmillan, New York, 1966.
5. For much of this section I am indebted to Hampden Jackson, J., *The Post War Decade*, Gollancz, London, 1961, pp. 30–33 and 60–63.
6. Stransky, *op. cit.*, p. 132

3. The Cold War up to 1955

Introduction

On 6 March 1946, in a speech at Fulton, Missouri, Mr Churchill put into words what most people in the West could not yet bring themselves to contemplate. He said:

> A shadow has fallen upon the scenes so lately lighted by the Allied victory. . . . From Stettin in the Baltic to Trieste in the Adriatic, an iron curtain has descended across the Continent. Behind that line lie all the capitals of the ancient states of Central and Eastern Europe. . . . These famous cities and the populations around them lie in what I must call the Soviet sphere, and all are subject . . . to a very high and . . . increasing measure of control from Moscow. . . . This is certainly not the liberated Europe we fought to build up. Nor is it one which contains the essentials of permanent peace.

The Cold War is the name given to the conflict between the Communist and the Western worlds which developed after the end of the Second World War. Three years after their life-and-death struggle against the common enemy, the Allies were split into two hostile camps. Soviet motives seem to have been composed of a complex mixture of power-politics and fanatical ideology. The Western powers reacted by playing the power-politics game too, but they also felt that they were struggling for the principles of economic freedom and of political democracy. On the whole, Western Europeans gave greater emphasis to the power-politics *motif*, and the Americans to the ideological. The bitter experience of Fascism had shaken West Europeans into what has been called the 'post-ideological' era. In most of their countries the Communists were free and tolerated. They knew that one may be a Communist for good and for bad motives; that one may think one believes what one does not really believe; that 'freedom' in our confused societies is at best relative and conditional. On the whole, they were more afraid of Soviet power than of Soviet ideology. The Americans tended, as did the Russians, to see politics in moral terms of right and wrong. They had trusted the Russians, and until 1949 the Chinese, and now they felt deeply let down. Disillusionment produced a tendency to 'over-react', to interpret every Soviet move as sinister and aggressive, and to overlook the defensive element in Soviet policy. The Americans became crusaders, regarding it as their mission to save mankind from the 'Communist conspiracy'. This attitude tended to turn them into fanatics who were fighting not *for* freedom, but *against* an enemy.

However, throughout the Cold War, the Americans tried very hard to work *with* the Russians in the United Nations and elsewhere, to establish world peace on the basis of international institutions. At their side were the British, providing the common sense and restraining hand of experience; and the French, who originally gave to the world the ideals of 'liberty, equality and fraternity'. So, for twenty-five years the Western Powers and the European Communists swung uneasily between conflict and collaboration.

The Cold War has two main phases. Here we are concerned with the first. The second will be discussed in chapter 14.

The Soviet Attempt to Annex Azerbaijan

The first move in the Cold War occurred in Iran. In 1946, the Russians began to annex the province of Azerbaijan, where Soviet troops were temporarily stationed under the terms of an Anglo-Iranian-Soviet Treaty of 1942. The Iranian government appealed to the Security Council of the United Nations; the matter was given world publicity and the Russians withdrew their troops. The United Nations had scored its first success in a great power dispute.

The Truman Doctrine

In the next move, in March 1947, the American government decided to give economic and military aid to Greece and Turkey. After the Communist rising in Greece in 1944, the Communist guerrilla army had remained active in the wild mountains of northern Greece. Communist guerrillas infiltrating from Albania, Yugoslavia and Bulgaria were carrying on terrorist activities, including the abduction of several thousand Greek children. The United Nations Security Counil, at Greek request, sent an investigation commission, but the Soviet veto prevented them from taking firmer action. At a secret meeting in the Kremlin with Bulgarian and Yugoslav leaders in February 1948, Stalin had declared that the uprising must be stopped, fearing it would lead to American and British intervention. This cautious attitude went unsuspected by the Western Powers, who at the end of 1947 doubted whether an independent, pro-Western Greece could survive.[1,2]

Turkey also appeared to be threatened by Russia, which since the days of Peter the Great had been trying to control the Dardanelles. 'Turkey is weak,' said Stalin to General Bedell Smith, the American Ambassador, in March 1946, 'and the Soviet Union is very conscious of the danger of foreign control of the Straits, which Turkey is not strong enough to protect. The Turkish Government is unfriendly to us. That is why the Soviet Government has demanded a base in the Dardanelles. It is a matter of our own security.'[3]

In asking Congress to take over from Britain the commitment to give military and economic aid to Greece and Turkey, President Truman made a general policy statement which came to be called the Truman Doctrine: 'I believe it must be the policy of the United States to support free peoples who are resisting subjugation by armed minorities or by outside pressures. I believe that we must assist free peoples to work out their own destinies in their own ways.' The anti-Communist crusade was launched. George Kennan, a distinguished American diplomat, commented: 'Throughout the ensuing two decades the conduct of our foreign policy would continue to be bedevilled by people in our own government as well as in other governments who could not free themselves from the belief that all another country had to do, in order to qualify for American aid, was to demonstrate the existence of a Communist threat. . . .'[4]

The Truman Doctrine marked the beginning of the general handing over by Britain to the USA of the responsibility which it had assumed for 150 years for keeping order in the Mediterranean, in Africa and in South-east Asia. Yet the main factor in ending the Communist menace in Greece was not American aid but the defection of Yugoslavia from the Soviet Empire in 1948.

The Marshall Plan

The refusal of the Communist countries to accept Marshall Aid in the summer of 1947 began to divide the countries of Europe into hostile economic groups, one linked to the United States, the other to the Soviet Union.

The Cominform

Stalin decided in October 1947 to revive in a new form the pre-war Communist International, or Comintern, the organization of world Communist Parties under the leadership of the Soviet Communist Party, founded in 1919. He had dissolved the organization in 1943, for when the Soviet Union was fighting Germany in alliance with the Western Powers it was no longer politically expedient for it to be directing an organization aimed at subverting them. The new Cominform (Communist Information Bureau) consisted only of representatives of the Communist Parties of the Eastern European states, and of France and Italy, whose parties were so strong that a Communist take-over was, in both countries, a practical possibility. In Eastern Europe, Stalin's aim was undoubtedly to strengthen Soviet control of the local Communist Parties and governments. Only the Yugoslavs, confident enough in their own national strength to be unafraid of

Soviet domination, were whole-heartedly in favour of the new body. Its headquarters were therefore in Belgrade. In November 1947 the Cominform inspired the French and Italian Communist Parties to organize serious strikes, intended to bring down the government and the political system. They were, however, 'contained' and thereafter Communist electoral support began to ebb in both countries. Stalin was probably not excessively troubled by this lack of success, since he was generally indifferent to the fate of Communist movements outside the area of direct Soviet control.

The Communization of Czechoslovakia

The cynical subjugation in 1948 of this westernized, democratic country, described in chapter 2, aroused deep feeling of anger and guilt in the West.

The Defection of Yugoslavia from Stalin's Empire

On 28 June 1948, Moscow expelled the Yugoslav Communist Party from the Cominform and exhorted the people of Yugoslavia to overthrow Tito and his colleagues. The Western world was astounded.

After the foundation of the Cominform a quarrel which had been rumbling since the end of the War, blew up. Tito said:

The cause of the conflict is the aggressive tendencies of the Soviet Union towards Yugoslavia. The first State of the workers and peasants, which had roused such enthusiasm among the working masses of the whole world and achieved such material success, had reached stagnation point in its development. The trend towards state capitalism was disenfranchizing the workers and causing the loss of much that had been gained in the October Revolution. ... Stalin ... instead of expanding the rights of the working class ... relied on a state machine which had become not the servant of the community but its master. ... Stalin himself has become the slave of the intelligence service he created and developed. Consequently in the Soviet Union today no one trusts anyone else,

43

everything is a cause for suspicion ... and the Soviet Union has become an enormous terror state.

The fundamental question on which Stalin failed is the problem of the freedom of the individual. These two concepts are identical. ... The Soviet Union has betrayed the hopes put in it.[5]

The interpretation of 'Communism' implied in this speech, combined with the attitude that each Communist country has the right to experiment in new kinds of Communist institutions, may be called 'Titoism'. In 1948 it was a deadly heresy.

Minor issues – the behaviour of the Red Army, the espionage activities of Soviet officials in Yugoslavia, and, above all, the Soviet policies of economic exploitation (see chapter 7) brought the quarrel to a head. Tito's situation was perilous. His relations with the Western powers were very strained over the problem of Trieste (see chapter 2). The Soviet Union and all the other Communist states severed trade and diplomatic relations with Yugoslavia but did not invade it, probably because Stalin knew that the United States possessed the atom bomb.

After the winding up of UNRRA, Yugoslavia had become dependent on Soviet aid for the rebuilding of its economy. The Western governments now stepped into the breach. Between 1948 and 1961, Yugoslavia received from the United States economic and military aid amounting to $574,000,000[6] and from Britain £39,000,000.[7] Yugoslavia was also given a special status in the OEEC. The Yugoslavs responded by agreeing, in 1954, to the cession of Trieste to Italy. Yugoslavia began to play an independent role in international affairs, involving itself with the 'non-aligned' countries of the Third World.

The Division of Germany

With the onset of the Cold War the Potsdam plan to govern Germany through agreed four-power policies broke down. After months of deadlock in the Allied Control Commission, the Russians withdrew their representatives in March 1948. The Western Powers then merged their three zones into one economic and administrative unit of 48,000,000 people, dividing it into ten *Länder* or states, each with its own democratically elected parliament and responsible government. Federal elections were held in August 1949 and in September the constitution of the Federal Republic of Germany (henceforth referred to as 'West Germany') came into force. In 1955, the handing over of sovereign powers to the new German government was completed. The Allies reserved their rights to the occupation of Berlin, the stationing of troops in the Federal Republic and the ultimate responsibility for German unification.

On 18 June 1948 the Allies had introduced a currency reform into their combined zones and West Berlin, designed to lift West Germany out of an economic morass in which people had even been reduced to barter. The results were spectacular: production rose by 25 per cent within a month, and the shops began to fill up with goods. The Allies also announced that they were setting up an International Authority of the Ruhr to administer the Ruhr industries. The Russians were enraged. On the day that the currency reform was announced, they cut off the surface access routes to West Berlin, and six days later they cut off all electricity, coal, food and other supplies to the 2,250,000 West Berliners. This was the 'Berlin blockade'.

The Russians had good reason to be extremely sensitive about West Berlin, the one real hole in the Iron Curtain. Any East German could buy a subway ticket to West Berlin and travel thence to West Germany and beyond. Between 1949 when the division of Germany became definitive, and August 1961 when the hole was sealed up by the building of the Berlin Wall, some 3,000,000 East Germans departed by this route. (The population of East Germany in 1949 was 17,500,000.) A preponderant number of these refugees belonged to the professional classes and the intelligentsia. West Berlin, surprisingly quickly rebuilt with Western money into a prosperous and lively city, was, as Mr Khrushchev later put it, a bone in Moscow's throat, an enclave of capitalism and democracy inside the drab Communist world.

The Western Powers rejected the idea of breaking the

45

blockade by land forces. If they had reacted with conventional weapons, the Third World War might have broken out – with the Russians deploying immensely superior forces. If they had abandoned the West Berliners, they might have been responsible for another Munich – leading also, perhaps, to the Third World War. They decided, instead, to supply the city by air. For eleven months, American, British, and French pilots flew 277,728 flights to bring West Berlin 2,343,301 tonnes of food and supplies[8] at the cost of eighty lives. The West Berliners were calm and co-operative and the spectacular success of the enterprise astonished the world. In May 1949 the Russians (who had not yet exploded their bomb) tacitly admitted that their bluff had been called and lifted the blockade. The airlift gave new heart to the West Berliners in their dangerous outpost. Above all, it created a bond of solidarity between the West Germans and their former enemies, which prepared the way for the foundation of the European Community and the North Atlantic Community (see chapter 9).

In October 1949 the Russians responded to the establishment of the Federal Republic in West Germany by setting up the German Democratic Republic (henceforth referred to as 'East Germany'), with its capital in East Berlin, in their zone. They likewise granted it full sovereignty in 1955, while retaining the right to station troops in the country.

By 1955, the two new German states were, therefore, legally free to conduct their own foreign policy. West Germany was accorded diplomatic recognition by most countries in the non-Communist world, and by the Soviet Union, which then agreed, ten years after the end of the war, to repatriate its German prisoners-of-war. East Germany was recognized only by the countries of the Communist bloc. Officially the rest of the world treated the state as if it did not exist, but did increasingly brisk economic business with it (see chapter 11).

The Formation of NATO in 1949

In December 1947, recognizing that the Soviet Union's use of its veto power made the United Nations' Security Council virtually helpless in Cold War issues, the British persuaded France, Belgium, the Netherlands and Luxembourg to join them in forming a defensive military alliance, the Brussels Treaty Organization. By the summer of 1948, the Americans were also gravely worried by the Cold War developments. The result was the signature, in April 1949, of the North Atlantic Treaty Alliance, a defence alliance between the United States, Canada, and ten Western European countries. If one member of the alliance were attacked, all the rest would come to its aid. Greece and Turkey joined in 1952 and West Germany in 1955 (see below). It was the United States' first formal peace-time alliance in its history. Under the Marshall Plan it had involved itself temporarily in Europe. Now it was committed for an indefinite period.

In 1950 something like fourteen NATO divisions and 1,000 NATO aircraft confronted 175 Communist divisions and 20,000 Communist aircraft. The strategic justification for this disparity was provided by the concept of the 'shield' to hold up the Communists, while the United States unsheathed its 'sword', the unique weapon of the atom bomb.

Ernest Bevin, the British Foreign Secretary, told a friend that the signing of the NATO treaty was, 'one of the great moments of all my life' – the culmination of his policy of laying the basis for an 'Atlantic Community' in the economic and military fields; but other people had their doubts. 'All right, the Russians are well armed and we are poorly armed. So what? We are like a man who has let himself into a walled garden and finds himself alone there with a dog with very big teeth. The dog, for the moment, shows no sign of aggressiveness. The best thing for us to do is surely to try to establish, as between the two of us, the assumption that teeth have nothing whatsoever to do with our mutual relationship – that they are neither here nor there. If the dog shows no disposition to assume that it is otherwise, why should we raise the subject and invite attention to the disparity?'[9] This was the view of George Kennan, the American diplomat. In September 1949 the Russians exploded an atom bomb.

47

Anti-Communist Hysteria in the United States

By 1949 the benign glow of internationalism was fading from the American scene. Conscription was reintroduced in 1948 – and in Britain too – and the American Defense Department began to finance massive programmes of scientific research into nuclear weapons and delivery systems. In 1950, President Truman ordered the construction of a hydrogen bomb. It was dawning on the American public that they themselves were now for the first time vulnerable to bomber attack. The 600,000,000 Chinese as well as the 100,000,000 Eastern Europeans were now under Communist rule. All this seemed part of a vast and sinister plot, a 'world Communist conspiracy', directed by evil men in the Kremlin. An hysterical fear filled many American minds, and a crude and bigoted figure arose to exploit this fear. In 1953 Senator Joe McCarthy became Chairman of a Senate Sub-Committee, and instigated, with wide public support, 'investigations' – many of them based on slander and gossip rather than an objective evidence – into the public and private lives of hundreds of thousands of Americans to see if they were tainted with 'Communism'.

Since public opinion was demanding scapegoats, President Eisenhower and his Secretary-of-State John Foster Dulles looked the other way. The persecution spread through American society, poisoning the atmosphere of free discussion, and encouraging the very conformity of opinion which is the hallmark of Marxism. In 1954 McCarthy was discredited, but the attitude which he had focussed lingered on.

The Communist Revolution in China: 1949

From 1911 when the last of the Imperial dynasties which had ruled China for 2,000 years collapsed, until 1949 when the Communists gained control of the country, China was in a state of chronic civil war, combined with Japanese invasion. Until the early 1920s feudal war lords fought each other. Then two large authoritarian parties arose; the *Kuomintang*, led by Chiang Kai-Shek, and the Communist Party, led by the peasant scholar Mao

Tse-Tung. These parties co-operated to crush the war lords and then began to fight each other. The *Kuomintang* was recognised internationally as the legal government of China. Until 1927 the Chinese Communist Party was directed by Moscow; then it began to pursue an independent course. As in Yugoslavia, it was essentially a national movement basing its support on the peasants. During the years of the struggle with Japan, from 1937 to 1945, the Communists steadily gained ground because they put up a better resistance to the Japanese than the *Kuomintang*. To Stalin, however, Mao's movement, like Tito's, was a heretical movement with schismatic implications. He therefore gave it no support, and in 1945 even advised Mao to reach an agreement with the *Kuomintang*.

After declaring war on Japan in December 1941, the United States lavished military and economic aid on Chiang Kai-Shek. It overlooked the fact that Chiang's regime was dictatorial, cruel, corrupt, and militarily ineffective, and had lost the support of the peasants. The civil war was resumed with full vigour after the defeat of the Japanese in 1945, and by October 1949 Chiang Kai-Shek had crumpled up and withdrawn his forces to the island of Formosa (Taiwan), which the Japanese had ruled since 1912 and restored to China after the war. In 1970 Chiang Kai-Shek was still ruling the island, claiming to represent 'Nationalist China', and maintaining armed forces of nearly 500,000 Chinese to invade the mainland when the moment seemed propitious.[10]

It is normal international practice to accord diplomatic recognition to the established government of a country. Its nature and the methods by which it has come to power are considered the country's own affair. Most Western European governments therefore soon established diplomatic relations with the Communist government and advocated that Communist China should replace Nationalist China as a permanent member of the Security Council of the United Nations. The Americans, however, took a moralist line. They refused to enter into diplomatic relations with 'Red China' – and had not done so by 1970. Nor were American citizens, with very few exceptions, allowed by their government to visit the country. On the Chinese side, the 'faithful dog' relationship of the past[11] turned into hatred and fear, fomented when the American occupation of Japan ended in 1951. The Americans had induced the Japanese to declare in their post-war constitution that they 'renounced war forever'. They had therefore to assume responsibility for Japan's defence. The peace treaty which its ex-enemies (excluding the Soviet Union) signed with Japan in 1951 was accompanied by a Security Pact which gave the Americans the right to station armed forces in and around Japan.

In 1950 Communist China invaded and conquered Tibet, and Communist North Korea invaded South Korea. President Truman then sent the American Seventh Fleet to patrol the Straits of Formosa and prevent the Communists from invading that island.

The Korean War 1950-53

On 1 December 1943 Roosevelt, Churchill and Chiang Kai-Shek had declared that when Korea was liberated from the Japanese it should be 'independent and free'.

In the six days during which the Soviet Union was at war with Japan, from 8 to 14 August 1945, Red Army troops entered North Korea. A little later a small American force landed in South Korea. The Russians and the Americans respectively accepted the Japanese surrender along the line of the 38th Parallel, which runs through the middle of the peninsula. The Americans planned to withdraw after a government for the whole of Korea had been established by 'free elections'; the Russians insisted on dealing only with the Communist Koreans. No agreement could be reached; so the Americans held free elections in their zone, which endorsed the government of the aged and corrupt Syngman Rhee, and the Russians then set up a Communist government in their zone. Both great powers armed their *protégés*, and then withdrew their own forces.

On 25 June 1950 North Korea invaded South Korea. The invasion probably had the blessing of Stalin but, 'all the available evidence shows that (it) caught Mao unprepared.'[12] The

American reaction was immediate and strong. On 26 June President Truman brought the matter before the United Nations' Security Council and secured a resolution to send a United Nations' army to help the South Koreans. The resolution escaped the Soviet veto because the Soviet Union was boycotting the Council on account of the refusal to admit Communist China. This *ad hoc* international army, the first of its kind since the Crusades, consisted, by 1951, of nearly 500,000 men: 50 per cent American, 30 per cent Korean, 5 per cent British, and the rest drawn from 14 other countries. The American General MacArthur, who had been in charge of the American occupation of Japan, was placed in command.

After some tough fighting, the invaders were thrown out of South Korea by the end of September 1950. The Americans, in the grip of anti-Communist hysteria, now secured United Nations' support for the invasion of North Korea. Warnings that the Chinese would intervene were ignored. As the United Nations' army approached the Chinese frontier, a large Chinese army, equipped with Soviet arms and aeroplanes, invaded North Korea. The possibility of war between Communist China and the United States loomed up. Britain and France urged caution on President Truman, and the Soviet Union on the Chinese. When General MacArthur began to advocate publicly that the United States should bomb China the President abruptly dismissed him. Both sides drew back from the brink, and after very severe ground fighting and long drawn-out negotiations a compromise settlement was reached which left the frontier between North and South Korea at the 38th Parallel. The atmosphere had been eased by Stalin's death in March 1953. The settlement was only an armistice; by 1970 no peace treaty had been concluded. It is estimated that 3,000,000 out of Korea's population of 30,000,000 died in this war. American casualties amounted to 147,000 and those of the other United Nations' troops to 17,000.[13]

The French War in Indo-China: 1946-1954

In the post-war decade the French refusal to consider

decolonization involved them in two bloody colonial wars, in Algeria and in Vietnam. The Vietnam War was an important episode in the Cold War because the League for the Independence of Vietnam (Vietminh) was led by Ho Chi Minh, who called himself a Communist. Ho Chi Minh's Communism was of the Tito-ist type. He wanted national independence combined with a social revolution which would give the peasants a better standard of life. His movement was indigenous, and apparently received no encouragement from Stalin, at least at first, nor was it directly linked with the Chinese Communists.[14] The Americans gave the French money and supplies; and when the French finally suffered a disastrous defeat in the battle of Dien Bien Phu in May 1954, Secretary of State Dulles considered military intervention but was restrained by Churchill, now Prime Minister of Britain again. The British and Russians acted as mediators at a conference held at Geneva in June 1954, at which the Communist Chinese and the Americans as well as the French and the Vietnamese were represented. It was agreed to divide Vietnam temporarily along the 17th Parallel. The French would evacuate North Vietnam and Ho Chi Minh would evacuate South Vietnam, where the French had already set up a puppet government. A separate Declaration, from which the American Government disassociated itself, called for 'free elections' throughout the country in 1956 as a prelude to its reunification. Since Communist North Vietnam contained the greater part of the Vietnamese population, and since there were also a number of Vietminh supporters in the South, the elections would have produced a Communist government. The Americans then began to replace the French as the dominant influence in South Vietnam, and to pour in economic aid and military advisers. South Vietnam was strategically important in the policy of 'containing Communism'.

The Re-arming of West Germany: 1950-55

Now that the Americans were becoming deeply involved in the Far East they began to take a fresh look at their commitments in Europe. The Europeans, whose economies were miraculously recovering after the injection of Marshall Aid, must, they felt, assume greater responsibility for their own defence. (The Americans were bearing 75 per cent of the costs of NATO.) They therefore demanded that West Germany should be re-armed, and threatened, if Britain and France refused, to with-draw from their military commitment to Europe. To many Europeans who only five years earlier had been released from the Nazi hell the thought of a renewal of German militarism was traumatic; the Germans themselves wanted to remain disarmed.

In October 1950, the French Government made a far-sighted and imaginative proposal: they suggested that a Western *European* army should be formed, in which officers and men of the various nationalities, including the Germans, would wear a European uniform and serve under a European flag. Since in democratic countries armies must be under civilian control, the European army would require a European government to give it orders, and a European parliament to control the European government and vote the army's budget. The European Defence Community (EDC), as it was to be called, would thus be a device for promoting the creation of the United States of Europe. The West German, Italian and Benelux Governments responded en-thusiastically, and after long negotiations a treaty was signed in Paris by the six governments in May 1952. Five parliaments duly ratified the Treaty but in August 1954 the French Parlia-ment rejected it, partly because Britain had refused to join, and the French wanted British support to counterbalance the Germans, and partly because of a failure of nerve, deepened by the defeat in Indo-China, at the prospect of the substantial surrender of sovereignty involved.

Dulles had already threatened that if the EDC project were rejected, the United States would have to make an 'agonizing reappraisal' of its policies towards Europe. The situation was saved by Sir Anthony Eden, the British Foreign Secretary, who proposed the use of the Brussels Treaty Organization as an alternative to the EDC. West Germany was to recreate its army and place it entirely under NATO, which it was now invited to join; it was to be forbidden to manufacture atomic weapons;

and Britain agreed to commit four divisions of troops and a tactical air force unit to the defence of the Continent for the duration of the Brussels Treaty, i.e. fifty years – a commitment which if made a year or two earlier might have saved the EDC.

An imaginative project had foundered on the rock of national emotion. In rejecting their own plan the French had conjured up again the ghost of German militarism. By 1955 they were no longer really afraid of this ghost; but the Russians were. To the Soviet Union the combination of German military prowess and American technology was menacing. The re-arming of West Germany must be considered a central factor in the development of the Cold War in Europe.

Seato and Cento

By 1955, Dulles had crowned the policy of 'containing Communism' by negotiating two more military alliances to supplement NATO. The South-East Asia Treaty Organization (SEATO), formed in 1954 after the French defeat in Vietnam, comprised the United States, Britain, France, Australia, New Zealand, Pakistan, Thailand and the Philippines. (The United States' military intervention in Vietnam was based on a protocol to this alliance which offered South Vietnam, Cambodia and Laos 'protection' in somewhat ambiguous terms). The Central Treaty Organization (CENTO), formed in 1955, consisted of the United States, Britain, Pakistan, Persia, Turkey and Iraq – the latter withdrew in 1958. It will be noted that most of the newly independent countries in the Middle East and South East Asia refused to join either organization.

The Communist world was now ringed around by the American military presence. From bases in West Germany, Greece, Turkey, Iran, Thailand, South Korea and Japan American aircraft, armed with atom bombs, ceaselessly encircled the Communist frontiers. The fleets of the United States and its Allies patrolled the Pacific, the Persian Gulf, the Mediterranean, the Atlantic and the Arctic seas. There were, however, no Russian or Chinese bases within 2,000 miles of the populated industrial centres of America, and only the Russian fishing fleet (probably spying as well as fishing) came near its shores. Many a decent Communist citizen, indoctrinated to think the worst of Western motives, may have felt that *his* country was threatened by a sinister capitalist conspiracy directed by evil men in the Pentagon.

The Warsaw Pact

The re-arming of West Germany provoked the Russians into making a counter alliance to NATO. In May 1955, the Warsaw Pact was concluded between the Soviet Union and all the Eastern European Communist states except Yugoslavia. (Albania withdrew in 1961 when it became a satellite of China). The Pact was, however, in a sense a formality, since all these states except Albania already had bilateral security treaties with the Soviet Union.

Conclusion

In 1955 the Russians agreed to withdraw their forces from Austria and to allow that country to be established as an independent democratic state which, though technically neutral, had its frontiers wide open to the West.

The Cold War was now stabilized. Between 1955 and 1970, the only new country to join the 'Communist world bloc' was Cuba. In Europe the Iron Curtain froze into rigidity, cemented by the building of the Berlin Wall in 1961 and the occupation of Czechoslovakia by Soviet troops in 1968. But the character of the Cold War changed greatly after 1953, when Stalin died, and when the Russians exploded a hydrogen bomb.

REFERENCES

1. Djilas, Milovan, *Conversation With Stalin*, Penguin, London, 1963, pp. 140–1.
2. Woodhouse, C. M., *A Short History of Modern Greece*, Praeger, New York, 1968, p. 259.
3. Smith, Walter Bedell, *Moscow Mission 1946–49*, Heinemann, London, 1950, pp. 41–2.

55

4. Kennan, George F., *Memoirs 1925–1950*, Brown and Co., Boston, 1967, p. 322.
5. Tito's speech to the Sixth Congress of the Communist Party of Yugoslavia in November 1952. Quoted in: Dedijer, Vladimir, *Tito Speaks*, Weidenfeld and Nicolson, London, 1953, pp. 262–3.
6. US Agency for International Development Statistics, 1967.
7. Figures supplied by the Central Statistical Office, London.
8. Heater, Derek, *The Cold War*, Oxford University Press, London, 1965, p. 28.
9. Kennan, *op. cit.*, p. 408.
10. Institute of Strategic Studies, *Strategic Survey*, 1970, p. 137.
11. Halle, Louis J., *The Cold War as History*, Harper and Row, New York, 1967, p. 194.
12. Lukacs, John, *A History of the Cold War*, Doubleday and Co., New York, 1961, p. 89.
13. *Ibid.*, p. 90.
14. Halle, *op. cit.*, p. 291.

4. The democratic countries of Western Europe

The Background

In the past two hundred years all Western European countries have been confronted with the problem of transforming a feudal into a modern society. In government this has meant replacing religiously sanctified customs, and the Divine Right of Kings, by secular law and constitutional systems. Would this transformation be achieved by violent revolution – as Marx claimed was inevitable – or by gradual evolution?

Throughout feudal Europe there had been assemblies composed of 'houses' or 'estates', representing castes – clergy, nobles and burgesses; the peasants were never represented. In Britain, Scandinavia, the Netherlands and Switzerland these feudal assemblies were gradually and peacefully transformed into modern democratic legislatures in which all citizens were represented as individuals, and the executive power was controlled by the legislature. The civil rights of the individual were also peacefully secured. In Britain the process was so gradual that no written constitution was necessary. Peaceful change was possible because the majority of the privileged classes accepted liberal ideas and were willing to surrender power to 'the masses'. In the other countries of Western and Central Europe there was no such gradual evolution. Violent revolution or the upheavals of war were necessary to overthrow the great feudal hierarchies, supported, in many cases, by the hierarchic Roman Catholic

57

Church. Constitutional democracy was born in painful travail in the decades following the French Revolution.

In seeking to establish democratic constitutions the countries of Europe had two models, the British and the American: the one based on the cabinet system, which integrates executive and legislature by placing the government inside parliament, and making the government dependent on always securing a parliamentary majority; the other based on the presidential system, the separation of executive and legislature, each directly elected by popular vote. In the British system Parliament is sovereign, and statute law must be applied by the Courts as the law of the land. In the American system the written constitution is, in effect, sovereign, since the Supreme Court of nine judges can rule acts of legislature and executive unconstitutional.

The First and Second French Empires, the Second German Reich and the Austro-Hungarian Empire in its latter years were autocratic versions of the presidential system : rule by hereditary emperors whom the legislatures could not control nor the electors replace. Switzerland evolved a democratic constitution similar to that of the United States. The executive branch is outside the legislature although appointed by it. It consists of a seven-man Federal Council which acts as a unit, rather than an individual chief executive, like the President of the United States. The other European countries adopted the British model.

An essential feature of constitutional democracy is the freedom to form political parties. In Britain, where this freedom prevails, the two-party system which developed in the seventeenth century is basic to the constitution; the party which provides 'Her Majesty's Government' confronts the party which provides 'Her Majesty's Opposition'. The two-party system is underpinned by the electoral system, whereby each Member of Parliament is elected by a simple majority in each constituency, and small parties are thus discouraged. But more fundamentally, it depends on two factors: the reconciliation of particular interests *within* each party, so that each can offer the country broad national policies; and a kind of tacit agreement *between* the parties that on many major issues they will agree to differ, or even support each other, rather than fight each other to the death. British party politics is pragmatic in style, rejecting abstract ideologies in favour of seeking the common-sense solution in each situation.

Before 1945 the only European countries where the British model worked well were those of Scandinavia. The others imported the British parliamentary system into societies riven by deep-rooted conflicts between religions, regions, and classes, often sharpened by the shadow of the barricades and the execution yards. The result was a multiplicity of parties, representing the different sectional interests, and fostered by the system of proportional representation, by which each party gains seats in the legislature in proportion to the votes cast for it. In the early thirties there were sixteen parties in the French Chamber and twenty-eight in that of Germany, while even the little country of Latvia had twenty-four.

The multi-party system necessitates coalition governments. Often several weeks of bargaining would be required to reach agreement on the terms and composition of the coalition, and as soon as one of the members of the coalition felt its interests threatened it would break away, the government would lose its parliamentary majority and have to resign, and the process would start over again. The average duration of a government in the Third Republic of France, the Weimar Republic in Germany, and the other countries where this system prevailed was about nine months. Such extreme political instability made it almost impossible to carry out constructive, long-term policies. Politics became a game, often a dirty one; *le système*, the French contemptuously called it.

The Teutons and the Latins, less pragmatic than the Anglo-Saxons, tended to try to impose an intellectual system upon an actual situation, to claim a monopoly of revealed truth and to treat opposition as heretical. In the inter-war years the weak parties of the 'Centre' were in many cases flanked by powerful ideological parties of the 'Right' and the 'Left', which wished to destroy the democratic parliamentary system and establish a one-party state. On the Left were the Communist Parties, dedicated

59

to Marxism, and directed and financed by the Soviet Government through the Comintern, the world Communist organization set up by Lenin in 1919. On the Right were authoritarian parties which, as in Spain and Portugal, based their ideology on the theology of Roman Catholicism; or, as in Germany and Italy, on the Hegelian idea of the state as 'the March of God on Earth', a moral absolute embodied in the god-like figure of the leader.

Immediately after the First World War constitutional democracy and the civil rights of man were established, in however shaky a form, in all European countries except Russia and Turkey. The major challenge confronting these regimes was to deal with basic social and economic problems: to establish the social rights of man – the provision of work, housing, education, and care in sickness and old age; to cure the chronic economic sickness of recurrent booms and slumps; and to ensure the fair distribution of land and the products of industry. The parties of the Centre were broadly divided into two groups: those which believed that the economic structure should be grounded on uncontrolled private ownership and enterprise, and those which stood for socialist policies – for some public ownership of the means of production, distribution and exchange. In Britain and Scandinavia the socialist parties were non-ideological. Elsewhere they tended to draw their inspiration from Marxism while working through the parliamentary system. Most of these socialist parties were founded and financed by the trade unions.

Less clear-cut was the division between those who wished to promote the welfare state – the provision of social services by the state – and those who regarded it as a threat to individual freedom. The Papacy, for instance, while condemning democracy in the *Syllabus of Modern Errors* of 1864, and affirming that the rights of private property are ordained by God, had also enjoined governments to institute the welfare state in the Encyclical *Rerum Novarum* of 1891. In general, the socialist parties stood for the rapid introduction of the welfare state, while the non-socialist parties adopted a *laissez-faire* attitude to social reform.

In the inter-war years parties which stood for democratic

socialism, for carrying out programmes of nationalization and the promotion of welfare services within the framework of constitutional democracy, achieved effective power only in Scandinavia: in Denmark in 1929, in Sweden in 1932 and in Norway in 1935. The industrial revolution came late to these countries, and the Social Democrats were therefore able to launch them into the modern world without the slums and other horrors of 'exploitation'. And social welfare proved, in practice, a far larger component in their policies than nationalization. In 1960 ninety-five per cent of Swedish industry was still in private hands, four per cent was owned by co-operatives, and only one per cent by the state. So solid was this 'consensus' politics that in Sweden and Denmark the Social Democrats were still in power in 1970, and in Norway up till 1965, when they were replaced by a coalition of other parties with similar policies.

Elsewhere, in the inter-war years, there was only a foretaste of Social Democratic rule. The British Labour Party was in power for two short periods, but since it was dependent on the parliamentary support of the *laissez-faire* Liberal Party, it could carry out no measures of nationalization, and meanwhile the Conservative Party, which ruled Britain for most of this period, was developing the social services which the Liberals had started before 1914. The Social Democrats controlled the City Council of Vienna from 1919 to 1934 and carried out many reforms. In France the Socialist Party, led by Léon Blum, carried out more reforms between May 1936 and June 1937 with the parliamentary support of the Communist Party, than the non-Socialist parties of the Third Republic achieved in twenty years.

With these exceptions, parliamentary democracy meant *immobilisme*; and those who wanted movement and change – the underprivileged, the unemployed, the young – as well as those who looked back with nostalgia to the old caste system – the aristocracy (especially in Germany) and some of the Roman Catholic hierarchy – turned to the anti-democratic parties of the Left and the Right, both of which offered social reforms, the Communists with nationalization and the Fascists without it. In Italy, France and Germany, the local Communist Party's subservience to the Soviet Union split the working-class movement, crippled the forces of social democracy, and gave Right Wing dictators their cue to take over in order to save European civilization and the propertied classes from 'the Red Peril'. By 1939 parliamentary democracy had given way to Fascist dictatorship in Italy, Germany, Spain, Portugal and Austria, and to semi-parliamentary dictatorships in all Central and Eastern European countries except Czechoslovakia. And in France the Right Wing brought down Blum's 'Popular Front' government, although they did not destroy the regime. Parliamentary democracy had failed in Europe; and its failure made the Second World War more or less inevitable.

The terrible experiences of the war prepared the way for a new start. For people who fought together in the Resistance, who suffered together in the concentration camps, who lost all their property, the barriers of class, region and religion fell away. There was a new determination to make democracy work and to press ahead with economic and social reforms. The Right Wing parties were utterly discredited. Most of the other pre-war parties re-emerged, but there were two significant changes. First, the Roman Catholic Church, hitherto the bastion of conservatism, now threw its weight behind democracy as well as social reform. This led to the rise of 'Christian Democrat' parties in West Germany, Italy, France (called the *Mouvement Républicain Populaire* – MRP), Belgium, the Netherlands and Austria (the Austrian Peoples' Party). In Italy the Pope had forbidden the Popular Party, formed in the early twenties by an idealistic priest, to make an alliance with the Socialists which might have prevented Mussolini from coming to power. Elsewhere the pre-war 'Clerical' parties, which were allied to the Church, had pursued conservative *laissez-faire* policies. In general the new Christian Democratic parties stood for private ownership – although they were not opposed to the nationalization of the major public utilities – and for major measures of social welfare. They called themselves 'Christian' because they wanted to relate politics to morality, and to religion in the broader sense. In Germany and the Netherlands the Christian Democrats included many Protestants; and everywhere except in Italy these parties proclaimed themselves 'non-confessional'; that is, they rejected any control by the Roman Catholic Church over their affairs. They were pragmatic, non-ideological parties.

The second change lay in the situation of the Communist Parties. In all the occupied countries they had played a magnificent part in the Resistance. By 1945 they had therefore gained a sort of heroic respectability, which led to their inclusion until 1947 in the governments formed in France and Italy – the first time that Communist Ministers served in any Western European democratic governments.

France

When the French government surrendered to the Germans in June 1940 General Charles de Gaulle, a junior general of outstanding ability, fled to England and set himself up as the leader of the 'Free French'. During the war Churchill and Roosevelt gave him their support, but there were many emotional clashes, which were to influence his attitude to Britain and the United States many years later. When he made a triumphal entry into Paris on 26 August 1944 he was the acknowledged head of the French Resistance, but since there had been no French government-in-exile, his constitutional position was ambiguous.

Liberated France might have relapsed into civil war and chaos as the Resistance, in which the Communists had played an outstanding part, combatted those who had collaborated with the Nazis. De Gaulle succeeded in absorbing the Resistance leaders, including the Communist leaders, into a provisional government of National Union with himself as its head. He persuaded the semi-autonomous Resistance Committees scattered over France to hand over local administration to the prefects, the re-appointed agents of the central government. He thus saved France from the danger of anarchy, but at the price of restoring the traditional highly centralized administrative system.

The leaders of the Nazi's puppet regime (the Vichy regime), Marshal Pétain and Pierre Laval, and those Frenchmen who had worked directly for the Nazis, were tried for treason. About 800 people, including Laval, were executed (de Gaulle commuted the death sentence of the aged Marshal); some 40,000 were imprisoned, and minor collaborators were deprived of civic rights and expelled from the revived political parties. There were also a number of acts of private revenge.

The constitution of the Fourth Republic was drawn up in the most democratic possible way. Women were given the vote and then, in October 1945, the electors voted in a referendum to have a new constitution. A constituent assembly was elected, but the constitution which it drew up was rejected by the electors in a second referendum, mainly because it had certain features which might have enabled the Communists to come to power. Another constitution was drawn up, of a slightly more conservative nature, and was approved in a third referendum by a majority of 1,000,000 votes, with 8,000,000 electors abstaining. On this doubtful mandate the Fourth Republic came into being.

The new constitution was essentially the same as that of the Third Republic (1875–1940). The legislature consisted of two Chambers, the National Assembly and the Council of the Republic. The President, the Head of the State, was elected by both Chambers for seven years. He appointed as Prime Minister a Deputy (Member of Parliament) who could command a majority in the National Assembly. The Deputies were elected by proportional representation.

The parties of the Left, the Communists, the Socialists and the new *Mouvement Républicain Populaire* (MRP), dominated the two constituent assemblies – the Communists had won twenty-five per cent of the votes, the Socialists twenty-three per cent. They pledged themselves, in the Resistance Charter of 1944, to a programme of fundamental social and economic reforms. The provisional government immediately began to implement this programme. The mines, railways, main power stations, Air France and most of the banks were nationalized, together with the Renault motor works, which the Germans had taken over in the war. A major programme of social security was enacted and a planning commission was set up under Jean Monnet, later to be the chief founding father of the European Economic Community, to plan the modernization and expansion of French industry. 'Hundreds of professors, industrialists, trade unionists, civil servants and assorted experts served without salary on the twenty-five committees which made recommendations to the commission'.[1] The first of a series of Five Year Plans was launched in 1946. Finally, an Economic and Social Council was set up, representing all major sectors of production, whose advice had to be sought by the government on all measures of an economic and social character.

The first constituent assembly unanimously elected General de Gaulle as acting Head of State, and he included five Communist leaders in his first government, formed in November 1945. Then, in January 1946, he suddenly resigned, because neither the constituent assembly nor the electors wished to adopt the American-type presidential constitution which he advocated in order to provide for a strong executive and to prevent a return to *le système*. He proceeded to build up his own extra-parliamentary movement, the *Rassemblement du Peuple Français* (RPF), which stood for a kind of democratic paternalism, offering what the novelist André Malraux called 'the myth of a new type: the liberal hero'. In May 1947 the French Communist Party, directed by the Cominform, demanded the rejection of American Marshall Aid and of military alliances, and instigated nation-wide strikes involving about 3,000,000 people. The Socialist Minister of the Interior had to use armed force to crush them, collaborators raised their heads and, with others who feared Communism, threw their support behind the RPF. In the election of 1951 the two extremist parties polled a total of forty-eight per cent of the votes and the RPF was the largest single party in the country. If it had not been for the introduction of a new electoral system which favoured the Centre parties, one or other might have been able to form a government. After 1951, however, the threat of extremism subsided, partly because both these parties lacked the support of the press, the radio and the nascent television, and partly because of the economic recovery resulting from Marshall Aid. In 1955 de Gaulle severed his relations with the discredited and declining RPF, and withdrew into private life in his home in the village of Colombey-les-Deux-Eglises. In the election of 1956 the RPF vote fell to under four per cent of the total. The Communists were now the largest party in the National Assembly, since they were stealing the working-class vote from the Socialists; a stable government depended on their support.

Maurice Thorez, the French Communist leader, was a diehard Stalinist. The Party's organization was authoritarian, and its adherence to the Moscow Party Line dogmatic. 'As in Russia, those who rose to power in the Party were the natural bureaucrats rather than the natural revolutionaries . . . "fossilized" in their refusal to confront new ideas or recognize new circumstances'.[2] The Party was failing to lead the real revolutionary movement, the movement to secure the *participation* of the workers in the industrial transformation of the country. It clung to the fantasy of carrying out a Lenin-type revolution through a highly disciplined party machine – a revolution which no-one in France really wanted. 'All public opinion polls and all political science investigations . . . show that the majority of those who vote Communist are not Communists, but voters who simply want to express their opposition to the Government'.[3] Many of France's leading intellectuals were Marxists but in 1956 they were deeply disillusioned by Khrushchev's revelations about Stalin's crimes and by Soviet suppression of the Hungarian revolt.

Between September 1944 and June 1958 there were twenty-seven governments in France. The precarious balance of the fourteen parties of the Centre finally broke down under the impact of the Algerian war which had started in 1954. In a hideous conflict of terrorism, reprisals and torture 9,000,000 Muslims were fighting the French for the right to self-government. By 1958 hysteria prevailed. The supporters of the war included the army, determined not to suffer the humiliation of a third major military defeat within twenty years; the Algerian *colons* (the million French settlers in Algeria); the Right-Wing conservatives, and a great many ordinary Frenchmen who could not bear to think that their young men were being killed and their taxes spent for a bad cause (by 1958 there were 350,000 French troops in Algeria and the war was costing £1,000,000 a day). The opponents of the war included many intellectuals and academic personalities, such as Sartre, who regarded it as a betrayal of the ideals of liberty, equality and fraternity; the Communist Party; some members of the Socialist and MRP Parties, and many ordinary French men whose consciences were deeply troubled. France was being pilloried by the Arab states at the United Nations, and it looked as if the conflict might be 'internationalized'.

In May 1958, after four weeks without a government, Monsieur Pflimlin, a leader of the MRP, managed to form one with Communist support. Fearing imminent betrayal by Paris, the career army officers and the *colons* carried out a *Putsch* in Algeria on 13 May, setting up Committees of Public Safety to rule the country in defiance of the Paris Government. The conscripts, listening to the news from Paris on their transistors, did not believe what their officers told them and adopted an independent-minded position. Since the rebels were demanding the complete integration of *Algérie française* into France, their revolt implied that they would attempt to seize power in Paris. A few days later they took over Corsica unopposed. The Pflimlin Government knew that if the paratroopers landed on the mainland, the metropolitan army and police could not be trusted to obey orders to oppose them. France seemed to be on the brink of either military dictatorship or civil war.

In this hour of crisis the eyes of Frenchmen and of Algerians, both *colons* and Muslims, turned towards the inscrutable man at Colombey-les-Deux-Eglises. On 15 May de Gaulle issued a written statement to the press:

... Faced with problems too hard for the regime to tackle, France has, for the last twelve years, followed a disastrous road. In the past, the country from its very depths entrusted me with the task of leading it to salvation. Today, with new

67

ordeals facing it, let the country know that I am ready to assume the powers of the Republic.[4]

De Gaulle's terms were that he should rule by decree for six months and then submit a new constitution to the country. The only constitutional alternative would have been a 'popular front' government with the Communists – a solution which might have precipitated civil war. So on 1 June he became Prime Minister, with the support of a majority of a hundred Deputies in the Chamber, of the army and of the *colons*. His pronouncements on the Algerian war were couched in riddles, but the *colons*, the army and the majority of the French people all felt that he would somehow safeguard their interests and honour.

As a political system the Fourth Republic had proved even weaker than the Third Republic of the inter-war years because the extremist parties were more powerful. But in the Third Republic the political system had conditioned economic, social and foreign policy. Because the political system was weak, foreign policy was weak and there was little progress in economic and social affairs. In the Fourth Republic the political system seemed to flourish in a kind of vacuum. Foreign policy, until the middle of 1953 in the sole hands of two ministers of the MRP Party, Georges Bidault and Robert Schuman, was in general far-sighted and constructive. France was a solid partner in the Western Alliance and the imaginative initiator of the new Europe. In economic and social affairs there was great progress (see below), supervised by the Planning Commission, which functioned independently of the Assembly and the parties.

The constitution of the Fifth Republic was drawn up by de Gaulle and his Minister of Justice, Michel Debré, submitted to a referendum in September 1958, and approved by an eighty per cent vote. Since it was not open to the voters to comment on the ninety-two articles, the referendum was in effect a vote of confidence in the General. The institutions of the Fifth Republic were similar to those of the Fourth and the Third – a two-Chamber Legislature, a Cabinet headed by a Prime Minister, and a President as Head of the State. But de Gaulle's determination to create a strong executive produced certain important changes: the ministers could not be members of either Chamber of the Legislature, which made it possible to appoint to the highest executive posts technocrats instead of politicians; the office of President, hitherto mainly a ceremonial post, was transformed into that of an American-style Chief Executive. He took this office over himself in January 1959, and until his retirement in April 1969 his Prime Ministers (Michel Debré till 1962, Georges Pompidou till July 1968, and Couve de Murville till April 1969) were merely his chief assistants. In 1962 he further strengthened the position of the President by a referendum to alter the constitution by making the President directly elected by popular vote, as in the United States, instead of indirectly, by members of both Chambers and municipal councils. In the United States the enormous executive power wielded by the President is counter-balanced by the very strong powers of criticism, of legislative veto and of financial control exercised by Congress. De Gaulle's third change was to weaken the powers of the Legislature. The President could dissolve it at will; it was not allowed to sit for more than six months of the year and in times of crisis he could govern by decree for six months. The electoral system reverted from the proportional representation of the Fourth Republic to the single-member system with second ballot of the Third – a system which favours larger parties or the formation of coalitions by the smaller parties.

Although de Gaulle had gained the support of the *colons* and the army in Algeria by appearing to be on their side, he had no intention of fighting the war to a finish. In September 1959 he announced his decision to offer Algeria 'self-determination'. In 1961 the generals in Algeria staged another revolt, with which he dealt firmly, using his special constitutional powers, and then secured endorsement of his policy from seventy-five per cent of the electors in yet another referendum. Meanwhile the war had entered a yet more hideous phase. Some of the extremist *colons*, together with certain dissident generals and officers, formed the

Organisation de l'Armée Secrète (OAS), which fought the regular army and the Gaullist government as well as the Muslims by indiscriminate bombing, murdering and torture in France as well as in Algeria. All the latent chauvinist elements in the country came to the surface, and there were several attempts to assassinate de Gaulle.

In March 1962 Algerian independence was finally negotiated and overwhelmingly endorsed by the French people, who were now profoundly grateful to the General for bringing the war to an end. But the settlement drove the OAS to further frenzy in Algeria. Muslims were daily lynched, their property was bombed and burnt, and even *colons* who were trying to flee to France were attacked. The higher ranks of the army were split. One famous Free French general, asked to preside over the trial of his colleagues in the OAS for treason, committed suicide.[5] To have brought the army to heel between 1958 and 1962 was one of de Gaulle's major achievements; but it had been a bitter experience.

The Second World War did not, like the first, slaughter a whole generation of French youth. Instead, it discredited the reactionaries of the older generation and moulded, in the Resistance and Free French movements, a new generation who were more interested in promoting economic progress than in playing the political game. By 1970 the sixth Five Year Plan was in force. The Planning Commission and the Economic and Social Council had extended their scope into all economic and social fields, including productivity, marketing, housing, health and education. The new method of seeking co-operation between major interest groups was being employed to achieve an *économie concertée*:[6] the new technocrats were carrying out a technological revolution. 'In ... fifteen years French engineering had risen from a European sub-standard to the equivalent of the world's best'.[7] Industrial modernization was accompanied by agricultural modernization: the numbers living on the land fell from over forty per cent in 1940 to seventeen per cent in 1968 – although French agriculture still remained backward in comparison with that of Britain, where only three per cent of the people lived on the land. A social transformation was also occurring as a result of the introduction of the welfare state and the expansion of educational opportunities, providing secondary education for the masses. But economic and social change brings dislocation and insecurity in its train.

By 1968 the democratic paternalism of the Fifth Republic had given France a more stable government than it had enjoyed for a century. De Gaulle's complex and majestic personality dominated the political scene and he regarded himself as embodying the power of the French people in a unique way. His ministers' tasks were to carry out the decisions which he reached in consultation with himself. In 1958 a new Gaullist Party was formed, the *Union Démocratique de la République* (UDR). Its sole policy was to support de Gaulle's leadership, but it attracted many of the young non-political technocrats who were modernizing the country.

De Gaulle's foreign policies pleased the average Frenchman by restoring his *amour propre* after the humiliation of crushing military defeats. The partial disengagement from NATO and the friendly hand held out to the Communist bloc helped to reconcile the Left to the regime. Yet there was much criticism from the press, the intellectuals and the leaders of the traditional parties. De Gaulle won the presidential election of 1965 by only a small majority and in the parliamentary election of 1967 the Gaullist majority was also considerably reduced. After its decline in the fifties, the Communist vote had risen to twenty-two per cent of the total, partly because after Maurice Thorez's death in 1964 the Communist leadership adopted 'revisionist' policies. 'Of course we are a revolutionary party, but in France revolution can only be achieved by democratic means', said their new leader, M. Waldeck-Rochet, in 1967.[8]

Suddenly, in May 1968, a revolutionary situation developed. It started with the students, who since March had been disrupting the new university annex at Nanterre, outside Paris, and who in early May transferred their agitation to the Sorbonne in Paris. The student leaders belonged to the 'New Left' of 'Trotskyites, Maoists, Guevarists' and other extremist groups, but they expressed the genuine grievances of the majority. There were too many students in French universities – 700,000, twice as many as in 1960, and nearly three times as many as in Britain – for the available facilities. Classes were too large, teaching methods too formal, amenities inadequate, and the rigid, centrally-fixed curricula out of date. The drop-out rate was thirty per cent. But there was also a deeper cause for the demand for a 'cultural revolution': a protest against the depersonalization of modern society.

The Rector of the Sorbonne called in the police, who arrested the student leaders and were withdrawn only after many clashes over barricades erected by the students. Then 8,000,000 workers took advantage of the situation to go on strike. The public services and most of the larger industrial concerns were paralysed. Although the students were agitating among the workers, the trade unions were determined to keep the two movements separate, for they were interested only in securing concrete economic gains for themselves. The Communist Party was taken by surprise; here, it seemed, was the classic revolutionary situation for which they had been preparing for decades; but with some embarrassment they threw their weight on the side of law and order. The government was also taken by surprise and after consulting the army leaders, de Gaulle ordered a parliamentary election. Meanwhile, Prime Minister Pompidou granted the trade union leaders a thirty-five per cent increase in minimum wages and persuaded the employers to negotiate new collective agreements. The strikers slowly returned to work.

The election, held at the end of June 1968, produced an overwhelming Gaullist majority: the French people did not want revolution. It was not a victory for de Gaulle, but for Pompidou, the man who had held the situation steady. In July de Gaulle dismissed him, with sixty journalists of liberal views who worked for the government-controlled radio and television.[9] The 'faceless' Couve de Murville became Prime Minister.

De Gaulle now set in hand long-term educational reforms, involving some devolution of authority from Paris to the universities and high schools; a measure of faculty and student participation in their administration; the establishment of two new experimental universities, and the expansion of technical education. A phase of hopeful educational experimentation opened. Then early in 1969 he put forward the idea of *participation*, not of workers in management, which was strenuously opposed by the employers, but as the devolution of responsibility for many local matters to new regional councils of parliamentary Deputies and representatives of employers, workers and other interests. He also proposed that the Senate, the Upper Chamber of the Legislature, should become a purely advisory body. To many Frenchmen this savoured of dictatorship, since the Senate represented local interests and served as a curb on the Lower Chamber. In April 1969 the electors were asked to vote in another referendum on both proposals jointly; but when de Gaulle announced that if the proposals were rejected he would resign, it was clear that he was again demanding a vote of confidence in himself. Fifty-two per cent of the electors voted 'no', and on 28 April he went into final retirement. In the ensuing presidential election Pompidou, the Gaullist candidate, won by a large majority. The Communist candidate, who was reported never to have used the word 'Communist' during his campaign, did far better than expected, and the non-Communist Left far worse.

Under the Fifth Republic France seemed at last to have moved away from the multi-party system. But in 1970 the Gaullist majority party was not yet confronted by an effective parliamentary opposition, except for that provided by the Communist Party, now part of the establishment. The discontent which had exploded in May 1968 was still simmering near the surface. De Gaulle's large expenditure on armaments in support of his expansionist foreign policy had delayed vital internal reforms needed to keep pace with social changes.

In November 1970 General de Gaulle died. The verdict of history will surely place him among the great men of France: in the dark days of the German Occupation he kept his country's honour and resistance alive; in 1945 he united divided France and secured the relatively painless birth of the Fourth

Republic; in 1958–62 he performed the apparent miracle of granting independence to Algeria without civil war in France; during the eleven years in which he ruled the Fifth Republic France enjoyed an unprecedented political stability, which gave her new confidence. On the debit side, de Gaulle's old-fashioned nationalism was inconsistent with the realities of French power in the post-war world. His policies side-tracked France from the historic task, undertaken by the leaders of the Fourth Republic, of playing a major part in 'creating Europe'.

West Germany

When the 47,000,000 West Germans were allowed by the Occupation Powers to form the Federal Republic of Germany in 1949, they faced very formidable problems: a country destroyed by bombs; a 'lost generation' in 3,500,000 battle deaths; and an inescapable burden of shame. After the terrible failure of their first experiment in democracy (the Weimar Republic of 1919–33) would they be able to make democratic institutions work? How would relations develop with their ex-enemies, on whom they were now dependent?

The constitution of the Federal Republic was set out in the Basic Law of 1949. It confirmed the federal structure of the state which the occupation authorities had established. There were ten *Länder* or states, some of them states of the ancient German empire, some of them new creations. Bonn, a small university town on the Rhine, was to be the provisional federal capital pending the reunification of Germany.

The constitution, like that of the Weimar Republic, is based on the Cabinet system, but to avoid the danger of popular election of a hero-figure, the president is chosen, not by plebiscite, as in the Weimar constitution, but by the federal and state parliaments. The constitution, which is interpreted by a Constitutional Court, resembling the Supreme Court of the United States, guarantees the right to form political parties, provided that their structures and programmes are democratic. To prevent the proliferation of parties which debilitated the Weimar Republic, half the parliamentary deputies are elected by proportional representation, half by the simple majority system, and no party can be represented unless it gets at least five per cent of the votes.

The Basic Law guarantees freedom of the press; and the policy of the occupying authorities in appointing carefully selected anti-Nazi newspaper editors bore fruit. The radio and television network, which the Allies decentralized and placed in the hands of independent bodies representative of various sections of society, maintained its independence of the state and federal governments – in contrast to the situation in France, where both were government-controlled.

The number of political parties shrank from nine in 1949 to three in 1961. There are two major parties, the Christian Democratic Union (CDU) and the Social Democratic Party (SDP). Both are moderate and non-ideological in attitude, drawing adherents from all classes and sections of the nation. The CDU was born out of an alliance of Roman Catholics and Protestants forged in the war. It also contains trade unionists and others who want social reform, and capitalists and liberals who believe in a free-enterprise economy. The SDP, the only survivor of Germany's pre-war parties, finally substituted 'democratic socialism' for Marxism as the basis of its philosophy in 1959, and announced its support for a mixed economy, the revival of the German army, the linking of West Germany to Western Europe, and the churches. The Free Democratic Party (FDP), a small party which in 1965 switched from a conservative to a liberal orientation, has at times held the fate of the two major parties in its hands. Extremist parties – the tiny post-war Nazi Party and the Communist Party – were banned by the Constitutional Court in the fifties as undemocratic in structure and ideology.

In West Germany's first elections, held in August 1949, the CDU and the SDP each won about a third of the seats in the *Bundestag* (the lower house of the federal parliament). Dr Konrad Adenauer was elected Chancellor by a majority of one vote, his position depending on the support of the FDP and another small party. In the elections of 1953 and 1957 the CDU won a clear majority over the SDP and the FDP but in 1961 the CDU vote fell and the Party was again obliged to form a coalition with the FDP. Born in 1876, Adenauer had had a distinguished career of public service; his most important post being that of Mayor of Cologne from 1917 to 1933. A devout Roman Catholic, he was also a leader of the Roman Catholic Centre Party in the Weimar Republic. Under the Nazis he had lived in retirement and was for a time in a concentration camp.

West Germany's political, legal and economic institutions were imposed by its victors. Under Christian Democratic leadership they were administered in a spirit of benign authoritarianism. Adenauer was the wise, firm father-figure whom the Germans needed to guide them out of the morass. The fourteen years of his rule have been described as 'Chancellor-democracy'. He treated his Party, the ministers and the legislators as children, disliking independent personalities, such as Dr Gustav Heinemann who resigned from his post as Minister of the Interior in 1952. German politicians and people were unused to thinking of an opposition party as an essential part of the democratic system, and Adenauer, whose formative years were spent under the Second Reich (1871–1918), shared to some extent the Bismarckian attitude that the parliamentary opposition was unfit to rule. In 1963, at the age of 87, he reluctantly relinquished the Chancellorship to Dr Ludwig Erhard, the Minister of Economic Affairs who had promoted West Germany's 'economic miracle'. But Erhard was weak as a politician, and in 1966 he was succeeded by Dr Kurt Kiesinger who had been a Nazi propaganda official during the war and a loyal follower of Adenauer after it. Professor Theodore Heuss, a liberal of outstanding integrity and intellectual distinction, was President from 1949 till 1959 when he was succeeded by Heinrich Lübke, a man of lesser calibre.

The fundamental psychological problem confronting the Germans was to come to terms with what President Heuss called their 'collective shame' – since guilt, as the prosecutors at the Nuremberg trials said, may be regarded as inhering only in individuals.

The West German Goverment continued the occupation powers' policies of bringing Nazi war criminals to trial and of denazification – the weeding out of Nazis from public posts; but both processes moved slowly. By the mid-sixties only some 7,000 war criminals had been convicted, often with surprisingly light sentences – a man tried for major complicity in the murder of 400,000 Hungarian Jews was sentenced to only five years' imprisonment (the death penalty was abolished in West Germany in 1949). This may be contrasted with the action taken in East Germany, whose population was a little more than a third of that of West Germany. The East Germans convicted nearly 13,000 war criminals and gave most of them heavy sentences.[10] Thousands of SS and Gestapo murderers were known to be at large in West Germany, or to have escaped to other continents. The federal parliament was finally impelled to extend the time limit for the investigation of Nazi crimes from 1965 to 1975.

Denazification was also much less thorough in West Germany than in East Germany. The West German Government, unlike that of East Germany, had no ideological model for the creation of a new kind of society. It tended, therefore, tacitly to accept the existing situation, and as a result many of the ordinary officials who had been almost inevitably caught up in the Nazi movement remained in their posts. In the mid-sixties two-thirds of the judges and army officers and half of the officials had served in some capacity under the Nazis.[11] A few senior Nazis held high offices; the head of Adenauer's Chancery, for example, had taken a leading part in drawing up the Nazi racial laws. The problem of denazification particularly affected education:

In the post-war years nearly all teachers had been teachers in the Nazi era. As a result, education in West Germany has been until recently in the hands of people who experienced authority and obedience as the most important things in the world, who were hidden in their ivory tower of science and arts, escaping from political engagement, trying to forget their failure in those twelve years and to let it be forgotten. Only in the last few years has a new generation of teachers, free from mental repression, come on to the stage.[12]

The West German Government compensated the victims of

Nazi persecution and made particular efforts to make amends to the Jews. It paid the survivors of the holocaust seven billion dollars and established friendly relations with Israel, giving $800,000,000 worth of goods in 1952 to help towards the settlement of 500,000 Jews.

The defeat of 1945 was followed by a 'dumbfounded silence' of German writers. But the younger generation who grew up after the war began to ask questions, and a group of young writers, some of whom – Günter Grass, Heinrich Böll and Rolf Hochuth – achieved international fame, almost obsessively confronted the older generation with their past. The older generation did not like it and Dr Erhard called these writers 'yap dogs' who should keep their mouths shut. To reject one's national past is not easy. Here, the small German Resistance movement against Hitler was of great importance, for it offered the Germans national heroes and heroines whose lives and deaths were an inspiration in the creation of a new Germany.[13]

From 1945 to 1955, for the first time in their history, the Germans had no army: none of the military organizations or installations were preserved; the officer corps was 'discredited, dispersed, sunk in the anonymity of civilian life';[14] it was a criminal offence to carry weapons. The recreation of the German army in 1955 at the instigation of the Western Powers was not at first at all popular: *Ohne mich* – 'leave me out' – was the slogan. The Germans were put in a difficult position; they had been condemned for 'militarism' – the exaltation of the military profession and the habits of arrogant authoritarianism and blind obedience which it had inculcated. How could they give their new army a sense of professional pride without reviving some of these habits and thereby arresting the democratization of the country? Everything possible was done to make the new *Bundeswehr* as different as possible from the old *Reichswehr* (which Hitler had renamed the *Wehrmacht*): a homespun citizen army instead of an *élite* caste; an army whose soldiers were trained to defend and not to attack; to think for themselves instead of to obey like robots; to reason instead of to hate. Above all, it was an army under the control of the civilian authorities, an army whose soldiers were allowed to join trade unions.

West Germany's 'economic miracle' was brought about by various factors: political stability; industrial modernization, made possible by the aid given by the Allied occupation forces and the one and a half billion dollars' worth of equipment provided under the Marshall Plan; the fact that for the first six crucial years there was no defence budget; Dr Erhard's 'social market economy'; the absence of industrial strife; and the hard work of the German people.

Dr Erhard's policy was to combine development of the welfare state with free enterprise – the free play of market forces. The underlying attitude implied not so much a rejection of the democratic indicative planning which was being adopted by other West European countries with varying degrees of success (see chapter 8), as of the authoritarian governmental direction and control (though not ownership) of the economy which had underpinned the militarism of the Second and Third Reichs. A leading West German politician has described this economic policy as 'the most important *political* decision made in West Germany since the war'. The success of the social market economy showed the German people that, 'in at least one area of society, order can be brought about without an agency to maintain and regulate it. . . . Its success was the success of an idea that had been as alien to German thinking as democracy itself; and there may . . . be a connection between the two'.[15]

The booming economy made possible the integration of over 15,000,000 refugees – 9,000,000 from the 'Eastern lands' ceded to Poland, 3,000,000 from the Czech Sudetenland, and over 3,000,000 from East Germany. The work force which they provided pushed the economy to even greater strength. Industrial peace was promoted by the development of economic democracy. First, the trade unions, revived by the Allies, were non-political, modern and un-class-conscious in outlook. There were only sixteen, one for each major industry. (Ironically, this sensible reorganization was made on the advice of the British Trade Union Congress, which has been unable to reorganize the 160 chaotic

British unions).[16] Between 1949 and 1962 the unions made 34,000 wage agreements with the employers, which were legally binding on both sides, so that strikes which contravened them were illegal. Second, the principle of co-partnership of workers on boards of management was introduced into German industry. In 1947 it was established by the British in the German coal and steel industries in order to undermine the 'military-industrial power-complex' which had given such sinister support to Hitler. After the occupation the trade unions forced Adenauer, against his will, to make the system permanent. Third, workers were encouraged to hold shares in major industries, such as the partially denationalized *Volkswagen* firm, in order to create a 'property-owning democracy'.

A basic weakness of Christian Democratic rule was the failure to reform the education system, due, as we have suggested, to the fact that the older generation was still in charge. The system remained formalistic and rigid in content, and authoritarian in structure, geared to the formation of an *élite,* and unable to cope with the rapidly increasing number of students. In 1964 only seven per cent of university students came from working-class homes. Despite its affluence, the proportion of its GNP which West Germany spent on education was one of the lowest in Western Europe. In East Germany twice as many students, in proportion to the population, went on to post-school education.

The foreign policy of the Christian Democrats was probably their greatest achievement. Adenauer was determined to reconcile West Germany with the Western Allies, and in particular with France, so he responded at once to the invitations to join the OEEC, the European Community and NATO. The personal friendship which he developed with General de Gaulle helped to create the atmosphere for this reconciliation and thus, at the political level, the enmity which had existed between the two countries since 1870 was at last ended. Towards Eastern Europe Christian Democratic policy was reserved. Adenauer negotiated the return of German prisoners of war from Russia in 1955, but the determination of the Party's leaders not to recognize the legal existence of East Germany nor to accept the permanence of the

Oder-Neisse frontier (on this they pandered to the highly emotional refugee pressure groups) contributed to the Cold War deadlock in Europe (see chapter 3).

During the long period of Christian Democratic rule the Social Democrats, although treated by the CDU with scant respect, were gradually edging closer to their policies. Their leader, Willi Brandt, was a man of humble origin who, after a poverty-stricken childhood, had been launched into socialist politics by Julius Leber, a leading Social democrat subsequently executed by Hitler for complicity in the Generals' Plot of 1944. Brandt fled to Norway in 1933, became a Norwegian citizen, and took part in the Norwegian Resistance. After the war, anxious to help in the rebuilding of Germany, he resumed his German citizenship. From 1957 until 1966 he was Mayor of West Berlin where his steady courage and energy earned him an international reputation.

In 1966 the small FDP withdrew from its coalition with the ruling CDU, depriving the latter of its parliamentary majority. So the SPD stepped in. Willi Brandt became Vice-Chancellor and Foreign Minister under CDU Chancellor Kiesinger. Many people criticised the SPD for abandoning its parliamentary independence in order to gain power, arguing that the resulting 'consensus politics' would aggravate the excessively conformist and authoritarian attitudes which pervaded the country. But the SPD's main purpose was to demonstrate to the electors that a party which had been in opposition since the foundation of the new state was capable not only of ruling but also of 'drawing the carriage out of the mess'. One aspect of the 'mess' was that a new neo-Nazi party, the National Democratic Party (NDP), formed in 1964, was steadily gaining votes and seats in the parliaments of the Länder. In February 1969 Dr Gustav Heinemann, the Social Democratic Minister of Justice in the Coalition Government, was elected President. A deeply committed Protestant who had been an active anti-Nazi, he had shown exceptional political independence and integrity throughout his career.

In the federal elections of September 1969 the Christian Democrats still gained the largest number of seats in the *Bundes-*

tag; but the Social Democrats gained twenty more than in 1965. With the support of the FDP, they were able to form a government for the first time since 1930. The NDP gained no seats. The Social Democrats' victory was the culmination of a steady post-war trend. The party received twenty-nine per cent of the votes in the election of 1953, and forty-three per cent in that of 1969. Since there were no major differences of policy between the two great parties, except in foreign affairs, the significance of the 1969 election lay perhaps not so much in the change of party as in the change of man, indicating that the public was growing out of the need for the paternalistic 'Chancellor democracy'.

Willi Brandt declared that 'twenty years is enough'. The time of repentance was over. The way to face the past was to build a new future. In internal affairs he launched a ten-year educational programme which provided, among other developments, for building several new universities, doubling the number of students in higher education and widening the range of subjects and types of teaching in secondary schools as an essential element in the democratization of the educational system. In foreign affairs he initiated a reconciliation with Russia and Eastern Europe which could usher in a new and brighter age for all Europeans. This *Ostpolitik* will be discussed in chapter 11.

Italy

In 1939 Italy was a semi-developed country with a standard of living equivalent to that of the United States in 1914 or France in 1924.[17] Half the population gained their living from the land. The country's economic problems appeared to be insoluble: 50,000,000 people lived in a mainly barren peninsula lacking almost all basic raw materials, including coal and iron. There was, therefore, a chronic balance of payments problem. The medieval south was out of step with the relatively modernized north: in 1951 the *per capita* income of the south was only half that of the north, and a quarter of the southerners were illiterate, as compared with six per cent in the north.[18] The war had wrought great destruction. In 1945 agricultural production was forty per cent, and industrial production twenty-five per cent, of the pre-war level.[19] Communications were shattered, and some 2,500,000 people were unemployed.

There were now three major political parties, the Communists, the Socialists and the Christian Democrats. The Communist leader, the Sardinian Palmiro Togliatti, had been converted to Marxism at Turin university and had become, in 1935, the Secretary of the Comintern in Moscow. 'He worked daily with the heroes of the Russian Revolution, Zinoviev, Bukharin, Stalin, Molotov, Trotski ... [and] emerged as ... the most authoritative interpreter of Marxism-Leninism in the West'.[20] During the twenty years in which he led the largest Communist Party in Western Europe, until his death in 1964, Togliatti became the leading exponent of 'revisionism', the new moderate Marxism. His policies oriented West European Communism towards respectable, pragmatic parliamentarianism and gave moral support to the East European regimes in their attempt to implement Khrushchev's doctrine of 'different roads to socialism'.

The majority of Italian Socialists held Marxist views and, like the Communists, in theory worked through the 'bourgeois' parliament only as a tactical means of achieving the revolution. They were not linked with Moscow, as the Communists were through the Cominform, but the common experience of Fascist persecution and of fighting together in the Spanish Civil War and the Second World War, had brought about a 'Popular Front', or coalition between Communists and Socialists which was to last until 1962.

The situation of the revived Christian Democratic Party was different from that of the non-confessional Christian Democratic parties in the other West European countries because of the looming presence of the Vatican, and because ninety-nine per cent of Italians were at least nominally Roman Catholic. Before the war the Vatican had preferred to support Mussolini rather than come to terms with a secular democracy; now it could no longer evade the challenge. It had three choices: the Church could seek to exercise political control over the Italian Christian Democratic Party (the traditional policy); she could keep aloof from politics, allowing Roman Catholics freedom of judgment in political matters as she was doing in the other democratic countries of West Europe; or she could give a spiritual blessing to all political activities. Between 1945 and 1970 Vatican policy oscillated between these three policies but the emphasis was on the first. In 1945 the leader of the Christian Democrats was Alcide de Gasperi, a native of the German-speaking Southern Tyrol. After his release from a Fascist jail in 1939 he had worked quietly in the Vatican Library. He was determined to reduce the political influence of the Church over the Party.

These three parties dominated Italian politics between 1945 and 1970, polling among them seventy-five to eighty per cent of the votes. In contrast to the two parties of the Left, the Christian Democrats were deeply divided by 'factionalism' – groups of politicians competing for power and influence for personal and economic reasons. On the right of these parties were a number of small parties representing the pre-war *laissez-faire* liberalism of the industrialist classes, the neo-Fascists and the Monarchists.

After the war the three parties united in a coalition government under the leadership of de Gasperi. He prevented reprisals against the thousands of officials and business men who had carried on their careers under the Fascist régime, and Togliatti, who was Minister of Justice, amnestied many political prisoners. The partisans had already dealt with Mussolini and his henchmen and there were no war crimes trials. In this atmosphere of reconciliation Italy's second democratic regime was established. As in France, women were given the vote. Then, in June 1946, the electors voted by a small majority to abolish the monarchy – the kings of the House of Savoy had presided over Italy since its unification in 1870. Simultaneously they elected Italy's first constituent assembly. The republican constitution which it drew up resembled that of the Fourth French Republic: a bicameral legislature, a president elected for seven years by both Chambers, and a prime minister appointed by the President, who had to be a Deputy who could command a parliamentary majority. The constitution incorporated the Lateran Pacts of 1929 which recognized the Vatican City as an independent state, and in particular forbade civil marriage and divorce and provided for Roman Catholic religious instruction in state schools : to gain Catholic support the Communists supported this measure. The constitution aimed at turning Italy from a highly centralized into a semi-federal state by providing for the establishment of twenty elected regional governments, which would replace the system of administration by ninety-three prefects appointed by the Ministry of the Interior – a system implanted in Italy by Napoleon. 'Democracy and the prefects are profoundly repugnant to each other', said post-war Italy's first President, Luigi Einaudi.[21] The electoral system was that of proportional representation.

As in France, the advent of the Cold War led to the ejection of the Communists from the Government in the spring of 1947. With them went the Socialists, and until 1962 the two parties formed a powerful parliamentary opposition. The elections from 1946 to 1963 showed a steady trend: the Socialist vote fell from twenty-one to fourteen per cent of the total; the Communist vote rose from nineteen to thirty per cent, indicating that the Communists had replaced the Socialists as the main working class party, and the Christian Democratic vote fluctuated between thirty-five and forty per cent, with a sharp rise to forty-eight per cent in 1948 when there was a fear of a Communist take-over. The Christian Democrats thus became the ruling party but, except for the period 1948–53, they never had an overall majority in the Lower Chamber, and so had to govern with the support of other parties – which meant, until 1962, the small parties of the Right.

From 1945 until 1953, the year before his death, de Gasperi was Prime Minister. Between 1948 and 1953 he headed eight ministries and the average life of a government between 1953 and 1970 was nine months; Prime Ministers were drawn now from the Right and now from the Left factions of the Christian Democratic Party.

De Gasperi persuaded Pope Pius XII to accept the relative independence of the Christian Democratic party from clerical control and thus secured the support of the Socialists and the

Communists in carrying out post-war reconstruction. But after de Gasperi's death Pius XII, frightened by the threat of Communism, increasingly asserted the Church's right to give political direction to the faithful. Papal interference contributed to the disintegration of the Christian Democrats; in 1960 Italy was without a government for sixty-three days; then the right wing of the Party, which was prepared to accept Papal direction, formed a coalition government with the small parties of the extreme Right, including the neo-Fascists. Communist-inspired riots brought this government down. A Christian Democratic alliance with the Socialists, who were dissillusioned with the Communists by the events of 1956, seemed the only alternative. The path to reconciliation was smoothed by Pope John XXIII, who succeeded Pius XII in 1958. In two Encyclicals, *Mater et Magistra* of 1961 and *Pacem in Terris* of 1963, he amplified the teachings of his predecessors about social justice and harmony, giving his blessing to the concepts of the welfare state, of a mixed and a planned economy, and of political democracy:

> the first time that a Pope has formally committed himself to the view that, other things being equal, democracy is best. . . . Pius XII's root assumption (was) that the great apostasy, the withdrawal of so many from allegiance to the Holy See, leading to secularism and so on to Communism, has shrouded much of mankind in impenetrable darkness and divided humanity in two[22]

writes a Roman Catholic historian. John XXIII spoke with 'all-embracing affection' as the father of all mankind.[23] He made the revolutionary pronouncement, in *Pacem in Terris*, that movements such as Communism which profess false philosophies may in practice do good deeds. And as a token of this attitude he gave an audience in 1963 to Khrushchev's daughter and son-in-law, the editor of the leading Soviet newspaper *Izvestia*. This unprecedented Papal policy made possible a completely new climate in Italian politics. Finally, in December 1963, after the Communists had increased their votes all over the country, the Christian Democrats and the Socialists united to form a government of which the veteran Socialist leader Pietro Nenni was deputy Premier. This was called the 'Left-Centre Coalition'.

Meanwhile an 'economic miracle' was taking place. By 1949 UNRRA and Marshall Plan aid had restored productivity to pre-war levels. The problem of the raw materials deficiency was being solved by the discovery of natural gas in the Po valley, and by the liberalization of trade through the OEEC and European Economic Community. Through indicative long-term planning, started in 1955, investment in and rationalization of industry were promoted and the problems of unemployment and the adverse balance of trade were tackled. Between 1953 and 1962 real *per capita* income increased two and a half times.[24] By the mid-sixties Italy was exporting as much in value as it imported, and for the first time was on the threshold of a full-employment economy.

The rapid industrial development, which took place mainly in the north – the populations of Milan and Turin doubled between 1955 and 1965 – made it possible to tackle the problem of the medieval backwardness of the south, of Sicily and of Sardinia. In these places there were shepherd boys who said: 'I've heard tell of the Pope, but what sort of thing is it?' and who believed that Russia was a little island. Witchcraft was still practised and banditry still flourished. In Sicily one of the most sinister secret societies in the world, the 150-year-old Mafia, dominated the regional government and extended its tentacles into the highest places in Rome. The plight of the poor and the tyranny of the Mafia in Sicily were publicized to the world by Danilo Dolci, an architect from Milan, who went to the island in 1952 to study the ruins and stayed to become an Italian Gandhi, living with and helping the destitute. He was sent to prison at one point for organizing an 'upside-down' strike in which he set unemployed men to work making a road without payment.

Between 1950 and 1970 large investments by the Italian Government, major Italian firms, the European Investment Bank and the World Bank established in the three regions the basic infrastructure of a modern state: irrigation schemes, railways, roads, steel and chemical works, schools, hospitals and agricultural services. The age-old scourge of malaria was brought under control. A land reform act of 1950 divided up a major part of the unused land among landless peasants, compensating the landowners. Nevertheless, only a small proportion of the 6,000,000 landless labourers in the south received plots, and many were too small for adequate subsistence. Betwen 1950 and 1967 3,000,000 southerners left the south to seek jobs in the exploding industrial cities of the north, or in other countries.

The measure of the economic and social transformation of Italy was indicated by the fact that between 1945 and 1968 the population living on the land fell from fifty to twenty-four per cent – still too high a proportion for a fully developed country, since experts consider that half of Italy's agricultural area should be abandoned as economically unviable.[25] In 1965 the Minister of Finance declared that a quarter of the people had reached a good Western European standard of living.[26] The Italians owned nearly as many motor cars per head as the British: they were becoming a consumer-oriented society.

As a result of this transformation the gulf between the rich and the poor, the north and the south, was widening. Millions of Italians were being jolted, physically and mentally, from their medieval rut into the modern world, shattering the deep bonds of Church and family which had cemented their society for centuries. The autocratic, over-centralized, inefficient civil service, local government, and legal and educational systems were not equipped to cope with these social changes. Poverty, unemployment and the teachings of the Church had for centuries inculcated the attitude that in allotting jobs and contracts, one's first duty was to one's family and friends. The alternative to corrupt action was often inaction. By the end of 1967 a total of £3,445,000,000 of state funds allocated to economic development remained unspent.[27] The local authorities in Siena (who happened to be Communist) had, by 1965, waited eleven years for approval from Rome to start a home for abandoned children.[28] Because the Christian Democrats were afraid of giving power to the Communists, who dominated the populous 'Red Belt' in central Italy, only five of the twenty regional governments provided for in the constitution had been created: in Sicily, Sardinia, the Val D'Aosta, the Alto Adige (Southern Tyrol), and Venetia. The taxation system had become so antiquated that the Church declared that it was not a mortal sin to falsify tax returns. In 1963 there were nearly 2,000,000 cases awaiting trial and since there was no *habeas corpus* law, innocent people could remain in prison for years.[29] The system of social security was still based on piecemeal insurance schemes designed to supplement the charity of family and Church. As social changes undermined traditional family life, the continued prohibition of divorce was causing great suffering. The educational system also urgently needed reform: in 1962 school places were available for only two-thirds of the children aged eleven to fourteen.[30] A bill providing for state nursery schools was defeated because the Church declared that it would lead to the 'deChristianization of Italian children'.[31] The universities, governed under a law of 1933, suffered from antiquated and authoritarian teaching. They had an intake of less than five per cent from the working classes and a drop-out rate of over ninety per cent.[32]

Finally, the parliamentary system itself was proving inadequate to the challenges of the situation. The fact that it took the members of Parliament twenty-one ballots to elect a new President of the Republic in 1964 brought ridicule on the Legislature. The majority of the politicians of the sixty-nine parties which put up election candidates seemed incapable of comprehending the tasks confronting them.

Between 1963 and 1968 the Left-Centre Coalition initiated various major reforms. Nearly one billion pounds was allocated for education; a commission was set up to study the Mafia problem and the police started to purge Sardinia of bandits; a detailed Five Year Plan was produced. But these measures did not fulfil the hopes of the leaders of the 'opening to the Left' that the Coalition would be able to make radical changes in the structure of the Italian state. The magnetic pull exercised over the Socialists by the ever more powerful Communists, and over the Christian Democrats by the ever more frightened Church – for the wise words of Pope John could not dispel overnight the anti-Communist phobia of five decades – made it impossible for the alliance to be more than a delicate balance of forces reducing each partner to impotence. By the time of the elections of May 1968 students, workers and peasants were in a general state of unrest.

Under the leadership of Togliatti and his elderly successor Luigi Longi, the Italian Communist Party pushed ideology into the background and placed in the foreground of its programme, as the 'Italian way to Socialism', the practical reforms which the Coalition had failed to achieve: regional decentralization; legal, fiscal and university reforms; suppression of the Mafia; more land to the peasants; the legalization of divorce, legal rights and equal pay for women; and workers' participation in capitalist industry – 'nationalization is not an urgent problem' said Longi in 1969.[33] In foreign policy, hitherto a major matter of difference between the Communists and the Coalition, the Party flouted Moscow in giving its support to the European Community, in applying for membership of the Parliamentary Assembly of the Council of Europe and in muting its opposition to NATO. It also held out a hand to the Church; Longi praised the reforms of the Second Vatican Council of 1962–5 and declared that 'the Italian way to socialism (involves) a search for a new rapport with groups that face the same problems of work peace and aspirations to combat injustice'.[34] Most Italian intellectuals supported the Communists. The Party had lost its revolutionary fervour and become respectable.

In a country where Catholic beliefs and customs are ineradicable, the Communists have modelled their work of proselytizing on the Church's own. Thus, Communist fiestas resemble religious festivals, with processions, bands, placards and models of Communist leaders in place of religious images, bright lights resembling Church illuminations . . . Children sell Communist buttonholes – as on other occasions they sell images of the local patron saint . . . Catholicism and Communism, while officially irreconcilable, in practice live side by side. In . . . a small village near Bologna, where the Communist vote is almost 100%, the main industry is making rosaries : the leading Communist woman deputy ... regularly attends Mass: in another place the Communist trades union leader beat his daughter when she didn't.[35]

The election of May 1968 produced a marked shift of votes from the Socialists to the Communists, and severely shook the Left-Centre Coalition. Between May 1968 and the end of 1970 there were five governments. Italy had had thirty-two changes of government since 1945. Nevertheless, two major reforms were finally enacted. First, the regional governments for the remaining fifteen regions came into existence in 1970. The Coalition controlled twelve of the newly elected governments, but in the 'Red Belt' the Communists came to power in Tuscany and Umbria with Socialist support, and in Emilia they had a majority on their own. Second, in December 1970, against the stern opposition of the Pope, divorce was finally legalized. Under pressure of intense labour agitation, expressed in nationwide strikes, the government, in 1970, promised to provide state-subsidized housing for the poor on an adequate scale and to give Italy a proper state-financed national health service.

By the end of 1970 the Christian Democrats and the Communists were both being challenged to shed their connections with authoritarian ideologies – with Roman Catholicism and the Vatican, with Marxism and Moscow – and to set their hands to carrying out, through the existing parliamentary institutions, the vital reforms which Italy needed. Were the Communists to win a general election, or a large number of the regional elections, they would face the momentous decision of whether finally to renounce their revolutionary role, and agree to work with and through a parliament containing other parties. If their decision were 'yes', the implications would be momentous for the world Communist movement.

Other Countries

Between 1945 and 1970 the Scandinavian countries continued to develop peacefully under their Social Democratic regimes.

Switzerland, with full employment and 1,000,000 foreign workers absorbed into its population of 6,000,000, also made peaceful progress. Dutch politics suffered from the endemic problems of coalition governments, drawn from eleven parties; in 1963 it took sixty-nine days to form a ministry. By 1970 there were growing social, economic and political tensions in the Netherlands, symptoms of the protest of many people, especially the youth, against the excessive rigidity of traditional social and religious institutions and in particular against the clerical basis of the main political parties – in 1954 the Dutch Bishops forbade the 4,000,000 Dutch Roman Catholics to vote for any party other than that of their Church.[36]

Belgium was split in two by a linguistic conflict. The people of Flanders, which comprises the five northern provinces of the country, and contains over fifty per cent of the population, speak Flemish, a Teutonic language similar to Dutch. In Wallonia, which consists of the four southern provinces and contains a third of the population, French is spoken. Up to 1939 Flanders was culturally and economically backward, many of its peasants speaking mutually incomprehensible dialects. Wallonia with its coal and iron mines and steel and textile industry was modern and prosperous; French was the official language of the whole country till the late thirties, when it was agreed that Flemish should be the official language in Flanders, and French in Wallonia, and that Brussels should be bilingual.

Linguistic tensions flared up again in the late sixties under pressure from student riots, the ancient Roman Catholic university of Louvain was split into French and Flemish speaking sections, and in 1970 a plan was under consideration similarly to split Brussels, now a European as well as a national capital.

Ultimately, Belgium's best hope of containing its internal language divisions lies in the European Community developing a firmer political structure of its own. In a European Parliament the disputes between Flemings and Walloons will become of secondary importance – in the same way that the religious divisions of Holland's political parties have tended to disappear in the Community's Parliamentary Assembly. In a more united European Community, the European nations have an opportunity of integrating their own citizens more successfully than they could in isolation.[37]

One of the most remarkable transformations since the war has been that of Austria. The first Austrian republic, established in 1919, was a sickly plant, which succumbed to dictatorship in 1934 and fell readily into Hitler's arms in 1938. In 1945 the second Austrian republic was established under the auspices of the occupying powers, and the democratic constitution of 1929 was restored. In 1919 the majority of the Austrians were anxious to unite with Germany, and when this was forbidden by the victors, the country subsided into a state of apathy and despair. Seven years of unification with Nazi Germany changed their attitude; they were now determined to carry out their reconstruction and development on their own and on a social democratic basis. The two main pre-war parties quickly revived: the Social Democrats, who now called themselves the Socialists, and the Christian Socialists, who changed their name to the Austrian Peoples' Party. They emerged from the elections of 1945 almost equally balanced, so much so that measures opposed by either party often could not be put through. They ruled Austria in coalition until 1966, when the Peoples' Party gained an absolute majority. The Communists never had more than five parliamentary seats, and the single Communist minister resigned in 1947.

Steel, electricity and coal were nationalized, but other major industries, such as timber, textiles and the tourist trade, remained in private hands. Despite the fact that the Four Power Occupation lasted until 1955, the Russians did not try to prevent this evolution of a mixed economy, based on a parliamentary democracy.

Conclusion

The factors which caused democracy to fail in several West European countries in the inter-war years – the combination of the backward pull of sectional interests, with deep roots in the

93

pre-modern past, and economic depression – were generally overcome between 1945 and 1970. Despite their political limitations, such as excessive divisiveness in Italy and in the French Fourth Republic, and a tendency to authoritarianism in Christian Democratic West Germany and in the French Fifth Republic, the regimes of all these countries pressed ahead dramatically with economic and social development. The strains and stresses which, in the late sixties, erupted in massive strikes and student riots, seemed to represent, not a failure of nerve, as did the Fascist regimes of the thirties, but the travail of social transformation from a traditional to a modern, from a proletarian to a bourgeois society, fanned, perhaps, by a deeper uncertainty about the nature and goal of this new society itself.

REFERENCES

1. Cairns, John, *France*, Prentice-Hall, Inc., New Jersey, 1965, p. 131.
2. Williams, Philip M., *Crisis and Compromise: Politics in the Fourth Republic*, Longmans, London, 1964, pp. 85–6.
3. Duverger, Maurice, *The French Political System*, University of Chicago Press, 1968, p. 131.
4. Translation taken from Werth, Alexander, *De Gaulle*, Penguin, London, 1967, p. 33.
5. Werth, *op. cit.*, p. 287.
6. Gilpin, Robert, *France in the Age of the Scientific State*, Princeton University Press, 1968, p. 220.
7. Kindleberger, Charles P., The Post-War Resurgence of the French Economy in *In Search of France*, Harvard University Press, 1963, p. 150.
8. Werth, *op. cit.*, p. 418.
9. *The Observer Foreign News Service*, London, No. 26491 of 8 May 1969.
10. Dornberg, John, *The Other Germany: Europe's Emerging Nation Behind the Berlin Wall*, Doubleday and Co., Inc., New York, 1968, p. 289.
11. Elon, Amos, *Journey Through a Haunted Land: the New Germany*, André Deutsch, London, 1967.
12. A young German scientist in a personal letter to one of the authors.
13. Prittie, Terence, *The Germans Against Hitler*, Hutchinson and Co., London, 1964, pp. 274–7
14. *The Times*, London, 19 November 1965.
15. Dahrendorf, Ralf, 'Bonn after Twenty Years: Are Germany's Problems Nearer Solution?' in *The World Today*, April 1969, Royal Institute of International Affairs, London.

16. *The Observer Foreign News Service*, London, No. 25945 of 6 December 1968.
17. Barzini, Luigi, *The Italians*, Atheneum Publishers, New York, 1964, p. 106.
18. Mammarella, Giuseppe, *Italy Since Fascism: A Political History 1943–63*, Casalini, Montreal, 1964, p. 225.
19. Mammarella, *op. cit.*, pp. 121–2.
20. Barzini, *op. cit.*, p. 115.
21. Germino, Dante, and Passigli, Stefano, *The Government and Politics of Contemporary Italy*, Harper and Row, New York, 1968, p. 77.
22. Hales, E. E. Y., *Pope John and His Revolution*, Doubleday and Co. Inc., New York, 1966, p.71 and p. 80.
23. Hales, *op. cit.*, p. 104.
24. Salvadori, Massimo, *Italy*, Prentice-Hall Inc., New Jersey, 1965, p. 161.
25. *Observer Foreign News Service*, London, No. 26682 of 17 September 1964.
26. Kogan, Norman, *A Political History of Post-War Italy*, Praeger, New York, 1966, p. 158.
27. *The Times*, London, Special Report on Southern Italy, 3 February 1969.
28. *The Times*, London, 17 July 1961.
29. *The Times*, London, 8 February 1963.
30. *The Times*, London, 1 July 1969.
31. *The Observer Foreign News Service*, London, No. 22359 of 18 February 1969.
32. *Ibid.*, No. 25224 of 6 June 1969.
33. *The Times*, London, 12 December 1964.
34. *The Times*, London, 20 March 1964.
35. *The Observer Foreign News Service*, London, No. 10597 of 18 August 1954.
36. *Ibid.*, No. 27471 of 16 February 1970.
37. *Ibid.*, No. 27502 of 26 February 1970.

5. The Non-Communist countries of Southern Europe

At the beginning of the twentieth century the countries of Southern and Eastern Europe were still essentially in the premodern age. In general, except in the Soviet Union, only the beginnings of modernization were made before 1945. After 1945 events impelled most of the East European countries to modernize under Communist rule. Greece and Turkey embarked on the task under regimes modelled on those of the Western European democracies; Cyprus and Malta were still British colonies; and Spain and Portugal were ruled by 'Fascist' dictators of pre-war vintage.

Spain

The Spanish Civil War of 1936–9 was fought between the Nationalists and the Republicans. The backbone of the Nationalists was the army, led by General Francisco Franco. They stood for the power of the Church and the landowners (one per cent of the population owned fifty per cent of the land); for private enterprise in industry; for centralized government and for authoritarian rule. General Franco sidetracked the King, who had gone into exile in 1931, and called himself Caudillo, or leader, of an elite party, the Falange. The Republicans stood, in general, for secularization, expropriation of the great landlords and self-government for the Catalonians and Basques. Beyond this they were divided, for they consisted of a motley collection of groups ranging from liberals and moderate socialists to extreme anarchists.

During the Civil War the anarchists were for a time in control of Barcelona and of some rural areas. The official Communist element was small.

The Civil War was soon internationalized. Some 80,000 German, Italian and Portuguese troops came to the aid of Franco. The Republicans received equipment from Stalin and the services of the 40,000 men of the International Brigades organized by the Communist Comintern. Some were tough young professional Communists like Walter Ulbricht of Germany, Klement Gottwald of Czechoslovakia, 'Tito' and Milovan Djilas of Yugoslavia and Luigi Longi of Italy, who were to rise to great power in their countries after 1945. Others were idealistic intellectuals from Western Europe and the United States – George Orwell, Arthur Koestler, Ernest Hemingway, Martha Gellhorn, W. H. Auden, André Malraux, Louis Fischer, J. B. S. Haldane. 'The Spanish Civil War appeared the great moment of hope for an entire generation angry at the apparent cynicism, indolence and hypocrisy of the older generation'.[1] The Republicans were defeated because they were divided, because the Nationalists had far more effective foreign help, and because France and Britain pursued a policy of 'nonintervention', refusing to sell the Republicans arms.

The Civil War caused the death of 600,000 Spaniards and cost a desperately poor country £3,000,000,000 (in 1938 monetary terms). Nearly 200 towns were badly damaged, much of the railways and merchant fleet was destroyed and a third of the livestock was dead. Food rationing remained in force until 1952.[2, 3] Savage retribution was wreaked on the Republicans. During the war both sides had committed many atrocities, such as the execution of hostages. Now every Republican crime was investigated; some 100,000 Republicans had been shot by the end of 1939 and in 1942 there were 241,000 people in the damp and overcrowded prisons.[4] In 1945 political prisoners were finally given a general pardon, and exiles were invited to return, but many did not take the risk.

General Franco managed to keep Spain neutral during the

war, but repaid Hitler for his help in the Civil War by sending his Blue Division of 47,000 'volunteers' to fight in Russia.

A series of 'fundamental laws', promulgated between 1938 and 1947, established the basis of the Spanish 'New State', described as an 'organic democracy, Catholic, social and representative'. Like Mussolini in Italy and Salazar in Portugal, Franco grounded his dictatorship on the principles of 'social corporativism', largely inspired by Papal political theory. The Cortes (parliament), revived in 1942, was an advisory body, without power to control the government. It represented, not individuals, but functions. Some of its members were nominated by Franco, others elected, mainly by the syndicates, bodies composed of the representatives of the managements and workers in each major industry. The state remained highly centralized; the autonomy for which the Catalonians and the Basques had struggled in the thirties was withheld. The whole system was based on the principles of hierarchy and authority. A concordat of 1953 with the Vatican gave the Roman Catholic Church more power than she had ever before enjoyed in Spanish history. In particular, her control over education was reinforced, the 26,000 Spanish Protestants were denied freedom of religious propaganda and the right to publish Protestant versions of the Bible.

Franco's Spain was a police state, in which the press was censored, free discussion muted, and most strikes forbidden. But his Fascism did not have the aggressive dynamism of the regimes of Hitler and Mussolini. A cautious, uncharismatic man, when the defeat of Germany and Italy had discredited Fascism, he played down the Falange and the leadership cult.

For some years Spain was treated as an international pariah and the Americans refused it Marshall Aid. Only in 1955 was it admitted to the United Nations and in 1959 to the OEEC.

In the fifties two factors began to transform the country. First, under an agreement of 1953 Spain received a large influx of American economic and military aid, and granted the United States in return the use of several naval and air bases. It suited the United States to have some bases which were outside the control of NATO, and Cadiz had, by 1968, become the most important American naval base in Europe, equipped to accommodate Polaris submarines. Second, tourists were coming in their millions, bringing foreign currency. This injection of foreign aid and currency began to lift Spain's stagnant economy off the ground. Before 1936 fifty per cent of the population lived on the land. By 1970 the figure had fallen to thirty per cent. Before 1936 a quarter of the population was unemployed or under-employed. By 1968, in spite of a population increase from 24,000,000 to 32,000,000, there was almost no unemployment – but 1,000,000 Spaniards had emigrated to jobs in other European countries – and major land reform still had not been carried out. Economic planning started in 1963 on the basis of a survey made by the World Bank.

For the first time the Spaniards were rising above the level of malnutrition and becoming a consumer-oriented society, and this was beginning to transform the character of the political scene. In 1958 General Franco, dedicating a memorial to the fallen in the Civil War, said: 'The struggle between good and evil never ceases . . . Anti-Spain was beaten and routed, but is not yet dead.' By 1970 a younger generation had grown up which thought in different terms. Whether in the universities, in the trade unions or in the Church (for many of the younger priests, inspired by Pope John, were becoming very radical), they were demanding the kind of moderate practical policies which were being pursued in other Western European countries. A significant new factor was the influence of European public opinion. Organizations such as NATO, the Council of Europe and the European Community (with which it applied for association in 1962) were not willing to admit Spain until it liberalized its institutions. An ILO study group, invited by the Spanish Government in 1969 to investigate labour conditions, urged strongly that free trade unions should be allowed and political prisoners be brought to trial or released. In 1969–70 international pressure secured the commutation of death sentences passed on several Basque nationalists.

In 1969 the seventy-eight-year-old General nominated the thirty-one-year-old Prince Juan Carlos, the grandson of Alfonso

99

XII, to be King and Head of State on his death and replaced some of the old guard in his Cabinet by younger technocrats. In 1970 the country was seething with unrest as the feeling grew that real changes would occur when Franco passed from the scene. Yet during his long rule, repressive and anachronistic though it was, Spain had at last been brought into the modern world and in 1970 the prospects of the successful establishment of democratic institutions seemed brighter than ever before.

Portugal

Portugal became a Republic in 1908 after the assassination of the King and his heir. After a period of anarchy under constitutional democratic government, Dr Antonio de Oliviera Salazar became Prime Minister, and in effect dictator, in 1932. The son of a peasant, he was a professor of economics, learned, austere and deeply devout. Although Salazar's dictatorship was very similar in structure to that of Franco in Spain, it did not, after 1945, excite the same international opprobrium. Portugal was a founding member of NATO, OEEC and EFTA but was not admitted to the Council of Europe.

In 1970 Portugal was still poor and backward, with a *per capita* GNP, in 1970, of only $660 per annum – as compared with $1020 in Spain.[5] Economic planning was started in 1953, and some modernization had taken place, but Portugal remained essentially a country of rich industrialists and landowners, and poor factory workers and peasants, of whom twenty-five per cent were illiterate – compared with fourteen per cent in Spain. In 1970 the apparatus of the police state – censorship of the press, secret police, arbitrary arrest and dungeons filled with some 3–400 political prisoners – was firmly in force. Salazar's dogged determination to hold on to Portugal's colonies, from which it derived fifteen per cent of its imports and to which it sent twenty-five per cent of its exports, meant that it was spending half its budget on defence. Between 1963 and 1969 defence expenditure doubled.[6] All men over eighteen were conscripted for three years' military service, and in 1970 some 125,000 of the 185,000 strong army were permanently overseas. Hundreds were fleeing from 'the draft' through secret routes into France. The Pope implicitly rejected Portugal's claim to be fighting in Africa on behalf of Christian civilization when in 1970 he gave a friendly audience to three Resistance leaders from Portuguese Africa.

In 1968 the seventy-nine-year-old Dr Salazar fell ill. President Tomas appointed sixty-four-year-old Professor Marcelo Caetano to be his successor as Prime Minister. Although Caetano had been Salazar's chief assistant in moulding the institutions of the corporate state, he was more modern-minded and cosmopolitan than Salazar, who never in his life left Portugal. Between 1968 and 1970 Caetano travelled in Europe, southern Africa and Latin America. In elections held in 1969 he allowed candidates to stand who did not belong to the ruling National Union Party and the result was the election of a number of progressive young technocrats. The opposition groups, which were not yet allowed to organize themselves into parties, stood for liberalization at home and self-determination for the colonies. A number of political prisoners were released. When Dr Salazar died in 1970 Dr Caetano had relaxed the rigours of the regime, but he had not substantially changed it. It appeared that the old guard was afraid of relinquishing power because this would expose to the world the bankruptcy of their post-war policy: the failure to modernize Portugal for the sake of an outdated imperialism.

Malta

In 1945 Malta was a British colony with a naval base in a strategic position in the Mediterranean. In 1956 a majority of the Maltese voted for integration with Britain, which would have involved electing Maltese representatives to the British Parliament. The minority wanted complete independence. The tension between the two parties was so great that constitutional government was suspended until 1961. In 1964 Malta became independent, but continued to accept the British Monarch as Head of the State.

Between 1964 and 1970 the Nationalist Party was in power. It was supported by the Roman Catholic Church and it favoured the continuation of the link with Britain and with NATO, whose headquarters at Valetta were the Western Powers' last toe-hold in the central Mediterranean. The opposition party, the Labour Party, stood for non-alignment, which might mean granting the Soviet fleet the same facilities as those enjoyed by NATO units.

The small and rocky island cannot support its 300,000 inhabitants. Britain, no longer needing the naval dockyard, agreed in 1964 to provide £51,000,000 over ten years, to subsidize the conversion of the dockyard to commercial ship-repairing, and to help the 12,000 Maltese employed in the docks to train for other jobs. In 1969 the Church proposed to apply some if its great wealth to the relief of the island's poverty. Another possible source of aid was oil-rich Libya – but up to 1970 Malta had shown itself reluctant to be sucked into the maelstrom of Arab affairs.

Greece

The modern Greek is, in Aristotle's phrase, a 'political animal'. Intelligent, wily and fiercely individualistic, politics is his absorbing pastime.

In the century of independence up to 1939 the Greeks tried to make democracy work. But their parties were held together, not by principles and programmes, but by personal rivalries and antagonisms. Imported Western European kings added an element of stability but also periodically practised monarchical autocracy. And periodically the army intervened to establish military dictatorships and to make and unmake régimes. In 1936 General Metaxas abolished the parliament of wrangling politicians and, supported by King George II, who had been recalled from exile in 1935, established a military dictatorship which carried out some needed social reforms.

When the Germans and Bulgarians withdrew from Greece in 1944 the country was prostrate. In the winter of 1942 450,000 had died of starvation. Now the retreating armies seized what small supplies of food there were and destroyed the few factories. Three-quarters of the merchant fleet, Greece's main source of livelihood, was sunk.[7] The value of the currency had so collapsed that it cost several thousand drachma to buy a box of matches.

As in Yugoslavia, the main Resistance groups had been Communist-led. They did not want the return of the King, who was identified with the right-wing Metaxas dictatorship, but Stalin had agreed with Churchill that Greece should be in the British sphere of influence, and although the British were prepared to countenance a Communist regime in Yugoslavia, they were not in Greece. An attempted Communist coup in December 1944 was therefore suppressed with the help of British troops.

From 1946 till 1967 Greece was a constitutional monarchy of the British type. King George II, whose return was approved by referendum, was succeeded by his brother Paul I in 1947. The Greek Communists, supported by guerrillas from Yugoslavia, Bulgaria and Albania, simultaneously renewed the civil war, committing serious atrocities, and abducting 20,000 Greek children. Massive American aid and the cessation of Yugoslav aid to the Communists after Tito's breach with Stalin tipped the balance in favour of the Greek Government. By 1949 the civil war was over. It had deepened the country's political division and retarded its economic recovery. 'Some 700,000 peasants, a tenth of the population, were uprooted from their blackened and destroyed villages and ... huddled in barren refugee camps.'[8]

A period of relative political stability then set in. The Conservative National Union Party, led by Constantine Karamanlis, was in power from 1955 to 1963, a record period in Greek politics. He was succeeded by the National Radicals, led by Georgios Papandreou, whose policies were more radical and who in 1964 gained a large parliamentary majority. The elections of 1963 and 1964 were the most honest and impartial ever held in Greece.

Between 1949 and 1965 the economic situation was transformed. The currency was stabilized; private foreign investment promoted industrialization; the rebuilt merchant fleet was again one of the largest in the world; roads were being constructed, electricity was at last reaching the villages and tourists were pouring in. The United States government ended its economic aid in 1964 because it considered Greece to be 'an out-standing example of a successful assistance programme'.[9] Aid from the European Community had also helped. Yet half the people still lived on the land and the distribution of wealth remained very uneven.

Karamanlis had concentrated on economic development. Papandreou complemented his policies by releasing Communist political prisoners and reforming the education system. All children were to have free schooling till fifteen instead of twelve and for the clever there would be free schooling till eighteen, and free university education. Greater emphasis was to be given to science and technology – a reform vital to the country's further development.

Then this relatively sunny picture was suddenly darkened. In 1965 the young King Constantine II, who had succeeded his father in 1964, forced Papandreou out of office, partly because his son was alleged to be involved in a left-wing army conspiracy and partly because he wanted Greece to leave NATO. The King's action was unconstitutional, since Papandreou was the leader of a party which had a large majority in the parliament. Two years later, the King was forced to agree to a new election, which everyone expected would renew Papandreou's majority. In April 1967, on the eve of the election, a Junta of some 300 middle-ranking officers seized power. The King made an un-successful attempt at a counter-coup by appealing to the dis-placed generals and then, in December 1967, went into exile.

The Junta, composed of men from the provinces lacking cosmopolitan experience, proceeded to establish a police state. They suppressed the parliament, *habeas corpus* and trial by jury, dismissed the high court judges, imprisoned some 2,000 critics and tortured some of them, censored the press, dropped Papandreou's education reforms, rewrote the school text books and dismissed teachers who would not extoll the regime.

This 'fascist' behaviour produced an international outcry, and by the end of 1970 the rigours of the regime had been some-what relaxed. *Habeas corpus* was restored and most of the political prisoners released. A consultative legislative assembly was nominated by the Junta, composed of men under fifty, but there was no sign of the restoration of real democratic institutions: 'When we arrive at the time for elections', announced the Junta, 'there will be a new spirit in the country and there will be new men'.[10] It seems unlikely that a group of provincial soldiers will be able to mould the Greek political animal in the way they want, but the very harshness of their rule may prepare him to make democracy work effectively in the land which invented it.

The regime confronts the Western powers with a challenging moral issue. All the Western European organizations to which Greece belongs – NATO, the OECD, the Council of Europe, the European Community (with which it is associated) – are based on the principles of democracy and respect for human rights. In December 1969 Greece was forced to resign from the Council of Europe, but NATO, the organization formed to defend democracy against Communism, is the touchstone. Greece provides NATO with important bases, including a missile base in Crete. So there has been no question of forcing Greece out of NATO, and in 1970 the United States resumed military aid to Greece, suspended in 1967.

Meanwhile the Junta, who had justified their seizure of power by asserting that Greece was threatened with a Communist coup – an assertion which most impartial observers did not believe – began to develop relations with the Communist bloc, which offered to buy Greece's otherwise unsaleable tobacco surplus in return for agricultural and industrial machinery. The Greek Communist Party remained outlawed.

From 1947 until 1967 Greece was a political backwater, quietly recovering from foreign invasion and civil war and developing into modernity. The advent of the Junta had turned it, by 1970, into a political hotspot in European affairs.

Cyprus

Cyprus, ceded by Turkey to Britain in 1878, became independent in 1960. Four-fifths of the population of rather over half a million (in the sixties) is Greek and the remainder Turkish. Each community speaks an entirely different language, practises an entirely different religion (Greek Orthodox Christianity and Islam), and lives in separate villages or separate parts of each town.

In the early thirties the Greek Cypriots began to demand *enosis* – union with Greece. After the war this agitation, led by Archbishop Makarios, the son of a poor shepherd, became more intense. The Turks reacted by demanding the partition of the island. The British were not prepared to endorse any settlement which was not acceptable to both groups. By 1955 the Greek Cypriots were in open revolt; British troops were shooting insurgents on sight and 'cleaning out' villages. Finally the Greek and Turkish Governments decided at a conference at Zurich in 1959 that Cyprus should be independent and neutral, and Britain thankfully endorsed this decision. It was agreed that Britain should retain sovereignty over two military bases, which became NATO bases, and that Britain, Greece and Turkey should guarantee Cyprus's independence. A constitution was drawn up which gave each community an entrenched position in the state: the President was to be the Greek leader Archbishop Makarios, the Vice-President the Turkish leader; there were to be seven Greek and three Turkish ministers; seventy per cent of the Members of Parliament were to be elected by the Greeks and thirty per cent by the Turks; the civil service was to be similarly divided and the army was to be split in the ratio of sixty to forty.

These arrangements were more or less imposed upon the Cypriots and the constitution proved unworkable. Communal strife broke out in 1963 and threatened to spark off war between Greece and Turkey, both members of NATO. The Cypriot Government asked for a contingent of British troops to help to restore order, and then in 1964 placed the matter before the United Nations. The Security Council appointed a mediator to work out a solution, and sent a United Nations' peacekeeping force of 5,000 troops under an Indian commander, into which the British troops were absorbed. Small contingents were also sent by Canada, Sweden, Ireland, Denmark and Austria. By

1967 two mediators had had no success. The mandate of the peace-keeping force was renewed year after year, the Greek Government infiltrated 12,000 troops into the island and in November 1967 the Turkish Government threatened invasion. The Greeks were worried, for the Turks could mobilize 1,000,000 men as compared with their army of 100,000, and possessed an air force twice the size of theirs.[11] The Americans, whose Sixth Fleet was prowling around in the area, counselled caution on the Turks and the Greeks agreed to withdraw their troops. The Greek Cypriots, who had been somewhat disenchanted by the mainlanders in their midst, finally abandoned their demand for *enosis*. This led to the opening of direct negotiations between the two Cypriot communities to try to work out a new constitution, but by 1970 no agreement had been reached.

Despite these troubles the economic development of the island, stimulated by Five Year Plans, went ahead apace after independence.

Turkey

The Turks are a linguistic group speaking 'Turkish', an Asiatic language entirely different in structure from the Aryan languages spoken by almost all Europeans. In the eighth century they were converted to Islam, and in the Middle Ages they founded the Ottoman empire, so-called after Osman, the founder of the dynasty which ruled it until 1923. The Sultan or Emperor was also the Caliph of Islam, the head of the Islamic faith. The empire included not only Asia Minor, inhabited by Turks, but also the Balkan peoples of South-Eastern Europe and the Arab peoples of the Middle East. The Turks did not intermarry with their European subjects, the majority of whom remained unconverted to Islam. By 1914 the Ottoman empire had lost all its North African and almost all its Balkan territories. It was still essentially a mediaeval, despotic regime and its alliance with the Central Powers in the First World War brought about its collapse. The victorious powers created 'Turkey', the country where the Turks lived, retaining no Arab lands and only a small foothold on the European side of the Bosphorus. Simultaneously the Turks produced a great man, Mustapha Kemal, a young general who in 1923 abolished the Sultanate and made himself *de facto* dictator of the new Turkish Republic.

Mustapha Kemal set himself to make Turkey into a modern, secular, democratic nation-state. He brought a democratic constitution into force, abolished the Caliphate, and tried to divorce the state from religion. Since Islam has no institutionalized Church, but is rather a way of life which regards all human institutions as based on a unique divine revelation, secularization was a different matter than in the Christian countries of Europe. First, it involved a legal revolution, replacing the Islamic law of God, interpreted by the *Ulema*, the wise men, by man-made codes modelled on those of Switzerland, Italy and Germany, administered by secular judges. Second, it involved a social revolution: the prohibition of polygamy, the establishment of civil marriage and divorce, the opening of public life to women and giving them the vote, the insistence that both sexes should wear western clothes (the badge of modernity), and the order that all Turks should give themselves surnames. Mustapha Kemal took the name of Ataturk – 'Father of the Turks'. Third, it involved a cultural revolution: the replacement of the Arabic script, the sacred script of the Koran, by the Latin alphabet. A Turkish writer has described this as the most revolutionary change in Turkish history since the conversion to Islam, for it oriented the Turks decisively towards Western culture with its emphasis on science and liberalism. And liberalism and science cannot be easily married to Islam, a religion which emphasises man's impotence in relation to God's omnipotence and which asserts that the infallible revelation given by God in the Koran provides guidance for every human contingency. Fourth, it involved an educational revolution: education should no longer consist in learning the Koran by heart (in Arabic) under the direction of the *Ulema*, but in giving compulsory secular schooling to all boys and girls from seven to twelve (in 1923 only ten per cent of the Turks were literate). Finally, a beginning was made with the modernization of the economy, on the basis of state ownership of the basic public services, and state control over and investment in other industries, the whole directed by Five Year Plans, first launched in 1934.

To symbolize these great changes, Ataturk transferred the capital from the ancient cosmopolitan semi-European city of Constantinople (now to be called by its Turkish name, Istanbul), to the little town of Ankara in the remote interior of Asia Minor.

Although Ataturk wanted Turkey to be a western-type democracy, he found that he had to suppress all political parties except his own, the Republican Peoples' Party, lest they should undermine his basic reforms. On his death in 1938 the National Assembly unanimously elected Ismet Inönü, his Prime Minister and closest friend, to succeed him as President. Turkey was neutral in the Second World War, but this time its sympathies were with the Allies. When Turkey joined the United Nations, Adnan Menderes, one of the leading politicians, commented that 'Turkey, by signing the Charter, has definitely agreed to practise genuine democracy'.[12] Inönü agreed to allow opposition parties and the Democratic Party, led by Menderes, was formed. Freedom of the press and of assembly were granted; and as a result the new party won a large majority in a free and fair election held in 1950. The Republican Peoples' Party, after ruling for twenty-seven years, went over peacefully into parliamentary opposition. The Democratic Party also won the elections of 1954 and 1957 – in the latter there was some corruption and control of the press.

The leaders of the Republican Peoples' Party were the intellectuals and well-educated army officers who had formed Ataturk's entourage. The new party enlisted the support of the majority of ordinary people – of those very interests which the Peoples' Party had in some way thwarted: the big landowners, incensed by the distribution of some land to the peasants in 1945; the peasants, who followed the landowners and who deeply disliked the religious changes; the new middle class created by Ataturk's economic reforms who resented the element of state control in them; and the immensely influential *Ulema* – in 1970 the vast majority of the Turks were still devout Muslims.

By 1960 it seemed to the army leaders that the Menderes regime was betraying the ideals of Ataturk's revolution. It was threatening to develop into a one-party rule, based on the interests of big business combined with religious revivalism. The government was building new mosques, supporting thousands of fanatical popular preachers and countenancing polygamy.[13] Its policies were also driving the country towards bankruptcy. Its middle-class and peasant supporters were demanding more consumer goods; education and improved communications were rousing the peasants out of the isolation and apathy of centuries and since Turkey was a democracy, it was difficult to ask them to restrict consumption so that their savings could finance capital development. Imports of consumer goods vastly exceeded exports, and inflation developed apace. The population increase of three per cent a year absorbed almost all the increase in wealth. Industry produced only fourteen per cent of the national product, while on the primitive farms, half of which still used the wooden plough, some 9,000,000 peasants were unemployed or under-employed. In Eastern Turkey fifty to eighty per cent of the peasants were landless.[14] The illiteracy rate was about sixty-five per cent, and over thirty per cent of the children of school age were not in school. In 1970 Turkey's *per capita* GNP was a third of that of Greece.[15] Some $1,600,000,000 of American economic aid, poured into the country between 1947 and 1962, was sucked into the morass of the largely unplanned economy. A traveller going from Turkey to Bulgaria or Russia in the sixties was struck by the contrast. In the Communist countries everyone was busy; the shops were bleak and bare but they contained the necessities of life, and it was rare to see a ragged person. Turkey was full of ragged men lounging around, while the shops were stacked to the ceiling with attractive goods which no-one was buying.

In May 1960 a group of middle-rank army officers carried out a *coup d'état*. The Members of Parliament of the Democratic Party were arrested, the leaders tried, and, despite international protest, Menderes and two of his colleagues were executed; others were given long prison sentences. Menderes, like the Earl of Strafford in 1641, had committed no criminal act, but had pursued policies which were politically unacceptable to the opposition.

In contrast to the Greek Junta, however, the Turkish military rulers were anxious to restore democratic government as soon as possible. One incentive was the fact that Turkey had to withdraw from the Council of Europe while democratic institutions were suspended. A new constitution was drawn up by a nominated constituent assembly, and approved by referendum in July 1961; and in October elections were held. Seldom had a military dictatorship relinquished power more quickly. The irony of the situation, however, was that the Democratic Party, renamed the Justice Party, led by Suleyman Demiral, won the elections of 1961, 1965 and 1969 with increased majorities.

Demiral pursued moderate policies. Five Year Plans were started in 1963, and between that year and 1968 Turkey received aid channelled through a group of OECD countries amounting to nearly $2,000,000,000. After 1967 the American contribution was drastically reduced and Turkey began to turn to its Communist neighbours. Between 1964 and 1969 its trade with these countries trebled, despite the fact that the Communist Party had been banned since 1925 and the publication of Communist writings prohibited – in 1970 professors were receiving prison sentences for translating them into Turkish.

In 1970 the 500,000 strong army still held the keys to power. In contrast to the armies of Greece, Spain and Portugal, it was the most progressive force in the country. Its dilemma was how to continue Ataturk's modernizing reforms and at the same time to maintain democratic government, for the great mass of the peasants were not ready for these reforms, and when given the vote, voted for the party which was most willing to carry on the old ways. Meanwhile, partly inspired by the events of 1968 in France, the students were beginning to resort to violent protest against the lack of reforms. It remained uncertain whether the affluence and education needed to jolt the country into the twentieth century could be provided through democratic institutions. Some intellectuals, wrote an observer in 1970, 'secretly wait for another Ataturk ... others suggest Russian-style social-

ism or pragmatic authoritarianism to replace democracy ...
Turkish democracy has reached a critical turning-point'.[16]

Conclusion

By 1970 the six non-Communist countries of Southern Europe
were in a state of social and economic transformation. One –
Greece – had become a dictatorship and two – Spain and
Portugal – seemed to be nearing the end of a long period of
authoritarian rule. Perhaps the most striking development was
that all these countries were ceasing to be isolated backwaters
and were being drawn into the mainstream of European life
and affairs; and in this their membership of or association with
the Western European organizations played a significant part.

REFERENCES

1. Thomas, Hugh, *The Spanish Civil War*, Penguin, London, 1968, p. 772.
2. Thomas, *op. cit.*, p. 758.
3. Ayling, S. E., *Portraits of Power*, Harrap, London, 1967, p. 317.
4. Thomas, *op. cit.*, p. 760.
5. World Bank figures.
6. *The Observer Foreign News Service*, London, No. 27715 of 5 May 1970.
7. Carey, Janex and Andrew, *The Web of Modern Greek Politics*, Columbia University Press, New York, 1968, p. 131.
8. Carey, *op. cit.*, p. 146.
9. Carey, *op. cit.*, p. 4.
10. *The Economist*, London, 5 September 1970.
11. Foley, Charles, *Legacy of Strife: Cyprus from Rebellion to Civil War*, Penguin, London, 1964, p. 178.
12. Lewis, Bernard, *The Emergence of Modern Turkey*, Oxford University Press, 1968, p. 305.
13. *The Listener*, London, 14 September 1961.
14. *The Weekly Guardian*, 30 October 1971, p. 6.
15. World Bank figures.
16. *The Observer Foreign News Service*, London, No. 27836, 19 June 1970.

6. The Soviet Union

The Development of Communist Russia from 1917-1939

After the war, new systems or constitutions were established in most European countries. In the Soviet Union, however, the structure of the Communist system, as developed by Lenin and Stalin after the Communist Revolution of 1917, remained unchanged.

Russia was the first European state to establish a regime based on a modern ideology, that of Marxism. Marx had prophesied that the classless, Communist society would come about in highly industrialized countries through an inexorable, predestined process, arising, phoenix-like, from the ashes of capitalism.

It was therefore something of a dogmatic embarrassment to Lenin when the unexpected disintegration of the Czarist regime in the First World War opened up the possibility of establishing the world's first Marxist state in backward, primitive Russia. In 1917 there were only some 3,000,000 factory workers in a population of 175,000,000. The vast majority were illiterate peasants, the 'dark people'. Through the centuries Russia had remained outside the great currents of Western thought – the Renaissance, the Reformation and the liberalism of the nineteenth century. In its national experience there was a peculiar mixture of barbaric autocracy and mystical messianism, of cruelty and compassion, of backwardness and prophetic hope. Alexander Blok (1880–1921), one of the greatest poets of modern Russia, said in 1920 that he believed that the twentieth century was destined to alter the life of mankind in a way no less radical than the century of the Incarnation. The blend of violence and idealism in Marxism was perhaps relevant to Russia's situation.

Lenin seized power by force. The first freely-elected parliament in Russian history, which met for one day – 18 January 1918 – had a large anti-Bolshevik majority. Therefore Lenin evolved the doctrine that the 'dictatorship of the proletariat' would be necessary to educate the masses for self-government and the 'withering away of the state'. The 'vanguard of the proletariat', as Marx called it, was the Communist party, organized by Lenin on the principle of 'democratic centralism', that is, the subordination of the lower party organs to the higher. 'To keep on developing state power in order to prepare for the withering away of state power – that is the Marxist formula,' said Stalin in 1939. 'Marxism-Leninism' produced a peculiar combination of the principles of dictatorship and democracy – in contrast to Fascist ideologies, which explicitly denigrated democracy. Although Lenin's successors have apparently prolonged the dictatorship indefinitely, the democratic element remains embedded in Communist institutions, waiting to be brought to life.

A peculiar distinction was made between 'socialism' and 'communism'. Under 'socialism', the state would own the means of production and the workers would be paid, in money, according to their work; wage differentials would prevail. Under 'communism', 'each would give according to his ability, and receive according to his needs.' Money itself would 'wither away'.

Meanwhile, to Russia, the first Marxist state in the world, would fall the holy mission of promoting world revolution.

Economic and Social Policies

During his short rule, Lenin nationalized the industries and the banks, but gave the land, taken away from the Tsarist landlords, to the peasants in private ownership. In the late twenties, Stalin forced through the rapid industrialization of Russia at the expense of the consumers and the peasants for whose benefit the Revolution had taken place. We are fifty or a hundred years behind the advanced countries,' he said. 'We must make good

this discrepancy in ten years. Either we do it, or they crush us.'
Thus Stalin proceeded to push Russia into the industrial revolution by two major measures. First, he 'collectivized' the land.
In four years the 25,000,000 private farms were forcibly
replaced by some 240,000 'collective' farms (owned and organized by the 'collective' of all the members) and 10,000 'state'
farms (owned and managed by the state). Productivity was increased by mechanization and other modern methods to ensure
deliveries of foodstuffs to the fast-growing industrial towns and
to export markets – for at this stage, Russia had to earn foreign
exchange to buy basic capital equipment abroad. The cost of
ruthlessly enforced collectivization was the death of some ten
million peasants and over half of Russia's livestock. Second,
Stalin added to socialism – state ownership – the concept of
planning. Since the state owned the 'means of production', it
could plan and organize growth as it wished. Targets – a word
which hardly entered into Western economists' vocabulary at
this time – could be set and enforced.

The first Five Year Plan was launched in 1928. The procedure
was simple. The planners in Moscow decided what was to be
produced – quantities, styles and specifications – and what factories, enterprises and services were to be used or created; each
factory was assigned a target. The factory managers were
allowed virtually no initiative in planning their output but within the factory they themselves had dictatorial powers, setting
each worker his target. If a manager or a worker failed to fulfil
it he committed a crime against the state, punishable by forced
labour or death. Over-fulfilment of the target was rewarded by
decorations and public glory. Millions were reduced to a sub-
human state or done to death by the pressures and brutalities of
the system.

Stalin's plans gave priority to heavy industry and military
equipment. Consumer goods were reduced to a minimum. Industry was deliberately dispersed throughout the huge country, and
ninety new towns were built beyond the Urals (European Russia
is relatively poor in minerals, in comparison with the vast un-
tapped resources of Siberia). By 1940, Russia was self-sufficient

in basic industrial equipment and armaments, and the urban population had risen to a third of the total.

The Plans were accompanied by the most severe restrictions of economic freedom : prices and wages were fixed by the state; workers were directed to their jobs and, after 1940, tied to them; as under the Czars, the peasants could not move about the country without internal passports; the factory managers were civil servants, appointed by the state; the trade unions acted merely as welfare organizations, or as pressure groups to secure higher productivity; strikes, regarded as a form of sabotage, were illegal. Lenin's Communist principle: 'From each according to his ability, to each according to his needs,' was abandoned in 1931 and wage differentials were introduced. The planned economy insulated the Soviet Union from the great depression, which affected every other European country. There was no unemployment, but there was something worse: the forced labour of several million convicts.

Stalin inaugurated a system of social welfare which in 1939 was unique in the world. Comprehensive public health services, hospital and medical care, were to be provided by the State for everyone, as well as pensions for all State employees – collective farm workers were not given pensions until 1965. Some of these services, such as holidays in state rest homes, enjoyed by over 2,000,000 workers in 1937, were organized by the trade unions at minimal cost to the workers. However, in the pre-war years, the exigencies of the Five Year Plans made it impossible to finance these services properly.

The Soviet Constitution and System of Government

Lenin and Stalin gave Russia constitutional government for the first time in her history. In 1970, Stalin's Constitution of 1936 was still in force. After 1945 it became the prototype for the constitutions of all the other Communist states.

The Constitution is based on the fundamental Marxist principle that the political structure of a country is an expression of its economic and social structure. Its opening clauses state that the USSR is a socialist state in which all power is vested in the toilers and workers of the towns and villages. The land, transport system, communications, banks, factories, municipal enterprises, state farms and 'the bulk of the dwelling houses in the towns' are state property. Collective farms and co-operative societies may own the property – but not the land itself; individuals may own their houses and private farm plots. There is freedom to save and to bequeath but not to employ labour and 'the economic life of the USSR is determined by the state national-economic plan.' In the West, the political system, that of multi-party parliamentary democracy, is regarded as more fundamental than the economic system, which is a matter for regulation, in so far as it needs regulation, through the established constitutional machinery. Thus Western democracy can tolerate a multiplicity of political parties which advocate private or public ownership as long as they do not seek to destroy the democratic constitution. 'The most democratic constitution in the world', however, can tolerate *only* the Communist Party, the party which affirms that public ownership is right, and private ownership is wrong.

The USSR is a federal state, 'nationalist in form, but socialist in substance'. There are fifteen Union Republics (three of these, Lithuania, Latvia and Estonia, were independent states from 1919 to 1940). Within the Union Republics are twenty autonomous republics, eight autonomous regions and ten national areas. Since the republics have their own constitutions, there are in fact thirty-six subordinate constitutions in the USSR. The USSR is not a federation in the sense understood in the West. First, the Constitution reserves to the Federal Government almost all subjects of any importance, leaving to the republics and regions little more than the right to develop their own culture, and in particular, their own language (over 100 different languages are spoken in the country) side by side with the use and teaching of Russian. Second, in a country where all production is government financed, the Federal Government controls the budgets of the republics. Third, in practice, the Communist Party, which is not federal in structure, dictates policy throughout the Union. Fourth, since two of the republics, the Russian Soviet Federal Socialist Republic (RSFSR) and the Ukraine, contain between them two-thirds of the population and over three-quarters of the industrial wealth of the country, the federal structure is necessarily lop-sided. Finally, Soviet policy towards 'nationalism' has always been ambivalent, since Communism is essentially an international movement, preaching that the working classes of all nations should stand together. During the Second World War Stalin ruthlessly deported whole ethnic groups to Siberia, including five small Mohammedan nations, and the Volga Germans.

The administration is carried out through a hierarchy of Soviets (councils) elected by the villages, towns, districts, regions and republics, and culminating in the Supreme Soviet, the Federal Parliament. All men and women over eighteen have the right to vote. Each Soviet elects an executive committee to carry out policy, but the executive committee of the Soviet above it in the hierarchy can annul its decisions. The Supreme Soviet meets for only a few days twice a year. It elects the top executive committee, the Government or Council of Ministers, whose Chairman is the Premier, which amounts to approving names submitted by the Party leaders. It also endorses, by a show of hands, the decrees and policy statements made by the Government and Party. By 1970, no dissenting vote had ever been recorded. The hard-hitting debating conducted in the parliaments of Western Europe and the complex processes of legislation which they carry out are unknown. At elections to the Soviets there is only one candidate, nominated by the Communist Party and usually, but not always, a Party member.

The Communist Party is an elite, a sort of priesthood, and membership is regarded as a vocation, requiring careful testing and training. In 1939 its numbers amounted to under 2,000,000. Its structure consists of a hierarchy of elected congresses and committees. The lowest is the 'cell', composed of the Party members in each social unit – factory, farm, school or office; within it all are of equal rank. The other members of the social group may not know who the Party members among them are.

At the top of the Party hierarchy is the Party Congress, consisting of up to 5,000 members, which is supposed to meet every four years. The Congress elects the Central Committee, whose size may amount to about 170 full members. The Committee in turn elects a small standing committee of about twelve members, called the Politbureau. This is the real governing body of the Soviet Union. It is like a cross between the British Cabinet and the Curia of the Holy See. It determines doctrine – the 'correct' interpretation of the Marxist-Leninist scriptures – and the 'Party Line' – the policy decreed for particular contingencies. Since the end is held to justify the means, the Party Line may sometimes involve a strange juggling with doctrine as well as the distortion of standards of integrity.

Policy decisions taken in the Politbureau or Central Committee are binding on all lower Party congresses and committees down to the 300,000 cells. The hierarchy of Party organs is parallel to the hierarchy of Soviets; the Soviets carry out the administration, and the Party guides and supervises them. The two structures are interlocked because most of the people who run the Soviets are also Party officials. Thus, the vast centralised Party machine ensures political and ideological conformity throughout the country.

The Secretary-General of the Russian Communist Party (which unlike the Chinese Communist Party has no chairman) dominates the Politbureau and controls the appointment of Party officials throughout the country. Until 1964, the post of Prime Minister was either held by the Secretary-General of the Party himself (as it was by Lenin, and by Stalin from 1941 to 1953), or by administrators who took their orders from the Secretary-General.

In Soviet society, the concept of 'democracy' has a special meaning. It does not mean that individuals have a right to think as they like and do as they like: this might lead them into 'deviationism' – heresy – and 'counter-revolutionary acts' – treason – but it does mean that within the framework of Marxist theory and Communist practice, the whole community should *participate* in discussing the Party Line and the plans for 'building Communism'.

The Constitution, like most of those of post-war Europe, con-

119

tains an impressive statement of 'the Basic Rights and Duties of Citizens' – the economic, social and civil rights. It makes no provision, however, for enforcing them, seeming to assume that they are inherent in the system. In the written constitutions of the United States and of post-war Western European countries, the law courts, or a special court, such as the Supreme Courts of the United States and of West Germany, rule against the government, and can pronounce a law invalid if it violates these rights. The concept of judicial review is unknown in the Communist world. The legal systems of the Western democracies are concerned with the individual as such, in terms of a philosophic ideal of objective 'justice', from which spring his 'rights'. Soviet law is concerned rather with the individual as an integral part of Communist society. There is no real distinction between public and private law. Actions not regarded as criminal in the West, such as being late for work, are crimes against the state in the Soviet Union. The courts consider it their function to assist the deviant member of society to mend his errant ways – which may involve first extracting from him a confession of his sins. This may in part explain the erratic attitude to the death penalty – now abolished, now imposed for crimes such as the theft of state property.

Art, Education, the Family and Religion

Communism aims at a cultural revolution which will produce a 'new type of man'. The Communists reject Western, bourgeois, subjective art, concerned with private feelings. Their cultural policy is called 'socialist realism', and in 1934 the First Congress of Soviet Writers declared it binding on all writers. Since that date, all books – the government is the sole publisher – have to receive the imprimatur of the Union of Soviet Writers. After Stalin came to power, a deadly conformity spread over the Russian press. Many of Russia's most gifted writers committed suicide or died in concentration camps, or, like Boris Pasternak, fell silent. For over two decades, the creative literary genius of the Russians was suppressed. After Stalin's death the poet Olga Berggoltz, in an outburst to a Leningrad audience, attacked the essence of socialist realism. ' ". . . In these poems . . . there are operators of bulldozers and steam shovels; there are horticulturalists, all carefully described . . . but from the outside . . . and the most important thing is lacking . . . a lyric hero with his own individual relationship to events and the landscape." '[1]

Lenin coupled education and collectivity as the essential pillars of the Communist state. The liberal democracies increasingly aim at educating a child to 'be himself', without being clear what this self is, hoping that he will prove to be socially concerned as well as individualistically creative. The Communists believe that a person is only truly himself when he is a Communist, a member of the 'collective'; so they start, as it were, at the other end. Under Lenin, homework, examinations, textbooks and corporal punishment were abolished and the schools were run by the 'collective' of children, workers and teachers (whom the children could dismiss). The practical results were disastrous. Trained minds, particularly in the fields of science and technology, were essential to the success of Stalin's Five-Year Plans; so formal and authoritarian instruction was reintroduced. The study of science was complemented by ideological indoctrination and the cult of Stalin worship:

'He commanded the sun of the enemies to set.
He spoke, and the East for friends became a red glow.
Should he say that coal turn white
It will be as Stalin wills . . .
The master of the entire world . . . is now Stalin.'[2]

By 1939 all children were having four years of schooling, and seven-year schools were being developed in the towns. The literacy rate had risen to eighty-one per cent.[3]

Lenin and his colleagues virtually abolished legal marriage, which they regarded as a bourgeois institution – spontaneous love should replace legal contract – and abortion was legitimized. Stalin reversed this policy, and restored family life to a legal framework of Victorian strictness. In 1936 abortion was forbidden, high fines were imposed for divorce and since 1944 all marriages have had to be legally registered.

Finding that the measures taken by Lenin had not succeeded in stamping out religion, 'the opium of the masses', Stalin started an anti-God campaign, conducted in the class-room and through the radio, the press and the stage. No religious books – not even the Bible – were printed. Freedom of worship, guaranteed in the 1936 Constitution, was interpreted in the narrowest sense and all Church activities other than actual worship were suppressed. Stalin was therefore highly embarrassed when in the census returns of 1937, 50,000,000 Soviet citizens described themselves as 'Believers'. The returns were destroyed, the officials concerned arrested and subsequent censuses omitted all reference to religion.[4]

The Purges

Stalin's purges must rank with Hitler's concentration camps as one of the most terrible experiences in the whole tortured history of the human race. Lenin and his more intellectual colleagues tried to draw a distinction between counter-revolutionaries – bourgeoisie, capitalists, Czarists – whose 'liquidation' was regarded as a historical necessity, and comrades, who could be permitted the luxury of discussion and argument. It was considered an axiom that the death penalty should not be imposed for opposition within the Party. Justice was meted out to toilers, workers and comrades according to 'revolutionary' or 'socialist' legality. By the mid-thirties, the real counter-revolutionaries had been completely eliminated. Stalin's economic and political policies had, however, met with considerable criticism from some of the comrades. Stalin, the son of Georgian serfs, was terrified of rivals superior to himself in intellectual calibre and culture. In his key speech to the Twentieth Congress of the Communist Party in 1956, Nikita Khrushchev said of him: '. . . Everywhere and in everything he saw "enemies", "two-facers" and "spies". Possessing unlimited power, he indulged in great wilfulness and choked a person morally and physically. A situation was created where one could not express one's own will.'[5] Moreover, Stalin had antagonized the majority of the peasants.

From 1935, a daemonic paranoia impelled Stalin to jettison

'socialist legality' and launch the greatest 'purge' in history. It is estimated that 1,000,000 people were executed. They included all Lenin's closest comrades except Trotsky (who was in exile), a large proportion of the leading army officers, intellectuals and Party members and thousands of ardent foreign Communists who had sought refuge from persecution in the holy land of Communism. Many people, branded without evidence as 'sabotteurs' and 'wreckers', were sent to a slow death in forced labour camps whose average population has been estimated at 8,000,000. A special feature of the purges was the show trial, at which devoted Party personalities confessed, after torture, that they were in reality agents and tools of 'the enemies of the people'.

In the years 1935 to 1938, most of the bravest spirits and the best minds of a whole generation were wiped out. The majority of those who survived had collaborated with the Dictator, or sunk into cowed apathy.

Stalin's Last Years: 1945-1953

The German invasion wrought catastrophic damage in Russia. It must have seemed to the ordinary Russian that all the immense sacrifices which he had made since the Revolution to 'build Communism' had been in vain. Yet there were intangible gains. The Soviet Union was now the second greatest power in the world. The defensive fortress psychology was replaced by national self-confidence and pride. Russia could talk with the great capitalist powers on equal, if not superior, terms and this would gradually impel it to accept the realities of the non-Communist world. During the war and the occupation of East Germany and East Europe millions of primitive peasants in the Red Army saw with their own eyes what this world was like, and marvelled. (Many were punished for seeing what they had seen when they got home.) The war also had a profound long-term effect on the Russians' attitude to their own régime. To those who had fought and suffered under Stalin's leadership in 'the great patriotic war' it seemed monstrous to be made to suffer further at his hands. The Russians began to emerge out of their apathy.

Stalin was now sixty-six. His aims were to retain in his own hands the monopoly of power which he had established since 1928, to rebuild Russia's shattered economy, and to extend Soviet domination over as much of Europe as he could effectively control.

The Fourth Five-Year Plan was introduced in 1946. Like the pre-war Plans, it gave first priority to heavy industry and armaments – iron and steel were set at thirty-five per cent above the pre-war level, coal at fifty-one per cent and electricity at seventy per cent. The agricultural targets were more modest, and the consumer goods targets were low.[6]

The Western powers had given Russia three billion dollars' worth of aid during the war, but afterwards American Lend-Lease aid was cut off and Stalin refused to accept Marshall aid. Once again, the Russian people had to go it alone. They succeeded: by 1950 the industrial level of 1940 had been exceeded by forty per cent, by 1960 steel production had risen from 10,000,000 tonnes in 1945 (19,000,000 tonnes in 1940) to 65,000,000 tonnes – 5,000,000 more than the target – and by 1965 to 90,000,000 tonnes. (The United States in that year produced 125,000,000 tonnes).[7] In 1949 Russia exploded an atomic bomb and in 1953, a hydrogen bomb – proof to an astonished world that its technology was as sophisticated as that of the West. This 'economic miracle' was facilitated by booty from Germany and Eastern Europe, estimated at ten per cent of the total fixed investment of the state between 1945 and 1956, by the labour of some 2,000,000 German prisoners-of-war, not repatriated until 1955–6, and of the inmates of the labour camps, still numbering millions. Its basis was once again the will and muscle power of the ordinary Russian. The lazy, drunken, illiterate peasant of the Tsarist days had somehow been transformed. He was now literate, disciplined and 'motivated'; yet he retained the capacity, which had been inculcated through the centuries, to endure rough living.

Agricultural recovery lagged behind, as did housing and the provision of consumer goods. In 1946 there was the worst drought since 1890 and in 1947 Russia experienced her last famine.

Stalin had purged Russia's creative-minded economists, and he was ignorant of economics as a modern science. He was unable to identify the real problems of the Soviet economy as it moved into the age of the second industrial revolution. By 1953 '... the Soviet economy resembled an exhausted beast. It had been driven far and fast and was near collapse.'[8]

To achieve these economic results and to counteract the effect of Western influences, Stalin had to continue the pre-war reign of terror. The secret police, headed by Lavrenti Beria, controlled the Party as well as the people. Loyal citizens continued to be arrested and sent to labour camps. One among millions was Alexander Solzhenitsyn, a graduate in mathematics and literature, who had been decorated for bravery in the war, but was arrested in 1945 for making derogatory remarks about Stalin. He emerged in 1953 to become one of the greatest Russian writers of the twentieth century. The renewed purges particularly affected the Party and the intellectuals. A quarter of the population of the Baltic States (annexed by Stalin in 1940), comprising the middle class and the intelligentsia, were deported to Siberia. The great Marshal Zhukov, the popular hero who had led the Russian armies into Berlin, was sent to a minor post in the provinces. The numbers executed were not, however, on the scale of the thirties.

Fear of foreign influences fell particularly heavily on the artists. Two French students, the first students from a capitalist country to be awarded scholarships to study in Moscow University, described the atmosphere they found in 1954 as follows:

This was the time of library books with torn out pages and deleted names, when Western culture stopped at Dickens and Balzac, when science was either proletarian or bourgeois. Everything was judged by the crudest possible yardstick of its social context and its relevance to the final aim ... There were no half tones ... In spite of the traditional warmth of Russian and of Soviet hospitality, it was impossible to have a serious conversation with anyone. The exceptions ... I found were Sinyavsky and Daniel (young Russian writers) ... Knowing them was a revelation, ... they ... made me understand how and why, in spite of appearances, the Soviet Union was also, and deeply, a great modern experiment and not merely the clumsy, fraudulent, deliberately naïve piece of ambitious reck-lessness it seemed.[9]

As for the musicians, Prokofiev and Shostakovich, two of the greatest world composers of the twentieth century, were sup-posed to write songs which the workers could sing in the fields.

Science was also dragooned. A geneticist, Trofim Lysenko, put forward the theory that acquired characteristics could be trans-mitted genetically to future generations. In the face of all reputable scientific opinion Stalin supported the theory because it suited Communist ideology, thereby crippling Soviet genetics for two decades when the improvement of crop yields was vital for Russia's economy.

During these years, Stalin ruled Russia and its satellite empire in the style of an oriental despot. No Party Congress was held between 1939 and 1952, and there were few meetings of the Party's Central Committee. The Politbureau was his tool. This is how he appeared in 1945 to the Yugoslav Communist leader Milovan Djilas, who had come to Moscow in a spirit of hero-worship:

An ungainly dwarf of a man passed through gilded and marbled imperial halls, and a path opened before him; radi-ant, admiring glances followed him, while the ears of courtiers strained to catch his every word ... He knew that he was one of the cruellest, most despotic figures in human history, but this did not worry him a bit, for he was convinced that he was carrying out the will of history ... Poets were inspired by him, orchestras blared cantatas in his honour, philosophers in in-stitutes wrote tomes about his sayings, and martyrs died on scaffolds crying out his name. His power, absolute over a sixth of the globe, was spreading farther and farther. This convinced him that his society contained no contradictions and that it was superior to every other society in every way. He joked, too, with his courtiers – 'comrades' – I, too, was swept up by Stalin and his witticisms. But in one little corner of my mind and of my moral being I was awake and troubled: I noticed the tawdriness, too, and could not inwardly accept Stalin's manner of joking – nor his deliberate avoidance of saying a single human, comradely word to me.[10]

In 1952, Stalin finally summoned the Nineteenth Party Congress, at which a new Central Committee (Party Praesidium) were elected; and it appeared that he was planning to replace his old henchmen by younger men. A new purge seemed to be in the offing, heralded by an accusation that a number of Jewish doctors had poisoned some of the dead Soviet leaders. Then, on 5 March 1953, Stalin died. 'Trained to believe that Stalin was taking care of everyone, people were lost and bewildered without him. The whole of Russia wept. So did I. We wept sincerely with grief and perhaps also with fear of the unknown.' So wrote the young poet Yevgeny Yevtushenko in his *Autobiography*.[11]

The Khrushchev Era: 1953-1964
Khrushchev's rise to power

Stalin had not designated a successor, but shortly after his death Nikita Khrushchev emerged as First Secretary of the Party, and Georgi Malenkov (who in the pre-war purges had worked in Stalin's private office compiling the lists of victims) as Prime Minister. Marshal Zhukov was brought back to power as Minister of Defence. At first who held which post did not seem to be of vital importance since the top leaders immediately denounced the 'personality cult' as 'immature' and announced that 'collective leadership', the 'correct' Communist system, would take its place.

However, doctrine is one thing, practice another. Khrushchev, hitherto less close to the seat of power than Malenkov, engineered Malenkov's resignation from the premiership in 1955 and Bulganin succeeded him. In June 1957, a majority of Khrushchev's colleagues in the Party Praesidium (the renamed Politbureau), led by the Stalinist Molotov and the disgruntled Malenkov, conspired to oust him. Their plan was simple: to out-vote him in the Praesidium. Khrushchev countered this by an equally simple device: he summoned a meeting of the Central Committee of the party; his ally, Zhukov, supplied military planes to ferry the members into Moscow from all over the country, and in the Committee he secured a vote in his favour. Molotov and Malenkov lost their posts and were appointed respectively ambassador in Mongolia, and head of an electric power station in Siberia. Later in the year, Zhukov, also a poten-tial rival, was again dismissed. In January 1958 Khrushchev took over the premiership from Bulganin, who was made Chair-man of the State Bank.

Like Lenin and Stalin before him, Khrushchev now held both the most important posts in the country, although he had not achieved this by terror. The only leading Communist to be 'liqui-dated' after Stalin's death was Lavrenti Beria, the sinister head of Stalin's secret police, who was shot in June 1953. Khrushchev had not only established his position without bloodshed, but in Communist terms, by constitutional means.

The relaxation of the terror

Khrushchev and his colleagues realized that if the Russian peoples' energies were to be mobilized for the great tasks ahead, they must be freed from fear of arbitrary persecution. The apparatus of the Reign of Terror was largely disbanded. The powers of the secret police were considerably reduced, and most of the inmates of the labour camps were freed. Many of the victims of the purges, including most of the deported racial groups, were 'rehabilitated'; pre-war edicts which had authorized convictions without objec-tive evidence and tied workers to their jobs, were repealed. Censorship was relaxed, limited foreign travel was permitted for professional purposes and Russians began to talk to the foreigners who visited their country in increasing numbers. But the police, the prisons and the camps remained in the background, for arbitrary use when required. The recodification of the laws after 1953 in order to establish a solid structure of 'socialist legality' only added to the inherent contradiction in the situation. According to Marxist doctrine, as Communist society develops, ending exploitation and bringing with it increased material affluence for all, crime should 'wither away'. But Soviet citizens, and in particular Soviet youth, continued to get drunk, to steal and to profiteer. So disturbing was this failure of human nature to conform to the Marxist model that in 1961 the death penalty was introduced for a number of economic crimes, including indulging in private enterprise.

Khrushchev's personality and attitudes

During the crucial decade in which the whole aspect of world affairs was transformed by the technology of the second industrial revolution, the development of nuclear missiles and the emergence of the Third World, Soviet policies at home and abroad were essentially directed by Nikita Khrushchev.

Like Stalin, Khrushchev started life as a peasant. He was born in 1894 in the village of Kalinovka in the Ukraine. The meaning of peasant poverty and the horrors of pre-revolutionary capitalism at its worst, haunted him throughout his career. His first wife died in the Ukrainian famine of 1921. Barely able to read and write, Khrushchev worked for the Communist Party during the First World War and the Civil War, and finally, through the Party, received a technical college education. Emotionally an ardent Marxist, he was not interested in intellectual speculation or dogmatic interpretation. He took it for granted that Marxists were on the right side of history and concentrated on what really absorbed him: practical solutions to practical problems. Energetic, efficient, uncritical, he was just the type whom Stalin needed to carry out his policies in the twenties and thirties. From 1938 to 1948, Khrushchev ruled the Ukraine, first organizing a major purge, and then promoting the war effort, including the partisan warfare, and assisting in the battle of Stalingrad. He was deeply involved in the sufferings of the war, and in the

129

problems of the people. In 1949, Stalin brought him back to Moscow to a senior post in the Party Secretariat.[12]

Khrushchev continuously travelled about the country, inspecting, advising, chiding, joking, behaving not like an awesome father figure, but like a cozy and somewhat absurd uncle; not like a dictator who sat in the Kremlin, cold-bloodedly sending millions to their deaths for 'reasons of state', but like a human being who genuinely cared about the welfare of other human beings. Here is an extract from a speech he made in Vladivostock in 1959, a speech not intended for foreign ears:

> Here in Vladivostock we met a woman . . . walking along with her kiddies . . . 'Well, how are things going?' I asked. 'Not bad,' she said . . . and then added 'In connexion with your visit they've chucked a lot of shoes and boots and textiles into our shops. Come and see us more often; the shops will be full of stuff then!' So I said . . . 'since you live on the coast, do you get enough fresh fish in the shops?' 'Well,' she said, 'there's plenty of salt herring; as for fresh fish, sometimes we get it, and sometimes we don't.' No doubt salt herring is very nice with potatoes and onions, or *tsibulka*, as we call it in the Ukraine; but all this is not good enough. We talked about it to the local leaders. I told them it was no good 'chucking in' goods to mark the arrival of the top leaders; 'and when I have left, you'll no doubt begin to 'chuck out' the stuff.'[13]

Khrushchev was as curious about foreign countries as he was about affairs inside Russia. He visited Poland, Yugoslavia, China, India, Burma, Afghanistan, Egypt, Britain, France, Austria, Scandinavia and the United States. His attitude to the Western world was both friendly and suspicious, arrogant and touchy, and yet eager to be accepted. When he visited the United States in 1959, he exclaimed in astonishment, 'Where are the peasants?' He reacted warm-heartedly to the kindness of his hosts. (See chapter 14).

At a session of the United Nations' General Assembly in September 1960, he lost his temper when the Philippine delegate attacked Soviet policy, banged his desk with his shoe, and shouted out that the speaker was 'the lackey of American imperialism.' The next day, however, he apologized, saying: 'I am a young parliamentarian; he is an old hand. Let us learn from each other.'[14] In various ways Khrushchev's leadership was vital to the development of the Soviet Union and of world affairs. At home he did not change the basic constitutional, economic and social structures that Lenin and Stalin had established but he introduced a new atmosphere and style. In foreign affairs, he changed the whole direction of the Cold War, and in particular, the nature of the Soviet Union's relations with her satellites.

Internal political developments under Khrushchev

In 1956, in a famous speech to a secret session of the Twentieth Party Congress, Khrushchev passionately denounced Stalin's policies and his cult of the individual. To the astounded delegates he gave facts and figures about the purges of the thirties and moving accounts of the sufferings of the victims, and castigated Stalin's self-glorification. 'Comrades,' he said, 'the cult of the individual acquired such monstrous size chiefly because Stalin himself, using all conceivable methods, supported the glorification of his own person ... His "Short Biography", published in 1948' (a compulsory text for all schoolchildren, students, workers, and soldiers) 'is an expression of the most dissolute flattery.'[15] The speech was not published inside Russia until 1961 but was circulated to Party members; its text was smuggled abroad and its contents quickly became common knowledge. The immediate effect was shattering. 'After the text was read', wrote the young poet Yevtushenko, '... many among the older people tormented themselves with the question: had they lived their lives in vain? ... A part of the younger generation naturally looked with suspicion not only on Stalin but on the past as a whole, and this doubled the distress of their parents.'[16] A German journalist was told by a building worker: 'For years, since my earliest childhood, Stalin had been held up to me as Stalin the Great, the Benevolent, the Wise, and I believed it implicitly. Now the whole picture has suddenly changed, and I simply don't know what to believe.'[17] 'All my friends,' wrote one of the

French students referred to above, 'reacted in the same, typically Russian way. Ashamed for their country ... they were even more ashamed of their own inertia, ... due to the fact that they had confused patriotism with passivity.'[18] Out of the Russians' sense of collective shame a new sense of *positive* patriotism was born, which sought expression in a passionate desire to expose the double-think and deceit which permeated Soviet life.

In 1961 the embalmed body of Stalin was removed from the mausoleum in the Red Square where it had lain side by side with that of Lenin; his portraits and statues were torn down, and the famous city of Stalingrad was renamed Volgograd.

The attack on the personality cult and the debunking of Stalin may prove to have been a turning point in the history of the Soviet Union. After 1956, the claim of Russia's leaders to be the infallible interpreters of the revealed truth of Marxism was undermined, although they tried to shore up the damage by building up the remoter image of Lenin. Russia had perhaps begun to experience, in modern terms, the cataclysmic change of outlook started in Western Europe by the Reformation – the change from adherence to external authority to affirmation of the primacy of personal reason and conscience.

In the conduct of political affairs, the style was also changed. Khrushchev aimed at revitalizing the Party. Stalin had reduced it by his purges to an administrative machine, but Khrushchev began to fill its ranks with members of the intelligentsia emerging from the new schools and universities. Membership increased from 6,000,000 in 1953 to 10,000,000 in 1963. At the top, Party Congresses and Central Committee meetings were held regularly. At the bottom, the atmosphere was lively. A widely read novel of the period, *The Seekers*, described a Party meeting at a scientific institute at which the members staged an uproar when the Party Secretary tried to rig the election of officials.[19] As Soviet society rapidly became more sophisticated and affluent, the Party inevitably tended to become less the interpreter of doctrine, and more the harmonizer of interests and pressure groups; to appeal less to the authority of *any* prophet, be it Stalin or Lenin (Khrushchev never set himself up in this role) and more to 'scientific laws'. Since Communist policy was now producing scientists and amassing scientific information on a scale unequalled except in the United States, the basing of Party policies on scientific laws meant adjusting 'scientific' Marxist-Leninism to the facts of life revealed by economists, sociologists and psychologists as well as physical scientists. If science is by its very nature an undogmatic activity, where will this lead?[20, 21]

Khrushchev's economic policies

Khrushchev believed that Communism must provide material affluence. He took a long step forward in developing a bourgeois society in Russia. This was to prove a major cause of tension with the Stalinists at home and abroad, especially the Chinese, who accused him of the heresy of 'practicism' – to which Khrushchev replied: 'You cannot put theory into your soup or Marxism into your clothes. If, after forty years of Communism, a person cannot have a glass of milk or a pair of shoes, he will not believe that Communism is a good thing, no matter what you tell him.'[22] Immediately after Stalin's death, higher priority was given to consumer goods. According to Soviet figures, the production of leather shoes, woollen fabrics and knitted clothes was more than doubled between 1953 and 1963. The output of refrigerators rose during this period from 49,000 to nearly 1,000,000 and of radio and TV sets from nearly 1,000,000 to over 7,000,000. Nevertheless, for a country of 220,000,000 people, the figures were still pitifully low. The housing target only involved raising the allowance per person from 4.67 square metres to 6.8 square metres.[23] Khrushchev personally decided against a policy of producing 'peoples' cars'.

The Plans of the Khrushchev era brought the Soviet Union fully into line with the second industrial revolution. Stalin's great industrial achievements were based essentially on coal and iron. In the fifties the switch over was started to an economy geared to oil, natural gas and water power. By 1961, the Soviet Union was the world's second largest oil producer (the United States was still the first); huge pipelines were taking the crude oil from

the old Caspian and the new Volga oil fields thousands of kilometres east into Siberia and west into European Russia and Communist Eastern Europe. The Soviet Union's production rose from
134,000,000 tonnes in 1940 to 243,000,000 tonnes in 1965, and
66,000,000 tonnes were being exported. Vast reserves of natural
gas were discovered in Siberia and elsewhere, and the first main
pipeline from the fields near Bukhara to the industrial towns of the
Urals was completed in 1963. Giant dams were also being constructed on the Volga, and the Siberian rivers – the Krasnoyarsk
dam, on the Yenisei River, had in 1970 the worlds' largest generators (500,000 kw capacity). Khrushchev's planners transformed
Russia's electric power situation from a pre-war capacity equal
to that of Norway, into a system of huge generators linked by
high voltage transmission lines to industrial consumers.

Another Soviet technological break-through, paralleled in the
United States, consisted in upgrading low quality iron ore – the
richer ore was being worked out. Under Khrushchev's plans, the
biggest blast furnaces in the world were built at Magnitogorsk in
the Urals and Krivoi Rog in the Ukraine.[24]

Khrushchev took a number of steps to increase agricultural
production. The most spectacular was the ploughing up of
225,000,000 hectares (equivalent to the whole crop land of
Canada) in Khazistan and Siberia but the top soil blew off and
yields were variable. Khrushchev consolidated the 250,000 collective and state farms into some 50,000 huge farms of an average
size of 37,500 hectares, increased the production of agricultural
machinery and fertilizers, reduced collective farm quotas, raised
the prices of their deliveries, and relaxed the restrictions on the
private plots.

At first Khrushchev's industrial and agricultural policies were
successful. Production in both sectors rose fifty per cent between
1954 and 1958. (In agriculture this improvement was mainly
from the private plots!) The launching of Sputnik in 1957
symbolized the fact that in technology the Soviet Union was
coming abreast of the West. However, after 1959, the economy
began to get into difficulties. Investment in the missile and space
race with the United States drained off capital, and the mono-

lithic bureaucracy inherited from Stalin was unsuited to the complexities of the computer age.

The development of education under Khrushchev

Before the war, Stalin had laid the basis for mass education from primary school to university. During the war, 82,000 schools, which had accomodated 15,000,000 pupils, eight universities and 200 other institutions of higher learning were destroyed.[25] By the late fifties not only had this damage been repaired, but free education was available for the vast majority of country children from seven to fifteen, and for the majority of urban children from seven to seventeen. Forty universities and over 700 other institutions of higher learning were giving free education of a very rigorous kind (five years at the university) to over 2,000,000 students, sixty per cent of whom were studying science subjects.[26] In 1956, the Twentieth Party Congress proclaimed the goal of ten years' education for all children. Ten years later, the number of students in higher education had risen to 4,000,000.

Education continued to be carried out according to the rigid, didactic methods established by Stalin, but throughout their school life the children were exposed to the writings of the great Russian masters and to Soviet literature from Gorky onwards. Although the teacher would dutifully give the Marxist interpretation of the work in terms of the writer's social background,

> There comes the moment ... when (he) finally shuts his mouth and the pupil opens the book for himself. From the very first line, Pushkin speaks directly to the young. Whatever the comrade teacher may have to say about the class struggle at the beginning of the nineteenth century, or about the exploitation of the Russian serfs by the landlords, pales beside the shining creations of Pushkin's imagination; in the relation of his characters to each other it is not class but common humanity that plays the vital role.[27]

If the study of science is undermining Marxist dogmatism, the study of the immortal works of Russian literature is surely undermining Marxist philosophic materialism.

The cultural thaw

The result of the immediate post-Stalin 'thaw' was to unleash the suppressed energies of the writers and artists. Lyric poetry appeared again, such as the poems written by Pasternak for his novel *Dr Zhivago*, and by the young Yevtushenko, and there was also a spate of plays and novels which criticized the way Communism was working in practice. One of the most famous was Alexander Solzhenitsyn's *One Day in the Life of Ivan Denisovich,* in which he described life in the forced labour camp in which he had spent eight years. By 1957, Khrushchev was troubled by the results of his 'thaw'. Pasternak, believing that his novel *Dr Zhivago* was going to be published in Russia, had sent a copy to an Italian Communist publisher. In several Western countries it was hailed as a masterpiece and Pasternak was awarded a Nobel Prize. The Soviet authorities then informed him that his book would *not* be published in Russia; he was expelled from the Writers' Union – which condemned him to literary silence – and told that if he went to Sweden to receive the prize, he would not be allowed to return. He refused it and died free but ostracized in 1960.

Pasternak was a deeply religious man. 'The Kremlin leaders ... reacted violently, not because the novel is anti-revolutionary (it is not), but because it is wholly apolitical. Its main message is that it is the human soul that counts, rather than political events.'[28] After 1960, Yevtushenko (born in 1933) and Sinyavsky and Daniel (both born in 1930) deliberately sent to the West for publication books which they knew would be rejected for publication in Russia; books which directly indicted the tyranny, terror and deceit of the Soviet regime as a betrayal of the true ideals of Communism. The publication in 1963 of Yevtushenko's *A Precocious Autobiography* raised a hornet's nest of protest in the Soviet establishment, for the young poet had been allowed to travel freely in the Western world, where he had made a highly favourable impression and improved the Soviet Union's image.

If the reader believes in God I will ask him: 'Can you equate the substance of Christianity with the swindlers who made money by selling indulgences, with the inquisitors, the priests who got rich at their parishioners' expense or the parishioners who pray in church and do shady deals outside it?' Neither can I, a believing Communist, equate the substance of my religion with the crooks who climb on its band-wagon, with its inquisitors, its crafty, avaricious priests or its double-thinking, double-faced parishioners.[29]

In 1962, Khrushchev told several hundred intellectuals that 'peaceful co-existence in the sphere of ideology is treachery to Marxism-Leninism.'[30] But during Khrushchev's rule, the majority of the intellectuals, though temporarily subdued, were left free.

Khrushchev's downfall

Khrushchev's failures – his handling of the quarrel with China, the Cuban missile affair, and most of all, the failure of his economic policies – brought about his downfall. In October 1964 a group of Party bureaucrats and military men summoned the Party Praesidium (renamed the Politbureau in 1965) and the Central Committee, while he was on holiday, and on his return outvoted him in both bodies. For the first time in Russian history the government was changed, other than by death, in a peaceful and orderly way. Yet there was still no comparison with the method of changing the government in a Western democracy. In Britain, Khrushchev would have become the leader of Her Majesty's Opposition, or been given a peerage. Instead, he vanished into obscurity, becoming a political 'unperson'.

Internal Affairs Since Khrushchev

The Central Committee of the Party elected Leonid Brezhnev to succeed Khrushchev as Party Secretary; and Alexei Kosygin became Prime Minister. Born into working-class families in 1906 and 1905 respectively, they have been described as 'faceless organization men'. Brezhnev was a bureaucrat who rose to power as the henchman of Stalin and Khrushchev, conniving at Stalin's purges. Kosygin was the Soviet Union's first technocratic statesman, his career having been mainly devoted to trying to make Soviet industry work more efficiently.

These men felt that the independent, open-ended thinking which was beginning to bubble up as a result of Khrushchev's 'thaw' threatened the system which had moulded them and brought them to the pinnacle of power. They pressed ahead with economic and technological development, therefore, while clamping down on freedom in the field of ideas. In the economic sphere, Brezhnev and Kosygin continued Khrushchev's basic policy of 'goulash Communism' – the expansion of consumer goods production, which between 1960 and 1970 was given almost equal priority with industrial equipment. Special emphasis was given to housing – in 1968 11,000,000 people moved into new dwellings, mostly two-roomed flats. The Italian firm of Fiat was engaged to erect an £584,000,000 plant at Togliatti-on-Volga, which would produce 600,000 cars a year in twelve models. So great was the demand for the 'peoples' cars', that in 1969 the manager of the central retail agency in Moscow warned that 'signing up now on the privately circulating waiting list was like signing up for a plot of lunar real estate.'[31] Owing to the appalling condition of the roads, the average speed of state-owned vehicles was stated in 1969 to be twenty-nine kilometres an hour.[32]

The development of a consumer-oriented society in Russia made it essential to break through the log-jam in the economic bureaucracy, which employed some 2,500,000 officials and used the crude planning techniques developed in the thirties for the basic capital infrastructure. The great investment in scientific research and in education was not producing a commensurate rise in the level of production. An eminent Soviet economist estimated that a quarter to a third of potential output was being wasted.[33]

Between 1965 and 1970, Brezhnev and Kosygin began to reform the system. First, they introduced computer technology into the centralized planning administration.[34] Second, they generalized the 'Libermann system' launched by Khrushchev, based on the ideas of Professor Yevsei Libermann of Kharkov

University, under which factory managers were given some responsibility for planning their own production targets in relation to their own assessment of consumer demands, and for using their wage funds as they wished. This meant that they could fire redundant workers, pay those whom they employed higher wages, and distribute profits as bonuses. However, the reform did not involve a real 'socialist market economy' of the kind which was developing in Eastern Europe, because the government continued to control the fixing of prices and the allocation of materials, which, in a market economy, are left free to operate according to the law of supply and demand. Nor was there any question of introducing industrial democracy of the Yugoslav type, which the Soviet leaders branded in 1968 as 'revisionist'.

In 1964 thirty per cent of Russia's labour force was still employed on the land, as compared with ten to fifteen per cent in Western Europe and five per cent in the United States. By 1970, the Soviet leaders appeared to have achieved a breakthrough in solving the agricultural problem. Between 1956 and 1960, the average annual grain harvest was 121,000,000 tonnes; between 1966 and 1969, it had risen to 162,000,000 tonnes; and the target for 1971–6 was set for 195,000,000 tonnes. These results were achieved by raising productivity, in particular by a crash programme of fertilizer production; by giving farms a fifty per cent increase in payment for deliveries to the State above their quotas; and by State subsidies to private plots.[35, 36]

After 1964, the Soviet economy moved out of the recession of the last few years of Khrushchev's rule. Real incomes of farm and industrial workers rose steadily. There was a growing shortage of labour (in contrast to the United States, where in 1970 4,500,000 workers, six per cent of the labour force, were unemployed). There was also growing labour indiscipline, and in 1970, a new strict labour code was introduced, providing for exile to Siberia for work defaulters. In that year, a Georgian factory manager was condemned to death for 'economic crimes'; the first reported death sentence of this kind since 1956.[37] However, 'the experience of all advanced countries has shown that

139

once a nation has committed itself to economic rationality, as Russia has done, it has got to use incentives rather than coercion.[38] By 1970, it seemed that in economic matters the Soviet leaders were approaching a critical point. They would either have to go forward to a real socialist market economy, or turn back to real 'Stalinism'. Such turning back was in fact unthinkable, since it would mean turning back on the Soviet Union's role as a technological super-power.

Khrushchev's successors pursued a policy of 'creeping Stalinization' in regard to literature and political expression. Sinyavsky and Daniel were sentenced to several years in labour camps for slandering the Soviet system by publishing their books abroad. Solzhenitsyn's novels, *Cancer Ward* and *The First Circle*, about the anguish of human beings under the shadow of death, were refused publication in Russia but were published abroad. They were at once acclaimed as great works, and Solzhenitsyn was awarded the Nobel Prize in 1970. He had been expelled from the Writers' Union in 1969 for protesting against censorship of the Press, and he was told that if he went abroad to receive the prize, he would not be allowed to return to Russia. Like Pasternak, he did not go. A number of other young writers suffered the same fate as Sinyavsky and Daniel. A particularly sinister way of dealing with these dissenters was to confine them without trial to lunatic asylums.

The invasion of Czechoslovakia in 1968 sparked off open political protests for the first time since 1918. In October 1968, Pavel Litvinov, a physicist and the grandson of Maxim Litvinov, Soviet Foreign Minister from 1930 to 1939, and Larissa Daniel, wife of the writer Daniel, were arrested for demonstrating peacefully against the invasion, and sentenced to several years of banishment. At his trial Litvinov cited Article 125 of the Soviet Constitution, which guarantees freedom of speech and of assembly 'in the interests of socialism':

Who (he said) is to judge what is in the interests of socialism? Perhaps the prosecutor, who spoke with admiration, almost with tenderness, of those who beat us up and insulted us. And he is a legal expert ... Evidently it is these people who are supposed to know what is socialism and what is counter-revolution. That is what I find is terrible, and that is why I went to Red Square. That is what I have fought against and what I shall continue to fight against for the rest of my life, by all the lawful means known to me.[38]

This bold speech by a young man reared under Communism was a far cry from the abject 'confessions' extracted from the victims of Stalin's purge trials of the thirties.

Other victims of neo-stalinism included the Baptists and other Christian sects, and the Crimean Tartars, who had been deported by Stalin to Siberia in 1944 and were being persecuted for protesting at the refusal of the authorities to allow them, twenty-five years later, to return to their homes. One estimate in 1969 put the numbers in prison camps at 1,000,000.

Something new was happening. A vast amount of underground literature called *Samizdat* was circulating from hand to hand, informing Soviet citizens of the fate of these people and discussing what reforms were needed. A Western reporter commented that:

> The political ideas aired in this underground way are becoming much more sophisticated and outspoken. They range from the Christian personalism of the All-Russian Social-Christian Union, whose leading members were imprisoned in 1967, to the more straightforward liberal ideas of the Democratic Movement of the Soviet Union ... Their factual tone and realistic approach betrays none of the senseless fear of Stalin's time.[39]

Even highly respected voices of the Soviet Establishment weighed in. Academician Andrei Sakharov (see p. 291) known as 'the father of the hydrogen bomb', was reported in 1970 to be forming a 'Committee for Human Rights' in the Soviet Union, and to have warned the Kremlin that the régime must institute democratic reforms or court international disaster.[41]

The members of the Soviet Civil Rights movement were citing

the provisions of the Soviet Constitution and legal system. They were also citing the United Nations' Universal Declaration of Human Rights. They were appealing to the conscience of the world. The intellectuals of the world, including members of the Communist parties of the West, made an extraordinary response. Suffering and sympathy were forging one more bridge across the Iron Curtain.

Conclusion

In bringing education and bourgeois affluence to the Russian masses, the 'dark people' of 1917, the Communist regime was sowing the seeds of its own transformation. In the Introduction we drew attention to the basic contradiction in the Marxists' claim to be 'scientific' and at the same time to possess a unique and prophetic revelation of truth. By 1970, the tension produced by this contradiction was becoming acute in the minds of many intellectuals and young people reared under Communism. In this context, the sudden emergence of the 'New Left' on a world-wide scale in the late sixties deeply disturbed the Soviet leaders. For behind the smokescreen of the 'Maoist', 'Neo-Trotskyist' and other confused ideas, what seemed to be emerging was the specific demand for socialism combined with freedom, the 'socialism with a human face' of Czechoslovakia. To the 'New Left', the Soviet Establishment was as conservative and repressive as any capitalist regime.

The tide of affairs is surely bearing the Russians into fuller contacts of all kinds with their fellow Europeans in the West. The West offers them the fruits of freedom and of sophistication. What will they offer the West? Yevtushenko suggests an answer:

The Russian people have suffered throughout their history as perhaps no other. Suffering might be expected to blunt and degrade the human spirit, destroying its capacity for faith in anything. Yet if we look attentively at the history of nations, just the opposite seems to be the truth. It is the prosperous nations of today ... which seem to show a grosser spirit and a weaker hold on moral values ... Why was Russia, so backward industrially, the first country to enter upon the path of socialism? Because ... she was perhaps ahead of all the others where her people's tears and sorrows were concerned ... We have paid for our ideal with so much blood that the cost itself has made it all the dearer and more precious to us, as a child born in torment is dearer and more precious to its mother ... For me a communist is a man who puts the common good above his own interests, but who would never wantonly destroy the lives of others in the name of the common good.[42]

REFERENCES

1. Crankshaw, Edward, *Khrushchev's Russia*, Penguin, London, 1963, p. 100.
2. Gordon, Manya, *Workers Before and After Lenin*, E. P. Dutton and Co., New York, 1941, p. 448.
3. Grant, Nigel, *Soviet Education*, Penguin, London, 1968, p. 21.
4. See Grose, Peter: 'God and Communism,' Article in Salisbury, Harrison, ed. *The Soviet Union: The Fifty Years*, The New York Times Co., New York, 1967.
5. Verbatim text in *The Observer*, London, 10 June 1956.
6. Pethybridge, R. W., *A History of Post War Russia*, Allen and Unwin, London, 1966, p. 62.
7. Salisbury, Harrison, *Russia*, Atheneum Press, New York, 1965, pp. 68–9.
8. Judy, R. W., article on 'The Soviet Economy: Commissars to Computers' in the *International Journal of the Canadian Institute for International Affairs*, Vol. XXII, No. 4, autumn 1967.
9. Labedz, Leopold and Hayward, Max, ed., *On Trial: The Case of Sinyavsky (Tertz) and Daniel (Arzhak)*, Collins, London, and Harvill Press, 1967, pp. 324–5 and 332.
10. Djilas, Milovan, *Conversations with Stalin*, Penguin, London, 1963, pp. 84–5.
11. Yevtushenko, Yevgeny, *A Precocious Autobiography*, Penguin, London, 1965, p. 95.
12. This account of Khrushchev's background is taken largely from Frankland, Mark, *Krushchev*, Penguin, London, 1966, pp. 68–9.
13. Quoted in Werth, Alexander, *Russia Under Khrushchev*, Fawcett Publications Inc., Greenwich, Connecticut, 1961, p. 33.
14. Halle, Louis, *op. cit.*, p. 390.
15. *The Observer*, text, see 5 above.
16. Yevtushenko, *op. cit.*, p. 109.

17. Mehnert, Klaus, *The Anatomy of Soviet Man*, Weidenfeld and Nicolson, London, 1962, p. 252.
18. Hélène Zamoyska, essay in Labedz, Leopold, and Hayward, Max, *op. cit.*, p. 56.
19. Mehnert, Klaus, *op. cit.*, pp. 269–70.
20. See Crankshaw, Edward, *op. cit.*, p. 41, pp. 68–9.
21. See Skilling Gordon, 'The Party, Opposition and Interest Groups', article in the *International Journal of the Canadian Institute for International Affairs, op. cit.*
22. Frankland, *op. cit.*, p. 194
23. *The Observer Foreign News Service*, No. 26666, London, 26 June 1969.
24. These paragraphs are based on Thabad, Theodore, article on 'The Resources of a Nation' in Salisbury, Harrison, ed., *op. cit.*
25. Grant, Nigel, *op. cit.*, p. 21, and Pethybridge, *op. cit.*, p. 70.
26. Grant, *op. cit.*, p. 70.
27. Grant, *op. cit.*
28. Mehnert, *op. cit.*, p. 228.
29. Yevtushenko, *op. cit.*, pp. 41–2.
30. Conquest, Robert, ed., *The Politics of Ideas in the USSR*, The Bodley Head, London, 1967.
31. *The Times*, London, 2 February 1969.
32. *The Economist*, London, 8 August 1970.
33. Miller, Margaret, *The Rise of the Russian Consumer*, The Institute of Economic Affairs, London, 1968, p. 21.
34. Sullivan, Walter, article on Soviet Science in Salisbury, Harrison, ed., *op. cit.*, p. 361.
35. *The Observer Foreign News Service*, No. 27901, London, 10 July 1970.
36. *The Economist*, London, 11 July 1970.
37. *Ibid.*
38. *The Economist*, London, 25 July 1970.
39. *The Times*, London, 15 October, 1968.
40. *The Economist*, London, 15 August 1970.
41. *Ibid.*
42. Yevtushenko, *op. cit.*, pp. 39–42.

7. Communist East Europe

1949-1956: the Grim Years

Between 1945 and 1949 one-party regimes, modelled on the Soviet Constitution and led by men trained in and subservient to Moscow, were established in Communist Eastern Europe, except in Yugoslavia and Albania. Some of these men were to remain in power for many years. Walter Ulbricht was still, in 1970, the boss of East Germany at the age of seventy-six. In Czechoslovakia, Antonin Novotny, a bricklayer's son, who had spent the war in a German concentration camp, became First Secretary of the Czech Communist Party in 1953 and effectively ruled the country till January 1968. In Rumania Gheorghe Gheorgiu-Dej, a railway worker who educated himself and directed resistance from his prison cell from 1933–44, ruled Rumania from 1952 till his death in 1965. In Poland and Hungary the 'Muscovites' Boleslaw Bierut and Matyas Rakosi respectively, were in power till 1956. All political opposition had been crushed, all non-Communist writers silenced. The way was clear to make these countries 'communist' on the model of Stalin's Russia, to introduce centralized economic planning, state ownership of industry and collectivization of agriculture.

In the thirties Russian citizens had been asked to renounce a rise in the standard of living for a generation so that the country's heavy-industry infrastructure could be established. After 1945 the Soviet Union set itself to exploit the Eastern European countries in order to restore its own economy. Their industries

145

were to a large extent geared to its own: for example, the Soviet Union bought 200,000 tonnes of sugar a year from Poland at half the world price and uranium mines in Czechoslovakia, Hungary and Rumania were sequestered. In 1956 Khrushchev admitted that the Soviet Union had robbed Poland of $500,000,000 worth of goods during this period.[1] Hungary was despoiled on the same scale. Rumania poured oil, raw materials and wheat into Russia, and from East Germany the Russians took eighteen billion dollars' worth of equipment, nearly double the sum allotted to them under the Potsdam Agreement, amounting to about forty per cent of the state's industrial capacity – including the parallel track of every East German railway. By contrast West Germany, between 1945 and 1950, paid the Allies some two and a half billion dollars, mainly for occupation costs, but received from the USA three billion dollars in Marshall Aid.[2]

The centralized Five or Six-Year Plans introduced into all these countries aimed not only at gearing their existing industries to the needs of the Soviet Union, but at developing new heavy industries suited to Soviet needs. The East Germans, for example, attempted to raise production under their first Plan ninety-two per cent above the 1950 level. Thousands of the good technicians and administrators who should have implemented the Plans were branded as 'enemies of the people' and replaced by incompetent Party stooges. Huge uneconomic steel plants were erected in Hungary, Slovakia and Poland, and heavy industry was started in Bulgaria for which raw materials were not readily available.

In East Germany, Hungary and Poland, where there were still large landowners in 1939, the land was distributed to the peasants in the immediate post-war years. By 1949 East Europe was a region of land-owning peasants. Then the order went forth to collectivize. The process was carried out by less brutal means than in Russia in the thirties – by material inducements and propaganda rather than by the firing squad. By the early sixties the farms had been more or less fully collectivized in all these countries except Poland and Yugoslavia – though, as in the Soviet Union, private plots could be retained. The years 1949 to

1956 were particularly grim. Food and consumer goods were very short; hours of work were increased and wages reduced, in order to finance capital investment. The standard of living declined. Everyone knew who was responsible for the grey misery of their daily lives – the glorious Soviet Union, which their leaders were daily exhorting them to love and thank.

In the face of growing popular hostility the 'Muscovite' leaders increasingly resorted to intimidation and terror. The press was heavily censored; contacts with the West were forbidden, except through Berlin, and the Churches, the only institutions not under Communist control, were deprived of nearly all their property. Church schools were taken over by the state and priests were imprisoned. In East Germany, where the population was seventy-five per cent Lutheran, a third of the Lutheran livings were vacant by 1953. Cardinal Mindszenty, the Primate of Hungary (sixty-seven per cent of the population were Roman Catholic) was arrested on Christmas Day 1948, and sentenced to life imprisonment. Cardinal Wyszynski, the Primate of Poland (the population was ninety-five per cent Catholic) was put under house arrest in 1953. On 26 August 1956, 1,000,000 pilgrims gathered at the Shrine of the Virgin at Czestochowa before his empty throne, filled with flowers.

Special efforts were made to indoctrinate the young people and to intimidate the intellectuals. In Hungary, in 1950–52, some 100,000 members of the middle classes were sent without trial to forced-labour camps. An outstanding East German Communist intellectual, Professor Wolfgang Harich, was arrested in 1956 for 'ideological rebellion' and sentenced to ten years imprisonment. He had published the following parable in a weekly paper:

Once upon a time, in the village school of Schilda, children were taught that 2 plus 2 $= 9$ . . . One day the authorities came to the conclusion that the mathematical fallacy involved in this ideologically educative theorem was in danger of becoming a bit obvious. Yet how to correct it? They could not risk too serious a reverse to law and order; at the same time they could not subject young brains to a jarring surprise. So the schoolteachers ... were told ... to explain, at first, that 2 plus 2 = only 8. They could then, in a purely bourgeois manner, reduce this sum to its drearily correct proportions. The children (and this, after all, was after eleven years of Communist compulsion) learned that 2 plus 2 = 7, they went to the lavatories and chalked up '2 plus 2 = 4.' It then became shockingly apparent that they had known the right answer all the time.[3]

Hundreds of thousands were imprisoned, and thousands were tortured and executed. In a series of dramatic trials a number of Communist leaders who refused to be Soviet stooges were purged as 'Titoist revisionists'. They included the Czech Foreign Minister, Vladimir Clementis, and Party Secretary, Rudolf Slansky; the Hungarian Minister of the Interior, Laszlo Rajk, who was hanged just outside the window of his wife's prison cell, and the Bulgarian Prime Minister, Traicho Kostov, who at his trial made a sensational repudiation of confessions exacted under torture. In 1951 the Polish Communist and war-time Resistance leader, Wadislaw Gomulka, was accused of ideological heresy, and imprisoned. His courage and integrity as well as his popularity saved his life. He would not 'confess' and his inquisitors were afraid of questioning him, and so he was not tortured or tried. But Stalin clamped down on the Poles. One measure was to force them, in 1949, to accept the Russian Marshal Rokossovsky as Minister of Defence and Commander-in-Chief of the army.

The majority lived in cowed fear and bitter humiliation. Society was permeated by agents of the secret police. Hungarian schoolboys would be blackmailed into becoming agents in order to save the lives or jobs of their parents.

The dark deeds were committed in the name of Stalin. His Eastern European henchmen likewise turned themselves into demi-gods. An observer in the mid-sixties noted that:

Ulbricht's birthdays are celebrated with fawning tributes in the press and pledges of higher output in his honour. Delegations of factory workers, children and party functionaries troop to his office to offer congratulations. Ulbricht's framed likeness adorns every office, clubhouse, and factory bulletin board in the country. Chemical plants, pigfarms, and trawler fleets are named after him.[4]

The Revolt against Stalinism: 1953-6

Stalin's death in March 1953 caused the solid ice of Stalinist terror in Eastern Europe to crack. The first rumble occurred in East Germany.

On 17 June 1953 a spontaneous workers' rising was triggered off by a demonstration of building workers in East Berlin, calling for a reduction of work norms and free and secret elections. Workers in coal mines and factories responded; crowds took over public buildings, burnt down Communist Party headquarters, opened the prisons, and formed 'Committees of Public Safety.' Martial law had to be proclaimed in three-quarters of the country and Soviet troops were called in to restore order in almost every town. Afterwards there were forty-two death sentences and 25,000 arrests.

In their Eastern European Empire, as well as inside Russia, the new Soviet leaders were confronted with three choices: to continue Stalinist repression, involving, probably, the direct use of the Red Army, as in East Germany; to let these countries tread the path that *they* wanted to tread, which would mean, in the end, allowing them full national independence and internal liberalization – the slippery road to the collapse of Communism; or to tread a middle path, retaining the essential structure of the Communist state and empire but to try to make it more acceptable to the people in various ways. This was the path they chose, at home and abroad, and they were still treading it in 1970.

The first move in the new Soviet policy for Eastern Europe was to achieve a reconciliation with the excommunicated heretic Tito. Secretary Khrushchev and Premier Bulganin visited him in Belgrade in June 1955 to make amends. A year later Khrushchev proclaimed the doctrine of 'different roads to socialism', implicitly renouncing the Soviet Union's claim to infallibility. The Cominform, which had excommunicated Tito, was dissolved in April 1956. Tito, for his part, made friendly noises but gave nothing away; he refused to join the Warsaw Pact, concluded in May 1956, or the newly refurbished Comecon. In 1970 he was still pursuing this policy of more or less friendly neutrality towards the Soviet Union, while the Russians increasingly sought his support in their quarrel with China. The combination of Tito's triumphant stand, the proclamation of the doctrine of different roads to socialism, the denunciation of the cult of personality and Khrushchev's condemnation of Stalin caused revolt to break out in Poland and Hungary. Khrushchev's speech, in particular, was a bombshell. In both countries a slight thaw had already set in after Stalin's death. Greater priority was given to consumer goods, collectivization of agriculture was slowed down, the police terror was reduced, and the censorship relaxed. The writers were the first to react. The Polish poet Adam Wazyk, a dedicated Communist, published, in 1955, a *Poem for Adults*:

> They ran to us shouting:
> A communist never dies.
> It never happened that a man did not die.
> Only the memory abides.
> The worthier the man, the greater the pain.
> They ran to us shouting:
> Under socialism a cut finger does not hurt.
> They felt pain,
> They lost their faith.

Michael Bruk, an eighteen-year-old student, published a letter in May 1956. At ten, he wrote, he believed in his country, for which his beloved brother had been killed in the Warsaw uprising against the Germans in the war. Told that this rising, inspired by the anti-Communist Polish government in London, had been wrong, he turned to God. At fifteen he lost faith in God and was converted to Communism. But now after the revelation about Stalin's wickedness: 'I no longer know how to raise my head . . . For I have no basis for believing in anything.'[5]

After the writers came the workers. On 28 June 1956 a spontaneous strike for better pay which broke out among the workers of the locomotive factory at Poznan turned into a mass demonstration against the government, the Russians and the secret police. 'We want bread and freedom'; 'Give us back our religion', shouted the crowd. Barricades were raised, the Soviet flag was torn down, troops were called in, and forty-two people were killed. The leaders of the riot were given a fair and open trial and 30,000 prisoners were released.

The Plenum of the Central Committee of the Polish Communist Party was summoned for 19 October to deal with these matters. The Polish leaders were suddenly informed that Khrushchev, Molotov (Soviet Foreign Minister) and other Soviet leaders, including several generals, would attend it. They quickly summoned the one man who had the moral courage and mass support to stand up to the Russians – Gomulka, who had been released from prison in 1954.

The Polish leaders were waiting for the Russians at the airport. Khrushchev immediately began to shout at Gomulka, charging him with wanting to sell out Poland to the imperialists, and demanding that the Russian leaders should join in the Polish discussions. But Gomulka stood firm. He told Khrushchev calmly that the Polish Plenum was meeting in private session but that as soon as it was over they would be glad to talk to the Soviet comrades. Meanwhile Russian troops were closing in on Warsaw. But Mao, Tito and the Italian Communist leader Togliatti made their support of the Poles clear. So the Russian leaders gave in. They halted the troops, agreed to withdraw Marshal Rokossovsky from Poland and went away without attending the meeting.

Gomulka affirmed that 'the road of democratization is the only road leading to the construction of socialism in our conditions' and immediately set major reforms on foot. Political prisoners were released, and the 'traitors' of 1945–56 were 're-habilitated'. Cardinal Wyszynski was reinstated, and threw his weight behind Gomulka. Religious freedom was restored, and the Catholic Church, for its part, agreed not to organize any

151

political party. The collective farms, which covered only twenty-five per cent of the farm land, were allowed to disintegrate; small private shops were permitted; factory managers were given more freedom, and workers' councils were encouraged. Contacts with the West were restored; radio jamming stopped; compulsory study of Marxism and the Russian language in the universities ended. In the elections of 1957 to the Sejm (parliament) some genuine choice of candidates and parties was allowed, and the result was a majority of only eighteen Communists over the rest.

The Russian leaders accepted these reforms because there were certain demands which Gomulka did *not* make. He did not try to take Poland out of the Warsaw Pact, ask that all Russian troops should be removed from the country, or allow full freedom of the press, which would have meant freedom to criticise the Soviet Union, and he made it clear that all parties and persons must operate within the framework of the Communist system. There could be no question of freedom to change or overturn that system.

In the spring of 1956 the Hungarian intelligentsia, students and workers were beginning to revolt spontaneously against Soviet exploitation and the tyranny of the Rakosi regime. In July the Russians ordered Rakosi to resign and called to the helm Imre Nagy, an honest and popular nationalist Communist, who stood for 'democratic socialism.' On 23 October 300,000 people marched past the coffin of the 'rehabilitated' Laszlo Rajk in Budapest, as a demonstration of solidarity with the Poles. The giant statue of Stalin was chopped down. Then the Hungarian secret police fired on the huge crowd as it flocked to the radio station to pursue its demands. Locally stationed Soviet troops failed to crush the revolt and in fact fraternized with the Hungarians. 'Once we came upon a Russian armoured car at a street corner, with a crowd round it, half hostile, half curious. The Russian soldiers were grinning as if embarrassed, trying to talk, even to exchange cigarettes ... Even the soldiers of the Russian proletariat knew ... that the revolt was working class.'[6] But then Nagy overplayed his hand. He announced that there would be free elections in which non-Communist parties would have full rights and that Hungary would withdraw from the Warsaw Pact and become neutral. Internally Hungary would cease to be Communist and externally it would withdraw from the Communist bloc. The Soviet Union reacted at once. On 31 October fifteen Soviet divisions with 6,000 tanks, which had been sent into Eastern Hungary, began to move into Budapest, while Soviet fighters screamed overhead. The moral strictures of the Western powers froze on their lips, for the British and the French were simultaneously invading Egypt. (See chapter 13). Many of the Russian troops were Mongolians, and some had been told that they were going to fight Germans. The realization that they were being sent to suppress the *workers* of a fraternal country came as a shock. Disconcerted, they turned savage and in ten days of serious fighting 25,000 Hungarians and 7,000 Russians were killed. There were many scenes of extraordinary heroism. Schoolboys threw Molotov cocktails into the Russian tanks and punctured their petrol containers. At 6:30 a.m. on 4 November the last message from Radio Budapest reached the outside world.

> This is the Association of Hungarian Writers (said a voice in English, almost overcome with emotion), we are speaking to all writers' associations and scientific unions of the world who stand for the leaders of intellectual life in all countries. Our time is limited. You know all the facts. No need to expand them. Long live Hungary! Up the Hungarian writers, scientists, workers, peasants and intelligentsia. Up! Up! Up![7]

The Russians appointed Janos Kadar as Premier. Cardinal Mindszenty, released from prison during the revolution, took refuge in the American Embassy. The deposed Nagy was abducted by the Russians and secretly shot on 16 June 1958. Some 16,000 young Hungarians were deported to Russia, and some 200,000 fled to the West (about 60,000 of these later returned). Tito gave the Soviet intervention his grudging approval. The Hungarian revolution showed the Russians and the Western world that with the exception of the secret police, the Hungarian nation was solidly united against the Stalinist Communist regime. It showed the Eastern Europeans that despite brave words about liberating Eastern Europe, the Americans, who had condemned the Anglo-French invasion of Egypt, would not risk war with the Soviet Union to help them and it showed the whole world that the Russians would use force to prevent any of the satellites from rejecting their system and leaving their bloc.

The Gradual Thaw: 1956-1970

The events of 1953–6 altered the whole course of Eastern European Communism. On the one hand the scales of ideological certainty fell away, and thinking began, again, to be open-ended; and on the other, the difficulties and dangers of ruling by brute force were revealed. The Soviet Union could hardly deny to the Eastern European countries the mild thaw which it was allowing at home. In all the countries, therefore, greater freedom of speech, of the press, of foreign travel and of religion, was allowed. (The last East German pastor was let out of prison in 1964). The powers of the secret police were reduced, and the victims of the purges of 1949–55, dead or alive, were 'rehabilitated'. Because of the 1956 revolts, this mild liberalization was greater in Poland and Hungary than elsewhere: for example, Poland was the only country which was able to abandon the collectivization of agriculture. But Gomulka and Kadar had to tread the same tight-rope as that which the Russians had established for themselves. A little liberty is a dangerous thing. Gomulka soon found that he had to clamp down, particularly on the intellectuals. In 1957 six prominent writers, including Adam Wazyk, turned in their Party membership cards as a protest at the reimposition of censorship; friction developed again with the Roman Catholic Church, and in March 1968 a student uprising was suppressed. Finally, in December 1970, workers' riots, sparked off by the sudden announcement of price increases, forced Gomulka to resign in favour of the younger technocrat, Edward Gierek. In other countries the old Stalinist leaders remained in power, ensuring that there was no political change.

There was, however, real economic progress. The Russians not only stopped despoiling these countries, but started sending them aid. In 1956–7 Poland and Hungary received some $1,700,000,000 worth of Soviet aid, and East Germany a lesser amount. Poland was the only one of these countries to receive American aid, which by the end of 1952 amounted to over $500,000,000 in credits and foodstuffs. Heavy industry was still given top priority, and collectivization of agriculture was completed everywhere except in Poland, but since basic industrialization had been achieved consumer goods were now appearing in larger quantities. The lean years were over. In Hungary, for example, real income rose thirty-four per cent between 1956 and 1963, and the government proclaimed its intention of supplying every third household with a TV set and forty per cent with washing machines.

At the same time there was a massive development of education, particularly in technology and science. The combination of liberalization, relative prosperity, education, and the passage of time, produced a new generation of men and women whose modes of thinking were very different from those of the elderly professional revolutionaries like Ulbricht, Kadar, Gomulka and Novotny. They were self-confident professionals, administrators and technocrats. 'The new breed is pragmatic. They have shed the old social democratic belief in the ultimate perfectibility of man... Unlike the old guard, (they) can laugh at themselves and at Marxism',[8] wrote an American observer of East Germany. By 1970 these new men were beginning to introduce a 'socialist market economy', which involved giving managers of state enterprises flexibility in the application of the national plans: freedom to hire and allocate labour, to borrow money at interest, to allocate investment capital from earnings, distribute profits among the workers, and to deal directly with domestic and foreign customers. Salaries and prices were related to profits. And these men were travelling around the world. An East German engineer 'handed me two of his calling cards – one in German, the other in English. "I need both kinds," he said, "I make three or four trips abroad a year – Poland,

Moscow, West Germany, Canada, Japan . . . Now we can travel abroad and learn from everyone." [9]

Leaving aside the special cases of Yugoslavia and Czechoslovakia, these economic reforms had, by 1970, been taken furthest in Hungary. They had received Soviet blessing because in theory the Party remained in firm political control. But by 1970 it was becoming apparent that in the long run economic policy cannot be separated from political policy. At a certain crucial point economic liberalization involves a shift of responsibility from the Party functionaries at the centre, to the factory managers in the field, who are concerned with consumer needs, and with making money. As such men shed ideology, they will inevitably want to liberalize the political system. By 1970 the rulers of East Germany, Poland, Rumania, and Bulgaria, scenting the danger, had not allowed their economic reforms to reach this crucial point in the shift of power from the centre.

In culture the same phenomenon was occurring. The new generation of intellectuals, who had not had their spirits crushed by the horrors of war, prison and torture, could not be suppressed. 'By the end of 1965 the flood of critical novels, plays, films and TV programmes (in East Germany) had reached the proportions of what one Communist Party cultural commissar called a "counter-revolution".'[10] 'Young Hungarians of today', wrote a Hungarian expatriate, 'are serious, modest and truthful, idealistic and unselfish . . . This great change is the joint product of Communism, education and the reaction to it.' The Communists had given the younger generation self-confidence, discipline and a sense of community; but at the same time their incessant lying had provoked a burning love of truth – the young people felt the lies to be an intolerable insult to their intelligence.

Yugoslavia: 1945-70

Tito's Yugoslavia, the Communist non-conformist, is a unique phenomenon in post-war Europe.

Before the break with Stalin in 1948, Tito 'communized' Yugoslavia rapidly and ruthlessly. The Soviet-type constitution of 1946 gave the Yugoslav Communist Party, consisting of

500,000 members out of a population of 17,000,000, a monoply of power. The secret police, assisted by spies and informers, imprisoned thousands of middle-class people as 'capitalists' and Nazi collaborators. Industry and commerce were nationalized and the first Five Year Plan of 1947 concentrated on the development of heavy industry to the detriment of agriculture. Enforced collectivization further discouraged agricultural productivity – during these years Yugoslavia was saved from famine only by $425,000,000 worth of UNRRA aid.

Yugoslavia's expulsion from the Cominform in 1948 forced it to reconsider its internal policies. Its situation, as a small, backward and shattered country, sandwiched between two hostile blocs, seemed desperate. It had, however, a unique asset: a degree of national unity under the leadership of a great man not enjoyed by any other European Communist state. Joseph Broz was one of the fifteen children of a Croat peasant. Born in 1892, he was brought up in Russia and returned to the new state of Yugoslavia as a Communist. In the inter-war years he spent over five years, off and on, in prison, barely escaping murder by King Alexander's police. He travelled extensively through Western and Central Europe for the Party, often in disguise – 'Tito' was one of his aliases. He became Secretary-General of the Yugoslav Communist Party in 1937.

Tito emerged from the war with something of greatness about him, courageous, tough and ruthless, but also humane, possessing the self-confidence and vision to bend dogma to experience and experiment. Blood-baths and purges were not necessary because Tito was accepted by the majority of the Yugoslavs as their national leader. He was not a 'Muscovite'.

Yugoslavia's second asset was the willingness of the Western powers to come to its help after the breach with the Soviet Union. Western aid made possible an industrial revolution in the twenty years after 1948. By 1964 industrial production was five times as great as in 1939, and *per capita* income had risen from $70 to $500.[12,13] It is the only Communist country whose economy depends upon good relations with the Western powers.

In the great quarrel with the Stalinist 'dogmatists' in the Soviet

157

Union, and later with the Maoist 'dogmatists' in China, the Yugoslavs asserted that *they* were the authentic Marxist-Leninists and 'the only creative innovators in the field of Communist theory and practice.'[14] The fundamental innovation was the deliberate attempt to secure the active participation of the whole people in the government and development of the country. In 1953 the peasants were allowed to revert to individual land ownership and farming, but were then persuaded to join voluntary co-operatives for the purchase of seed, the use of machinery and the pooling of knowledge about new farming methods. Each industrial enterprise is managed by the collective of the workers and by a board on which sit elected workers' representatives. The Yugoslav system of workers' councils is unique in Eastern and Western Europe – a prototype of 'socialist democracy'. At any given time fifteen per cent of the working population are sitting on these bodies. The enterprises themselves function within the framework of the pioneer socialist market economy, part free, part controlled by planning which is more 'indicative' than imposed.

Tito aimed at healing the deep pre-war divisions in the country, the divisions between the Croats and the Serbs, and between the Roman Catholics, the Greek Orthodox and the Muslims, by establishing Yugoslavia as a federal state in which the six constituent republics had a large measure of autonomy. Under the constitutions of 1953 and 1963 executive power was decentralized. The elected councils in the communes, the districts and the republics were given real powers and responsibilities – to plan production, raise taxes, and so on. They were assisted by a large number of committees elected or co-opted for special purposes. By 1970 one Yugoslav in a hundred was sitting on some committee. No minister or official, except Tito himself, could serve for more than two terms. At all elections at the various levels there was a choice of candidates – though not of parties – and the parliamentary bodies debated major topics, such as the Five Year Plans, with a seriousness and vigour unknown in any other Communist country.

The powers of the secret police were reduced, almost all

political prisoners freed, censorship of the press *before* publication removed, and workers allowed to seek work in Western Europe: 1,000,000 out of a population of 20,000,000 had gone by 1970.

In September 1970 Tito, aged seventy-eight, announced that he would shortly retire, leaving the future allocation of his powers to be decided by a large body representing not only the Communist Party but all the various interests in the country.

The Yugoslavs claim that their system represents a more advanced stage in the 'withering away of the state' than that achieved by any other Communist country. They have provided a model for other Communist countries, as the events of 1968 in Czechoslovakia were to show.

The Czechoslovak Crisis: 1968-70

In order to understand the extraordinary ferment of the Czechoslovak revolution of 1968, two factors must be borne in mind. First, in the inter-war years Czechoslovakia had developed as a democratic, well-educated, relatively prosperous country which felt itself to be part of Western Europe. Whereas for the backward peasant peoples of the other Eastern European states (leaving aside the special case of East Germany) two decades of Communist rule brought progress for the masses, Communism partially retarded Czechoslovakia's natural development. Second, the stolid Czechs had, in general, remained passive since their great betrayal by the West in 1938. They had put up little military resistance to the Nazi occupation, and had remained unmoved by the Polish and Hungarian risings of 1956. The long-delayed outburst, when it came, was all the more passionate.

In January 1968 Antonin Novotny, the Stalinist Party Secretary and Head of State, was voted out of office by the Central Committee of the Czech Communist Party, and the forty-six-year-old Alexander Dubček, one of the youngest men to lead a Communist country, was elected Secretary. He was a second generation Communist, the son of a worker. Brought up in the Soviet Union, in the mid-fifties he returned to Moscow to study at the political school of the Soviet Central Committee which trained Communist leaders. He had never visited the Western world. He was a sort of Communist Gandhi, 'gentle and saintly, with a strong compassion for humanity.'[15] In his modest and open way of life, he identified himself with the people to an extent unique among Communist leaders.

In March 1968 Novotny was replaced as Head of State (President) by the seventy-two-year-old General Ludvik Svoboda, a 'Hero of the Soviet Union' who had commanded the Czech legion in the Soviet army; and Oldrich Cernik became Prime Minister. They began to transform Czechoslovakia. First, a number of reforms were started or completed whose aim was to establish human rights: freedom of the press, of assembly and of religion; the right to strike and to travel abroad; 'rehabilitation' of the victims of the Stalinist purges and autonomy for the four million inhabitants of Slovakia. Second, the reforms aimed at 'giving socialism a human face' by introducing uninhibited discussions and secret elections in every branch of the Party and government, from workers' committees on the shop floor to serious debates in the national parliament. Third, the liberalization of the economy, started in 1963, was greatly accelerated. Fourth, while not proposing to withdraw from the Warsaw Pact, the Czechs now suggested that all member states should have an equal say in its direction.

Although these reforms were being initiated by sincere and dedicated Communists, who thought they were improving, not destroying, Communism, they aroused panic in the leaders of the Soviet Union and of some of the other Communist states. The future of Communism as a system must have seemed at stake, even more so, probably, than in 1956, because Dubček and his supporters represented the new, educated, idealistic younger generation. Moreover, Czechoslovakia, like Poland, is of special strategic concern to the Soviet Union. As the only satellite state, apart from East Germany, which has a common frontier with West Germany, it is 'the dagger in the heart of Europe' – vital to their defence needs.

On 20 August 1968, 650,000 Soviet, Polish, Hungarian, Bulgarian and East German troops invaded Czechoslovakia.

They encountered a stunned and sullen hostility. Throughout the country street signs were removed. Arrows were put at cross-roads marked 'Mosckba (Moscow) 2,000 miles.' The names of villages were obliterated – except for one. 'We thought that even the Russians would respect it. We suffered under Fascism with them, together. Why should they believe that Lidiče has changed now?' said Vaclav, a miner who was one of the few children who survived the Nazi massacre of the people of Lidiče.[16] Russian tanks were daubed with Swastikas and bombarded with bags of flour. The tank crews needed water to mix their 'concentrate', a kind of powder which is very nutritious but highly unpalat-able', but when they approached a tap they would be warned sympathetically by the local inhabitants that the water had been poisoned by 'counter-revolutionaries'.

The Czechs improvised a clandestine radio service, and the world's first clandestine television service, on which their star reporters and newscasters appeared. Colonel Zatopek, the former long-distance runner, announced: 'We were getting the socialism going real nice here before these bloody Russians came.'

On 21 August the Russians arrested Cernik and Dubček. As Soviet soldiers entered the Czech Communist Party head-quarters, Dubček was trying to telephone to the Soviet Ambas-sador, saying 'How can they do this to me? I have devoted my whole life to co-operation with the Soviet Union. This is my pro-found personal tragedy.' The three Czech leaders were trussed up and driven to a remote place in the Carpathian mountains, to be executed as soon as a Czech government subservient to the Russians had been set up; but it proved impossible to find Czechs who would serve in such a government.

Instead, President Svoboda agreed to go to Moscow to negotiate with the Soviet leaders, on condition that Dubček was present. They were forced to accept a permanent Russian military presence, and to agree to re-establish rigid control over all means of communication and over the country's intellec-tuals.[17] The alternative was some tougher form of Soviet occupation and control.

When he returned to Prague, President Svoboda told the weeping people that 'senseless bloodshed must be avoided at all costs,' and that the only realistic future lay in moral and intellectual resistance. The Czech people obeyed their leaders, but continued to express their non-violent protest in various symbolic ways. The most famous was the suicide of the student Jan Palach, who set himself on fire as a human torch. The Red Army, in striking contrast to its behaviour in 1945, comported itself during the occupation with great self-discipline and correctness.

In April 1969 Dubček was forced to resign the Secretaryship of the Czech Communist Party, and was replaced by Dr Husak, a tough Slovak willing to do the Russians' bidding. Under his rule 'socialism with a human face' had withered and died by the end of 1970. The Party, the trade unions, the press, radio, television, and the staffs of schools, universities and the law courts were purged. Dubček was disgraced in July 1970 by formal expulsion from the Party; the other liberal leaders were allowed to resign. Under laws introduced in 1969 against 'subversion' and 'anti-socialist propaganda', certain leading intellectuals were arrested for protesting against the invasion. Some 60,000 Czechs sought refuge abroad. Authoritative economic planning was restored. Yet Husak did his best to keep repression within limits and to avoid a return to Stalinism. As far as was known there were no executions and relatively mild penal measures. Even the 'Muscovites' realized that Czechoslovakia could not afford to suppress her 'technological intelligentsia'.

The eight exhilarating months of freedom showed the whole Communist world what Communism could become; and the spectacle of the Communist super-power deploying over half a million troops to suppress unarmed 'toilers and workers' led by a dedicated Moscow-trained Communist, profoundly undermined the moral prestige of the Soviet Union.

REFERENCES

1. Singleton, F. B., *Background to Eastern Europe*, Pergamon Press, Oxford, 1961, p. 156.
2. Dornberg, John, *The Other Germany*, Doubleday and Co., New York, 1968, pp. 16–17.
3. Prittie, Terence, *Germany Divided*, Little, Brown and Co., Boston, 1960, pp. 120–2.
4. Hangen, Welles, *The Muted Revolution*, Alfred A. Knopf, New York, 1966, pp. 37–8.
5. Lewis, Flora, *The Polish Volcano*, Secker and Warburg, London, 1959, pp. 131–2.
6. Aczel, Tamas, ed., *Ten Years After: Hungary 1956*, MacGibbon and Kee, 1966.
7. Mikes, George, *The Hungarian Revolution*, Andre Deutsch, 1957, p. 152.
8. Hangen, *op. cit.*, p. 100.
9. Hangen, *op. cit.*, p. 209
10. Dornberg, John, *op. cit.*, pp. 16–17.
11. Mikes, *op. cit.*, p. 13.
12. Auty, Phyllis, *Yugoslavia*, Thames and Hudson, London, 1965, p. 135.
13. Rusinow, Dennison, 'Understanding the Yugoslav Reforms', in *The World Today*, February 1967, Chatham House, London.
14. Bromke, Adam, ed., *The Communist States at the Crossroads*, Praeger, New York, 1965, p. 180.
15. Chapman, Colin, *August 21: The Rape of Czechoslovakia*. Cassell, London, 1968, p. 113.
16. Chapman, *op. cit.*, p. 73.
17. Chapman, *op. cit.*, pp. 67–8.

8. Economic developments in Non-Communist Europe

During the inter-war period, most of the leaders of economic opinion believed in *laissez-faire*; that is, they believed that governments should not interfere with economic forces. These forces, it was held, would automatically operate through the law of supply and demand to ensure the best interests of mankind. Booms and slumps, involving a measure of unemployment, were an inevitable feature of the economic process.

The booms and slumps of the early twenties, and the inflation which accompanied them, particularly in Germany, were serious enough to disturb the economists' complacency. The Great Depression of 1929–33 shattered this complacency completely and discredited the easy optimism of *laissez-faire* philosophy. The shrinkage of the volume of world trade by a third in four years, and the unemployment of a quarter (as in Britain) or a third (as in Germany) of the labour force, were catastrophic experiences. It was realized, also, that the chronic disequilibrium of the capitalist world economy had been exacerbated by the exacting demands for the payment of reparations and war debts. The policies of autarchy pursued in the years 1933–9 which, combined with rearmament, produced a limited recovery, were essentially policies of defeatism: the major countries of Europe found themselves unable to make a system of international trade and monetary exchange work, and fell back on primitive methods of barter. As a result, there was, between 1919 and 1939, relatively little economic growth in Europe outside the Soviet Union.

The New Economics

The *laissez-faire* approach to economic policy presents certain difficulties. First, it assumes that there will be full employment of resources; but in the inter-war years there was unemployment of labour and of other potentially productive resources, and unemployed workers cannot just be written off as having no economic value, like unproductive land or capital equipment. Workers have at least to be kept alive; the unemployed will not be satisfied with their lot. Second, the 'natural' forces of downward change, expressed in bankruptcies and unemployment, will be resented by producers and merchants, who do not like having to cut the prices of goods, and by workers, who do not like having their wages cut. Governments will also tend to resist reducing agricultural production in favour of cheaper imported supplies. Third, even if depressions are only temporary disturbances which, if left to themselves, will 'in the long run' automatically be redressed by the forces of supply and demand, many people will not be prepared to wait. As John Maynard Keynes of Cambridge University once retorted: 'In the long run we are all dead.' In the inter-war years he launched a new and more dynamic approach to economic theory. He and his followers argued that by suitable planning of investment in relation to available savings, it would be possible to *influence* demand and thereby to keep factors of production, and especially manpower, in useful employment. The economic system could be *managed*, while leaving scope for the play of supply and demand in the determination of prices and encouraging freedom of enterprise. The amount of money available for investment by public authorities, private firms or individuals, and for spending by consumers, could be controlled through government investments, taxation and credit supplied by the banks and hire-purchase financing. National budgets need not necessarily be balanced in any given year. When the private sector was slack, government expenditure, and especially government investment, should

165

be increased – normally, it had been reduced. When the private sector was overactive, that is, when competition for labour and other factors of production pushed incomes up to the point where people were trying to buy more than could be produced in the period under consideration (over-full employment), governments should step in to keep prices down by measures designed to restrict purchasing power. These would include incentives to save, higher taxation, cuts in government expenditure and credit restrictions.

Before 1939 these ideas were largely ignored in Europe, although they influenced President Roosevelt's New Deal policies in the United States. After the war, however, they came into their own. The men responsible for the economic affairs of post-war Western Europe had learnt the bitter lessons of the twenties and thirties; they had noted how the Soviet Union's planned economy had grown in the inter-war years, unaffected by the depression; and they had gained practical experience in the war of operating economic 'controls'. They were therefore now determined to use governmental powers to prevent booms and slumps and to foster economic growth and full employment. And since the actions of one country affect the economies of others, international economic co-operation was essential.

Planning

During the Second World War the belligerent countries had to use their resources to the full. They therefore had to plan in detail the allocation of men, supplies, transport and funds. Rationing was introduced throughout Europe. Worldwide arrangements for purchasing food and raw materials were made by Britain and the overseas Allies, and speculative prices were controlled. Allied shipping movements were carefully planned, and civilian supplies to certain areas, such as the Middle East, were programmed. Inflation was curbed by controlling the supply of money and plans for the relief of liberated countries were initiated.

After the war these policies were adapted to peace-time conditions. The governments of Western Europe began to plan how their economies should 'grow', and to use instruments of economic and political control to steer this growth. When men ceased to abandon themselves to the allegedly automatic working of blind economic forces and began consciously to control their economic and social progress, a turning point in history had been reached.

The Netherlands, Norway and France led the way in working out modes of economic planning suited to societies based on political democracy and free private enterprise. The plans were drawn up by the governments in partnership with the great independent organizations – the associations of employers and trade unions. They were not centrally imposed, as in the Communist countries, but 'indicative', involving broad guide lines rather than rigid targets. The independent organizations also collaborated in the execution of the plans. This introduced a new atmosphere into relations between labour and management, and between them both and the government. So many interested parties would join in the exercise that the mere existence of these indicative targets would influence private investment programmes, especially those of larger firms, and thus they helped towards their own fulfilment. The plans also provided guide lines for the government and the financial authorities, who could take corrective measures when trends diverged from the targets. They enabled the government to forecast its expenditure and to relate it to tax yields. 'The effect of the series of plans on France was revolutionary. Within 15 years France had, in large sectors of her economy, caught up with the 20th century.'[1]

By the mid-sixties most Western European countries, with the major exception of West Germany (where such planning evoked Nazi practices), had adopted some form of indicative planning. In 1967 the European Community started reviewing the short-term plans of its members. The next move may well be toward the twenty-year forward look.

Planning necessitates certain statistical tools and techniques. Before 1945 there were few statistics of national income. The United Nations tackled the task from the outset, establishing a quick and comprehensive statistical service which is continuously being improved. By 1970 European planners were also well served with data provided by the United Nations' Economic Commission for Europe, the OECD and the European Community.

Armed with such statistical data, supplemented by the computer, economists became more numerate. In the twenties economics was taught in most European universities in terms of broad principles, indicating long-term tendencies to which no values were given and which bore little resemblance to what was happening in the real world. Since 1945 a new science of 'econometrics' has developed, which seeks to measure the effect of particular factors on each other, such as the impact of particular 'inputs' of resources on output, or the cost-effectiveness of certain investments. Such phenomena as rates of investment, inventories, trade, and supply of money and unemployment, are closely watched for they serve as 'indicators' for assessing the general state of the economy, and deciding whether corrective action is required. Before 1945 only rough approximations were possible. By 1970 governments and economic and trade organizations were arguing about half per cent differences in rates of growth.

The development of indicative planning between 1945 and 1970 was, therefore, a basic means of applying the Keynesian theory that man should steer his economic growth. The main danger in this development was that planning would become an end in itself, and that planners would become 'organization men', organizing everybody. In 1970 the position of the consumer in the process was not clear. He often had little real say in determining prices or in influencing priorities of production according to his needs. All he could do was to refuse to buy.

Public Ownership

In all European countries, certain public services such as posts and telecommunications, roads, water supply and sewage disposal, had long been generally regarded as suitable for ownership by the state or the local authorities. A real difference of opinion, however, existed on the desirability of public ownership of the means of production. Left-wing political parties wanted large-scale nationalization but most of the other parties believed in private ownership. In the Soviet Union, everything was nationalized; elsewhere there was, in 1939, some nationalization of public utilities. Main-line railways were publicly owned in most European countries – in Austria, Belgium, Czechoslovakia, Germany, Italy, the Netherlands, Poland, Scandinavia and Switzerland; in France, one of the several regional networks was nationalized. Electricity and gas were under public control in many countries. There were also a number of state monopolies, such as those manfacturing tobacco in France, and broadcasting in Britain. In Turkey, where capital was scarce, important basic industries like coal, iron and textiles were controlled through state-owned banks.

After 1945, there was a substantial increase in the public sector in Western Europe. War-time and post-war circumstances necessitated the nationalization of certain industries such as the Renault motor works in France. The Austrian Government took over many of the undertakings handed back by the Russians in 1955. Certain basic industries regarded as essential to the functioning of the economy were nationalized as a matter of deliberate policy. In the late forties, for instance, the British Labour Government nationalized the railways, the generation of electricity and gas, cable and wireless communications, long and medium distance road transport, the coal and steel industries and the Bank of England. Only in the case of steel and road transport was there a major conflict of views between political parties. Steel was returned to private ownership in 1953 and re-nationalized in 1967. Road transport was also offered back to private owners, though there were takers for only part of the nationalized sector. The French government took over all the railways, and also coal, electricity and gas generation and distribution, cables, wireless and television. The aircraft industry and the production of local petroleum and natural gas were later brought under public control. In Italy important industrial undertakings which had come under the control of certain banks before the war were taken over or reorganized by the State. The state corporations thus set

169

up later acquired other concerns, so that by 1963, through various holding companies, the Italian Government owned, in whole or in large part, a variety of nationalized enterprises, including steel, shipping, shipbuilding, engineering, petroleum and petro-chemicals, telephones, electricity production and toll-paying motorways. In West Germany, on the other hand, the tendency was to return to private ownership some of the undertakings which had come into the government's hands after the war, including the Volkswagen motor works. The private interests expropriated by nationalization were always compensated.

The result of these measures was to establish in these countries a 'mixed economy', consisting of a public sector of nationalized industries and a private sector of privately owned industries. All the national political parties except the Communists accepted this situation.

International Trade

The liberal or 'free trade' view held by most Western economists is that international trade should be developed, because it enables each country to concentrate on the production of goods in which it has the greatest relative advantage, while buying from abroad goods in the production of which it suffers from the greatest relative disadvantage. It also enables production to be carried out on an economic scale.

This theory, however, assumes a high level of employment of the factors of production. Many economists argue that when a recession sets in, it is better to produce the goods needed by the use of unemployed local resources and labour than to import them. If any major country adopts this policy and reduces its buying from abroad by protectionist methods, the likelihood is that others will do the same. In the end all will be losers, because the benefits of large-scale production and marketing, and the particular advantages held by some countries in the production of certain goods, will have been sacrificed.

Since the First World War there have been frequent conflicts between these two approaches. Between the wars protectionist policies prevailed, producing a serious set-back in world trade and 'the export of unemployment.' But from 1945 to 1970 the liberal approach was dominant. The principle was generally accepted that no country should take unilateral action in international trade. Restrictive measures should only be taken in consultation with trading partners, and in accordance with commonly agreed rules. By 1970 international machinery for examining trade policies had been well established; but international co-ordination of such policies, in order to avoid inflation and the imbalances which impel governments to take restrictive measures, had not yet been achieved.

Between the wars international trade was stifled by tariffs and import quotas; barter agreements partially replaced multilateral trade. During the depression of 1929–33 world trade shrank by one third. After 1945 steps were taken to prevent this situation from arising again. A treaty setting up an International Trade Organization to liberalize trade policies and control and steady prices of raw materials foundered in 1948 when it became clear that the United States Senate would refuse ratification. Meanwhile the General Agreement on Tariffs and Trade (GATT), consisting of rules to free international trade, came into force on 1 January 1948. The parties agreed that international trade should be conducted on the basis of non-discrimination: concessions made by any one country were automatically granted to all other trading partners – this is known as 'the most-favoured nation clause'. Protection should be effected only through tariffs, and not by prohibitions, quotas or other special measures, although temporary quantitative controls might be imposed in an emergency, such as a threat to the balance of payments. In general, there should be consultations before any measures were taken which would damage the trading interests of contracting parties – a very great change from the spirit of the pre-war situation. Finally, arrangements were made for 'rounds' of negotiation to take place between all the participating countries at the same time and place, with the assistance of a Secretariat at Geneva. The previous system, consisting of a vast number of separate negotiations between pairs of countries, conducted all

over the place and all interacting on each other because concessions made in one case had to be offered to others, had become
unworkable.

In the first round, in 1947, 123 bilateral treaties were
completed, affecting about half the world's trade. More
countries joined GATT, and in 1949 147 trade treaties were
simultaneously drawn up. Other rounds followed. Tariff rates
for tens of thousands of items in world trade were reduced on a
scale never before achieved. After a time, however, it became
difficult to continue on a commodity-by-commodity basis, since
low-tariff countries had few more concessions to offer, so the aim
became an over-all reduction in tariffs. This new approach culminated in the 'Kennedy Round' of discussions. The United
States, Britain, the European Community (acting for the first
time as a single negotiating entity) and other countries offered a
fifty per cent reduction in tariffs on industrial goods. The fifty or
so countries which accounted for about three-quarters of the
total world trade agreed to tariff cuts by 1972, valued at some
forty billion dollars for about seventy per cent of their dutiable
imports, excluding cereals, meat and dairy products. Two-thirds
of the cuts were at least fifty per cent. The OEEC countries had
also, by 1955, virtually eliminated quantitative import restrictions, and the members of the European Community and of
EFTA eliminated their industrial tariffs by 1968. In most
European countries national interests still demanded the protection of agriculture by price supports or subsidies; yet even
here trade had been largely freed. The developing countries,
however, suffered from restrictions on certain of their major
exports of manufactured goods, such as cotton cloth. In 1970
special tariff concessions for them were under consideration. The
result of all these measures was a remarkable expansion of international trade. Between 1948 and 1967 the exports of the
thirteen countries of the European Community and EFTA,
taken together, increased more than five times in terms of value,
while world exports trebled. The trend continues.

A number of factors made these far-reaching measures
possible. First, the evils of the pre-war competitive 'beggar-my-

neighbour' restrictions on trade, and excessive national protection by tariffs and quotas, were fully appreciated. Second, the need was felt to develop a Western European market large enough to face the huge economic power of the United States and the growing potential of the Soviet Union. Third, industries with new technologies and high capital investment could not develop on the basis of small national markets; it was recognized that it would be wasteful to set them up in many countries. Fourth, the difficulty which might have arisen in repaying debts incurred to the United States in the war was largely solved by the liberal attitude of the American Government – strikingly different from its attitude after the First World War – in giving Marshall Aid and in making many loans. Fifth, devaluations of many currencies in 1949 made it easier for the countries concerned to expand exports and secure dollars. Sixth, since Eastern Europe, under Communist rule, now aimed at self-sufficiency, Western Europe was no longer faced with the pre-war problem of absorbing the former's agricultural surpluses. Finally, the growth in production and trade was both the result and the cause of the liberalization of international exchanges.

Monetary Problems

A little background

After the First World War the gold standard system had ceased to exist, in the sense that gold coins were in circulation and that people could exchange notes for gold and export it to settle payments in other countries. Gold movements no longer operated to ensure that payments into and out of a country would remain more or less in balance.

Many people thought that a fixed price for gold produced a stable currency. In terms of purchasing power this was not so even before 1914. Periodic fluctuations in wholesale prices of over forty per cent took place. Sometimes the supply of gold would increase through a discovery of new goldfields or technical processes and prices would tend to rise. Sometimes the expansion of production and trade ran up against a limitation of media available to pay for it because the supply of gold had not kept pace and prices were then forced down.

Gold coin largely disappeared from use in Europe after the First World War. In practice, 'all sovereign states switched wholly to the creation of their own monies by simply printing it as needed.'[2] For monetary purposes, gold was used only in the settlement of balances between the central banks of the various countries. These arrangements were supplemented by what was known as the 'gold exchange standard', still largely in use in 1970. The reserves of a national bank might be held not only in gold but also in dollars, which were at the time readily convertible into gold, or in sterling.

In the sixties, there was a great expansion in the lending of balances expressed in dollars, but held in accounts in Western Europe outside the control of the United States, the so-called 'Eurodollars'. These funds, described as 'the money that knows no frontiers',[3] were used as reserves and could be moved freely from one centre to another. The market for them was largely centred on London.

Such devices, together with the greatly increased use of 'bank money' (that is, rights to draw on bank accounts and credits) in national transactions, made it possible to provide for a great expansion in the volume of credit and currency available within certain countries, and in the media available for the settlement of international transactions.

At various times, however, Britain was placed in a position where, in order to meet the claims made on it by holders of sterling abroad, it might have to pay sums quite out of proportion to its gold holdings or earnings from foreign transactions. On certain occasions the United States experienced similar difficulties.

A major drawback of the system was that its stability, and the economic fate of many countries using it, depended on the way in which the reserve currency countries managed their economic affairs. If they accumulated large reserves and did not correspondingly expand their purchases from or investment in other countries, they would retard development in other countries. If, on the other hand, they imported too much or invested too much abroad, confidence in their ability to meet the claims which might be made upon them would be shaken. In either case, other countries had no control over policies which vitally affected them and which might be based on national interests or internal political considerations. In the late sixties, France made a major protest at the excessive influence of the United States on the world's monetary system.

The Keynesian approach involved expanding output and expenditure until productive capacity was so fully employed that the supply of goods could not be increased fast enough to meet the rising demand. As a result, the money in circulation would exceed the value of available goods and services at the ruling prices. The latter would then rise. This idea of running the economy at a high level constituted a breakthrough in applied economics, designed to prevent the recurrence of a cumulative depression such as that of the thirties.

In the field of international monetary transactions this approach left at least three problems to be solved. The first was how to prevent prices rising beyond the point at which there was a satisfactory rate of employment of resources. The second was what to do when prices in one country or a group of countries got out of line with those of others with which it had close trading relations. The third was how to ensure that there were enough internationally-acceptable media of payment for the settlement of balances between currencies, particularly at a time when the volume of trade and prices was rising fairly fast.

1949–67: a period of relative stability

Initial readjustments in the values of the various European currencies after the war culminated in the devaluation of the pound and some other currencies in 1949. After this, relative stability in the exchange rates of the major West European currencies, and in their relations to gold and the dollar, lasted, essentially, until November 1967, in satisfactory contrast to the confused conditions which prevailed between the wars. (See table 1).

Many influences produced this stability. Almost all the

TABLE 1

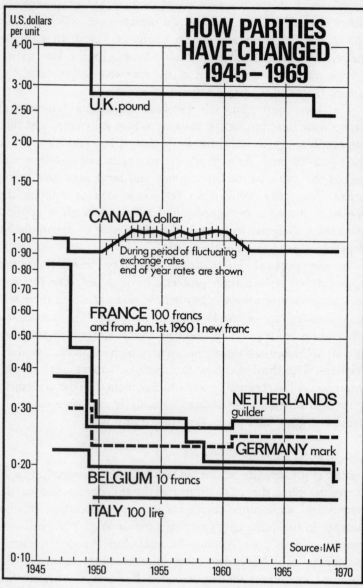

Published in *The Times Annual Financial and Economic Review, 1969,* The International Scene, 29 September 1969, p. II.

Western European states were members of the International Monetary Fund in Washington, which promoted exchange stability by allowing changes in par value to be made only to correct a fundamental long-term disequilibrium. It could then place resources in hard currency at the disposal of a member state to help it to cover itself against claims on its currency. In 1950 the European Payments Union was established under the auspices of the OEEC as a central clearance and credit scheme between all Western European countries and the countries of the sterling and franc areas (that is, the countries of the Commonwealth other than Canada, and the former French colonies, which link their currencies to the pound and the franc respectively). By 1961 all the Western European currencies could be mutually converted without difficulty, so the Payments Union was disbanded. Regular meetings of the financial experts of the member states of the OECD provided a forum for resolving financial difficulties on the basis of objective surveys. Exchange rate policies became a matter of common concern. In 1970 the European Community countries were even envisaging achieving a common currency by 1980, though in practice this would only work if there were an overall economic and budgetary programme (see chapter 9).

Western European price increases were kept within ranges sufficient to prevent unmanageable imbalances in the flow of payments from one European country to another, and between Europe and the United States. Even so, strains arose from time to time. When money was being spent at a rate which produced excessive inflation and income rises, often reflected in excessive imports, the government concerned had to take corrective measures. These would involve the siphoning off of money from the spenders by increased taxation, limiting purchases through the restriction of bank credit, tightening hire-purchase terms, raising interests rates, and cutting down government expenditure, including expenditure on social services – measures which were, naturally, highly unpopular.

Between 1945 and 1969 Britain experienced recurrent crises of confidence in the pound; the foreign holders of sterling would present withdrawal claims out of all proportion to the balances in gold and hard currency which the Bank of England could keep. France also encountered difficulties, largely because its internal prices rose too fast in relation to production. Heavy government expenditure on wars in Indochina and Algeria and the political instability which prevailed before 1958 were contributing factors. Drastic restrictive measures were taken in 1957 and in 1958, when the franc was devalued by about thirty per cent; and again in 1963 and 1968–9. On the whole, however, the French economy was prosperous; for many years the Bank of France held the world's second largest gold reserve. West Germany went ahead even faster than France. To correct an imbalance of exports in relation to imports, the value of the Deutschmark was raised by about five per cent in 1961. The Netherlands followed suit. The memory of the runaway inflation of 1923 prompted the West German government to take restrictive measures even at the risk of unemployment. In 1963 Italy also had to take restrictive measures, which caused a temporary setback in business and markedly increased unemployment. In 1964–7 Switzerland restricted credit for unessential purposes and forced employers to reduce the number of foreign workers employed. The United States also suffered from temporary recessions in 1953, 1958 and 1963, which affected other countries.

1967–9: years of crises

From the end of 1967 to 1969, the monetary system, which had worked fairly well since 1949, was severely shaken by a succession of crises.

For many years, Britain had been struggling with an unfavourable balance of payments. Reserves for the pound were sometimes down to the value of only a month's imports. The mere existence of a Labour Government, elected in 1964, aroused distrust among conservative-minded foreign bankers. To 'maintain confidence', the Labour Government was therefore driven to take a series of particularly drastic restrictive measures to prevent prices and incomes rising faster than productivity and to cut down public expenditure. They were ineffective and, in

November 1967, the pound was devalued by about fourteen per cent. A few months later, new restrictions and taxes were introduced, taking an unprecedented amount of over £900,000,000 off the market.

Large-scale international help was made available to enable the pound to hold its new rate. Short-term credits were granted by the United States, France, Switzerland, West Germany and other countries. The International Monetary Fund extended drawing rights up to $1,400,000,000. A stand-by credit of $2,000,000,000 was provided by central banks. In July 1968, a further stand-by credit of $2,000,000,000 was provided to support a scheme of guarantees to certain holders of sterling balances. Subsequently, further cuts were made in current expenditure in Britain, and to restrain imports, importers were asked to deposit for six months half the value of the goods imported.

Another crisis arose in February-March 1968. Some people were nervous about the dollar itself. United States reserves had been heavily drawn upon and its balance of payments was unfavourable, owing to heavy American investments in Europe and elsewhere and to the rate of inflation at home. They therefore bought large amounts of gold for hoarding and for speculation. The leading central banks agreed not to carry out transactions in gold above the official price, and left the non-monetary gold market to find its own level, the so-called 'two-tier' price system for gold.

In May 1968, severe political troubles in France led to a run on the French franc, which accentuated the financial imbalance between France and West Germany. The latter's exports were doing well and its reserves were rising fast. Speculators anticipated an upwards revaluation of the mark and, in November 1968, well over $1,000,000,000 worth of foreign currency poured into the country within three days, largely from France. The finance ministers and governors of the central banks of the ten leading financial countries met at once. The Germans refused to raise the value of the mark but they took steps to raise the costs of their exports and to facilitate imports. International measures to support the franc were urgently taken, and the French government introduced drastic cuts in public expenditure and other deflationary measures. Germany took steps to restrain exports. These measures, however, were not adequate to correct an imbalance which seemed to be more than temporary, and during 1969, in spite of strong political opposition in both cases, the French franc was further devalued and the German mark upvalued.

Problems ahead

The major crises which occurred between November 1967 and November 1968, and the subsequent readjustments in currency values, high-lighted the need for international machinery to ensure that one country would not accumulate reserves at the expense of its partners or allow its reserves to run down to a dangerously low level. If an organization for this purpose were set up it would need to have powers to influence national budgetary policies, investment programmes and credit expansion. This would amount to the creation of a federal government. By 1970 discussions on proposed changes had not faced the issue of how to manage an international monetary system. They had dealt merely with improvements in the machinery for consultation to enable changes to be carried out in an orderly manner.

In some countries the amount of currency and of credit which could be issued might still be limited by the amount of gold or of equivalent currencies held in the reserves. This forced several governments to adopt the kind of deflationary policies already described. Growth and employment could thus be hampered by adherence to the gold or gold exchange standard. Even in the United States, the fear that this might occur led in 1968 to legislation to reduce the amount of gold legally required as a minimum cover for the currency.

The total amount of monetary gold held in all the reserves of the world is not only unevenly distributed, but is inadequate to meet even moderate imbalances arising out of the quickly growing volume of international transactions; and the amount of new gold available is small. As the United Kingdom's and the

United States' balance of payments improves, there is a likelihood that reserves held in the form of sterling or dollars will decline rather than rise. There is a very real danger that the inadequacy of acceptable means of settling international balances may cause one country after another to restrict its programmes for internal expansion, when productive resources are all the time rapidly expanding. After pointing out that some countries were, in 1968, basing their plans on slower rates of growth, a leading British periodical commented: 'In an educated community of nations, in an age with such opportunities as the present, it is appalling that this counter-revolution of falling expectations should set in. It is not caused by any slowing down in the rate of accumulation of man's knowledge, or productive capacity, or technical innovation: it does not need to take place.'[4]

A first step to increase liquidity was taken by the creation by the International Monetary Fund of 'special drawing rights', which became available in January 1970. These promoted liquidity by providing additional reserves for certain countries, but the total amount involved was inadequate to provide a long-term solution, and the rights are not necessarily distributed according to real need.

A more drastic suggestion is that the value of gold should be raised in order to increase the money value of reserves and of means of settlement. This would, however, penalize countries which had not sought to convert all their reserves into gold; it would give a new lease of life to the gold standard, and a special bonus to gold-producing countries – mainly South Africa and the Soviet Union – and to gold hoarders and speculators. It would not of itself bring about a better system for the adjustment of international balances; in fact, it would strengthen the position of countries which held the largest amount of gold in their reserves.

Two other relatively minor reforms were advocated by some specialists. The first would allow a wider margin for adjustment between the points at which gold has to be imported or exported. The second would seek to make necessary long-term changes take place gradually, at, for instance, a pre-arranged rate of one per cent a month, rather than in sudden rather large jumps. This system is known as 'the crawling peg'.

Another method is to let the exchange rate 'float', or find its own level, at any rate during periods of crisis. This was done in Germany for a while late in 1969, and has since been extensively resorted to. However, this introduces a considerable measure of uncertainty into international transactions.

A more radical approach would be to abandon the gold standard altogether. It no longer acts as an automatic regulator, as it did to some extent before 1914. In 1970, it was, in fact, a system managed by the United States, with some help from the International Monetary Fund, which sometimes tends to constrict the expansion of production and trade.

There is, however, no agreement as to what to put in its place. Perhaps the time has come for the world to set up a monetary system which would be consciously geared to agreed objectives, and which would stimulate growth and social aims, while keeping inflation within acceptable limits.

Full Employment

In the inter-war years, the scourge of widespread unemployment which haunted the lives of millions of workers was generally regarded as unavoidable in the industrialized countries of Europe. In the agrarian countries the problem was partly disguised, because superflous industrial workers could return to the farm. (This situation still applied in France, West Germany and Italy even in 1970. Some countries could adjust to change by varying the numbers of immigrant workers employed.)

During the thirties, Keynes and his colleagues had maintained that unemployment could be largely avoided, and the war had shown what could be done in finding work for all.

After 1945, 'full employment' became a major element in government policy throughout Europe. In May 1944, the United Kingdom government set out in a 'White Paper'[5] the policies to be pursued after the war to maintain a high and stable level of employment and to combine this with a rising standard of living.

Similar statements were issued in the United States and Canada. The concept of the 'right to work' came into being. The United Nations' Universal Declaration of Human Rights of 1948 stated that 'everyone has the right to work, to free choice of employment . . . and to protection against unemployment.' In 1964, The International Labour Conference adopted the Employment Policy Convention, by which governments agreed 'to declare and pursue, as a major goal, an active policy designed to promote full, productive and freely chosen employment.'

A high and stable level of employment was, on the whole, achieved in Western Europe between 1945 and 1970 by applying to technologically dynamic economies the various measures of planning and control which we have discussed. It does not necessarily mean that the figure for unemployment was 'nil'. Two per cent unemployment is normally reckoned to indicate a healthy economy, since this figure will cover people who are changing jobs, or who are unemployable. Up to 1970, levels in most European countries remained under three per cent, in Britain under two per cent, and in Switzerland, and in West Germany after it had absorbed some 15,000,000 refugees, under one per cent.

Problems also arise when a full employment economy policy runs up against anti-inflationary measures, as in Britain. There, considerable anxiety was expressed in 1968, when the drastic measures taken to curb inflation caused unemployment to rise to two and a half per cent – a level formerly regarded as below the minimum necessary to ensure mobility of labour in a dynamic economy. In 1970 there were still many areas where unemployment was serious, either because of backwardness, as in Southern Italy, Spain, Portugal, Greece and Turkey; or because employment policies had not kept pace with rapid technological change. As Europe swings into the age of automation, labour displacement may cause unemployment unless there is bold and imaginative planning for the rapid transfer and development of skills.

Growth

One of the most significant features of the period was the
remarkable and steady rate of growth. The term was not used by
economists in the twenties. It was simply assumed that there
would be progress and that the economy would automatically
grow. By 1970 politicians and civil servants as well as economists
had become acutely 'growth-conscious' and were constantly
measuring growth progress.

Rates of growth

In the inter-war years progress was slow, except in the Soviet
Union, which was already planning its growth. The potential
impact of technological change on standards of living was
hindered by unemployment, restrictions on international trade
and lack of confidence regarding investments. In the fifties and
sixties, however, there were exceptionally fast rates of growth in
nearly all the countries of Europe, both East and West. In 1968,
it could be said that 'among the dozen or so richest countries of
the world, it is now usual to secure a regular annual economic
growth rate of somewhere around 4 per cent.'[6] This applied to
nearly eleven countries in Europe.

The actual rates of growth from 1950 to 1970 are given in
table 2. The corresponding figures for the United States have
been added for comparison. The increase in income per head,
that is after allowing for the growth of population, was greater
than for any other period of European history. In some countries
of Western Europe there was, however, a tendency for the rate of
growth to slow down after 1964 – a result of the restrictive fiscal
and credit policies imposed to combat inflation and to improve
the balance of payments. Another deterrent was a slackening of
investment, both public and private, due to rising costs and the
restraints on demand, but 1968, 1969 and 1970 were years of fast
growth in most of these countries.

The figures given for national product, while reflecting
growth, do not mean that the standard of living necessarily rose
to a corresponding extent. This was partly because of the increase

TABLE 2

Average Annual Rates of Growth of National Product in Western and Southern Europe and the United States of America – 1960–1970

Country	*(Constant market price; per cent)*			
	1950–60	*1960–64*	*1964–67*[1]	*1965–70*[2]
		Gross national product		
Austria	5·5	4·6	2·9	4·3
Belgium	3·0 [3]	5·3	2·8	4·2
Denmark	3·3	4·9	3·3	4·1
Finland	5·3 [3]	5·3	3·3	4·1
France	4·5	5·6	4·4	5·4
Germany (Fed. Rep.)	7·8	4·9	2·6	4·3
Ireland	1·7	4·2	2·6	4·1
Italy	5·4	5·5	4·9	6·3
Netherlands	4·8	4·9	4·1	4·7
Norway	3·6	5·1	4·8	4·6
Sweden	3·3	5·5	3·4	3·5
Switzerland	4·4	5·5	2·9	3·5
United Kingdom	2·7	3·6	1·7	2·4
		Gross domestic product[5]		
Greece	5·9	8·1	6·3	7·0
Portugal	4·3 [3]	6·2	5·1	5·4
Spain	4·3 [4]	9·7	6·3	5·7
Turkey	6·3	6·2	6·6	7·3
		Gross national product		
United States	3·3	4·5	4·8	3·7

Sources: INTERNATIONAL LABOUR ORGANIZATION, SECOND EUROPEAN REGIONAL CONFERENCE, Report I: *Technological Change and Social Progress: Some problems and perspectives.* (Geneva, ILO, 1968) p. 6, where original sources for the first three columns of figures are cited.

(1) All 1967 data are provisional.
(2) Estimate of the Organization for Economic Co-operation and Development, 1970.
(3) 1953–1960.
(4) 1954–1960.
(5) The gross domestic product differs from the gross national product by the exclusion of incomes received from abroad in payment for national factors of production.

in population, and partly because proportions of the national income were invested in heavy industry or spent on armaments.

Structural Changes

The figures so far given are averages and these hide difficult problems of structure. Employment in agriculture was on the decline throughout Europe. Owing to improvements in techniques and productivity, production in agriculture increased faster than the demand for its products. In many countries, governmental measures cushioned agriculture from these changes. However, taking Europe as a whole, the proportion of the labour force engaged in agriculture, together with forestry, hunting and fishing, dropped between 1950 and 1960 from 39.2 to 31.8 per cent. In the long-industrialized countries of Europe, the drop was from 25 to 17 per cent.[7] The trend continued in the sixties. The transfer of low-productivity agricultural labour to other sectors with a higher productivity made an important contribution to growth.

Other declining industries were coal and iron ore, mining and textiles. On the other hand, there were many growing industries, such as those concerned with the manufacture of motor vehicles and their accessories, aircraft, chemicals, petrochemicals and plastics, synthetic fibres, household durables (washing machines, refrigerators, etc), radio and television, electronic equipment, as well as such services as petrol stations, car servicing and repair shops, banks, insurance and travel.

In general, these extensive changes were carried through smoothly, with little unemployment, and a minimum of hardship. This was partly due to the general expansionist trend, and partly to the positive measures taken by governments to ease the transition.

The position in 1970

Between 1945 and 1970 there was rapid reconstruction of war damage, followed by a period of unprecedented growth, with full employment and rapidly rising standards of living. The notion of a minimum living standard for all, whether at work or unable to work, gained ground. The welfare state was developed. International trade was liberalized and prospered greatly. Major advances were made in international economic co-operation, and the first steps were taken towards the real integration of the economic systems of the six countries of the European Community. This was an amazing achievement in the span of a single generation.

Nevertheless, by the end of the period difficulties were emerging. 1968 was a year of protest, of confrontation, of expressions of frustration and of dissatisfaction with the existing order. Some of the causes were political; but unsolved economic and social issues were also involved. These issues included the gaps in full employment; the fact that minimum incomes were not yet universally guaranteed; the inadequacy of the arrangements to help industry to adjust its resources and men to technological change; the problems of how to involve the consumer more fully in deciding the allocation of resources, and how to strike the right balance between control and initiative in economic planning; the need for greater international co-ordination of economic policies and programmes, and for improving the means of settling the balances of payments between countries.

Some of these problems will be further discussed in chapters 9 and 12.

REFERENCES

1. Cobban, Alfred, *A History of Modern France*, Volume 3, *1871–1962*, Penguin, London, 1965, p. 247.
2. Mendelsohn, Stefan, 'Gold, Double or Quits', in *The Economist*, London, 1968.
3. *European Community*, March 1969, pp. 9–12.
4. *The Economist*, 18 December 1968, p. 14.
5. *Employment Policy*, Cmd 6527, London, H.M.S.O., 1944.
6. *The Economist*, 28 December 1968, p. 13.
7. Bairoch, P., and Limber, J. M. 'Changes in the Industrial Distribution of the World Labour Force, by Region, 1880–1960', *International Labour Review*, Vol. 98, No. 4, October 1968, p. 326.

9. Towards the unification of Western Europe

Motives for Unification

'Europe' has never been a political entity since the days of the Roman Empire, except for the short periods of Napoleon's and Hitler's domination. Its separate states engaged for centuries in incessant wars. After the First World War the idea of a European government began to receive support from intellectuals and students and in 1929 Aristide Briand, the French Prime Minister, told the Assembly of the League of Nations that there ought to be 'some sort of a federal link' between the peoples of Europe – the first time in the twentieth century that such a proposal had been made by a statesman in power. But soon the storm clouds of political and economic nationalism blotted out these ideas.

In 1945 there was a deep desire in Western Europe to construct a new moral and political order which would make war between Europeans impossible. Unofficial groups sprang up at every level, from Members of Parliament and business executives to school teachers and students, to work to *faire l'Europe* – 'create Europe'. On two separate occasions one of the authors asked a young Frenchman and a young German what their nationality was. Each replied: 'I am a European'. Many Europeans felt that a federal Europe offered the only constructive solution to the problem of Germany. There were also economic motives: many believed that only through international action could slumps be avoided and trade expanded.

A measure of economic planning was a condition of Marshall Aid; and the second industrial revolution, the application of electronics to production, which was developing rapidly after the war, was revealing the possibilities of mass production and marketing, and making countries the size of France no longer viable in research and technology. Unification also seemed important for defence against the Communist threat from the East. Finally, after the war the United States consistently used its influence to promote a United States of Europe, partly as a bastion for its own defence against the Soviet Union, and partly because it agreed with the 'Europeans' that federation would prevent a recurrence of the European wars in which America had been reluctantly involved.

We must now define more exactly the term 'European unity.' In principle there are two alternatives: confederation or federation. A confederal organization would be an association of independent, sovereign states, similar to the United Nations, meeting for joint discussion and the planning of concerted action. A federal organization would involve a specific surrender of sovereignty in certain fields to a supranational body with powers to take decisions binding on member states which might disagree with them. If the United States of Europe were set up on the model of the United States of America, West Germany or any other federal state, such matters as foreign policy and defence would be the concern of the federal government and not of the governments of the individual member-states. These would, however, retain full control over matters of more local interest, such as education, health and law. In their public statements politicians often failed to make the distinction clear.

When confronted with the choice between federation and confederation, the countries of Western Europe split into two camps. West Germany, France, Italy and the Benelux countries, the six states to whom the solution of the German problem was most vital, were in favour of federation. Britain, the Scandinavian countries and other small states such as Ireland and Switzerland, wished to see Europe develop on confederal lines.

189

In the first decade after the war there was an unprecedented continuity in the foreign policies of France, West Germany, Italy and Benelux. From 1944 to 1954, French foreign policy was in the hands of Georges Bidault or Robert Schuman, members of the Roman Catholic MRP party; German foreign policy was presided over by Chancellor Konrad Adenauer, a Rhinelander; Belgian foreign policy was dominated by the international figure of the socialist leader Paul-Henri Spaak, who for the past twenty years has alternated between serving his country as Foreign Minister and holding high office in the United Nations and in NATO; finally, the post-war Dutch statesmen were enthusiastic Europeans. The chief architect of the new Europe, however, the backroom thinker whose ideas were translated by these states-men into treaties and institutions, was Jean Monnet, a small lively Frenchman, the son of a Cognac merchant who had never been a politician. He was a personal friend of many British and American statesmen, including Churchill and Kennedy. He prompted Churchill's dramatic offer to France in June 1940 that Britain and France should become one country, and launched Western Europe into new methods of economic planning. (See chapter 4). His philosophy was summed up in the word 'Community'. 'Most people,' he said, 'are well-intentioned, but they see only their own point of view. The thing is to bring them together round a table and make them talk about the same thing at the same time.' This 'same thing' is not a synthesis, nor a compromise, but a *new situation* arising naturally from a change of attitude. 'Work for common ends and means – create solidarity in practical matters, and ideas about class war, national rivalries and hereditary hatreds will disappear of them-selves.' Monnet's philosophy was an attitude, not an ideology. He inspired a large number of 'Europeans' to carry out the Community *process* – another key Monnet word.

In 1945 many people in liberated countries of the continent looked to Britain to lead them into the United States of Europe. But for the next sixteen years Britain repelled every attempt to persuade it to join in the creation of a European federation. First, the British had not experienced either the anguish of occupation or the humiliation of defeat; they had ended the war proud of their nation, not disillusioned with nationalism. Second, Britain's imperial and seafaring tradition had made it a world power in feeling and in fact; the eyes of British idealists were on the United Nations, not on a united Europe. Britain attached great importance to its 'special relationship' with the United States, built up by the personal comradeship between Churchill and Roosevelt in the war; and between 1945 and 1951 the Labour Government was preoccupied with transforming the Empire of subject territories into the Commonwealth of self-governing nations. For the next two decades the concept of the multi-racial *Commonwealth* was to evoke in the British the same kind of idealism which the concept of the multi-racial *Community* evoked in the Continentals. Third, the British, whose parliamentary institutions were among the most stable in the world, were reluctant to hand over any control over their affairs to European countries which had not made democracy work well. Moreover, the Labour Party, in power for the first time with an absolute majority, was preoccupied with internal reconstruction and social transformation.

The European Organizations

Between 1948 and 1960, eight major organizations were founded in Western Europe – we have already referred to some in chapters 2 and 3. Three of these – the European Coal and Steel Community (ECSC), the European Economic Community (loosely called the 'Common Market'), and the European Atomic Energy Community (Euratom), which by 1970 had been merged into the 'European Community' – were supranational; and five – the Western European Union (WEU), the Organization of European Economic Co-operation (OEEC), the North Atlantic Treaty Organization (NATO), the Council of Europe and the European Free Trade Association (EFTA) – were international.

The international organizations have an essentially simple structure. In each the directing body is a Council or Committee composed of representatives of the member governments, ministers or their deputies. On all matters of real importance these intergovernmental Councils take decisions by unanimous vote – necessarily so, since a country's agreement to abide by a majority vote which might go against its interests would imply a surrender of sovereignty. (The Committee of Ministers of the Council of Europe, which takes decisions by a two-thirds majority vote, is an exception; but in contrast to the procedure in NATO, these decisions are only recommendations to member governments and are not binding on them.) This procedure has its advantages; it eliminates the tensions which might arise from division into majority and minority groups, and encourages 'consensus', since individual countries do not wish to put themselves in the position of appearing to obstruct the general will. But essentially it means that progress proceeds at the pace of the least progressive member.

Working with each Council, and in some cases, for instance in NATO and in OECD, acting as its Chairman, is the Secretary-General of the Organization. He is a European civil servant, and heads a staff of administrators and experts drawn from all the member countries. The membership of these bodies is listed in Appendix 3. Here we will briefly describe their structure and achievements.

The Western European Union (WEU)

(Its Council of Ministers meets in Paris, its Parliamentary Assembly in London.)

This organization was originally a military alliance formed in 1948 between Britain, France, and the Benelux countries, to which Italy and West Germany adhered in 1955. Its military functions were largely absorbed by NATO, but it continued to serve a political purpose by providing an official meeting ground for Britain and member countries of the European Community after France had vetoed Britain's entry into the Community in 1963 (see below).

In addition to the usual Council of Ministers and international Secretariat, the WEU has a Parliamentary Assembly of 89 MPs, modelled on that of the Council of Europe (see below). It is the only European parliamentary body competent to discuss European defence problems.

The Organization for European Economic Co-operation (OEEC) and the Organization for Economic Development and Co-operation (OECD) (Headquarters, Paris)

The OEEC was established in 1948 to plan and administer Marshall Aid. The United States did not join in order to avoid exerting pressures on the recipients. By the early 1950s, when Marshall Aid was spent and economic recovery under way, the method of joint planning had been found so productive that the OEEC remained in existence to promote economic expansion through continuous international consultation, and through removing trade quotas and securing currency convertibility. By 1959 it looked as if the European Community and the European Free Trade Association (EFTA) (see below) would duplicate much of its work. (The only OEEC countries which were not members of the Community or EFTA were Ireland, Iceland, and Spain.) Moreover, the United States was then moving towards the concept of an 'Atlantic Partnership', between two independent but interdependent world powers, Europe and North America (see chapter 14). So in December 1959 it was decided to transform the OEEC into the OECD, The United States and Canada became members, Japan joined in 1964 and Australia in 1971. It thus became the meeting place of the main industrialized non-Communist countries. The substitution of the word 'Development' for 'European' in its title implied that one of its concerns would now be to relate the European economy to that of other continents. It has, in particular, assumed the task of co-ordinating, from the donor's end, the aid given by the rich to the poor countries.

The North Atlantic Treaty Organization (NATO)
(Headquarters: Paris until 1966, then Brussels)

We described in chapter 3 the founding of NATO in 1949 by twelve states, including the United States and Canada, as an organization based on a mutual defence alliance. In 1952, Greece and Turkey joined it; in 1955, West Germany was admitted; and in 1966, France withdrew from the military Organization, while remaining a signatory to the Treaty and a member of the Council and Secretariat.

Several NATO military commands were established in Europe and North America. Since Communist aggression was considered most likely to occur in Western Europe, the Supreme Allied Commander in Europe (SACEUR) was given a permanent integrated general staff, the Supreme Headquarters Allied Powers in Europe (SHAPE) – the first of its kind to be established in peacetime. General Eisenhower was the first Supreme Commander and all his successors have been American generals; under the Supreme Commander military officers of all the member states work together as a team. SHAPE is directed by a Council of Ministers or Permanent Representatives of the member states, who in their turn are serviced by a civilian Secretary-General and integrated Secretariat.

All the member states except Iceland (which has no armed forces) have placed units of their armed forces under the operational control of the various NATO Commands and the NATO Council. Belgium, Luxembourg, Denmark, and Turkey have placed *all* their forces under NATO, as did West Germany in 1955 as a condition of its rearmament. These forces remain national units commanded by their own officers and equipped with weapons of their own choice and design – the scheme for a European army having fallen through in 1954. This lack of standardization and of operational integration could be a serious handicap in war. NATO's chief practical achievement has been to develop an 'infrastructure' of airfields, pipelines, telecommunications and radar systems throughout its European member states.

The development of NATO's strategic policy will be discussed in chapter 11.

The Council of Europe (Headquarters: Strasbourg)

The WEU, the OEEC, and NATO were established as Atlantic bodies, and confederal, not federal, since there was no question of the United States surrendering any of its sovereignty. They did not meet the aims of the continental federalists, particularly the aim of the integration of West Germany in Western Europe.

An unofficial congress of 700 European enthusiasts held at the Hague in 1948 called for a constitution for some kind of a United States of Europe. As a result, ten countries signed the Statute of the Council of Europe in May 1949. It was based on a compromise between France, Italy, Belgium and the Netherlands, which wanted a real surrender of sovereignty, and Britain and the Scandinavian countries, which did not. The Council of Europe has no supranational powers. Its main organs are a European Parliament, called the 'Consultative Assembly', and a Committee of Ministers. Membership is open to all countries which, according to the Statute, 'accept the principles of the rule of law, and of the enjoyment of all persons within its jurisdiction of human rights and fundamental freedoms.' This provision disqualified Spain and Portugal, as well as the Communist states. By 1970, eighteen states were members. The Committee of Ministers has described the Council as 'a regional organization for the peaceful development of a European society'.

The Council of Europe is concerned with all topics except defence. In practice, in order not to overlap with OECD, its sphere of action, as distinct from parliamentary discussion, has been mainly concerned with legal, social, educational and cultural matters.

The Consultative Assembly is the first international parliamentary body set up in modern times. It consists of 147 Members of Parliament chosen from among their own members by the parliaments of the member states. Some 300 million people are thus indirectly represented in it. The MPs sit in the Assembly Chamber in alphabetical order of their names, regardless of nationality. The Assembly's function is to debate proposals, which are then put forward to the Committee of Ministers. It has no power to make laws which bind the peoples of the member states over the heads of their governments. The Council of Europe thus serves as a kind of holding operation pending the desire for real federal institutions. The regular visits to Strasbourg for over twenty years of MPs from eighteen countries, drawn from all political parties except the Communists, and including many of the most eminent statesmen in Europe, has fostered a European perspective and begun to promote a European public opinion.

The Council produces about forty studies, recommendations and agreements a year. As examples of its activities, it had, by 1970, negotiated a European Cultural Convention; promoted the reciprocal recognition of university qualifications in member countries; the teaching of 'European' civics; the revision of history and geography text books to delete nationalistic bias, and teacher and pupil exchanges. In social affairs it had secured the adoption of a European Social Charter, and promoted the application of international labour standards and social security. It had concerned itself particularly with public health and the defence of the environment, established a European Water Charter, and organized 'European Conservation Year' in 1970.

One of the Council's most important activities lies in the field of human rights. In 1948, the United Nations adopted the Universal Declaration of Human Rights, an affirmation that the civil, political and social rights 'of all members of the human family is the foundation of freedom, justice, and peace in the world'. In 1966, the United Nations approved two Covenants of Human Rights – treaties under which the signatory states would commit themselves to implement these rights. But a proposal for an International Court of Human Rights to which individuals could appeal if their governments violated civil and political rights, was rejected; and by 1970 very few member states of the United Nations had ratified the Covenants. The Council of Europe has, however, set a precedent. It has drawn up two Conventions, one dealing with civil and political rights, and the other with social rights, and has set up a European Commission and a Court of Human Rights to deal with violations of the first Convention. (Separate Conventions are required because the enforcement of the civil and political rights requires legal and constitutional action, while the establishment of social rights is an entirely different kind of activity, requiring, in fact, the development of the welfare state.)

By 1970, all member states except France had ratified the first Convention, thus affirming their determination to implement these rights, and eleven member states, including Britain but not including Greece, had recognized the right of their own citizens to address petitions to the Commission of Human Rights.

When the Commission has decided that a case of violation of human rights by a member government falls within its competence, and that the applicant has also made out his case, it hears testimony from both sides and tries to reach a friendly solution. If this fails, the Commission reports to the European Court of Human Rights at Strasbourg, or, in instances where the Court's authority has not been recognized by the defendant's government, to the Committee of Ministers. The verdict of either institution is final and binding. Two examples may be given.

In 1969 the Governments of Norway, Sweden, Denmark and the Netherlands prepared a report for the Commission indicting the Greek military régime for using torture 'as an administrative practice,' and for failing to prove its claim that the suspension of civil liberties had been justified by an internal emergency. A number of Greek citizens came to Strasbourg to give evidence to the Commission for and against their government. But in December 1969, before the Commission had considered the report, Greece withdrew from membership of the Council of Europe.

In October 1970 the Commission decided that East African Asians who had opted for British citizenship when Britain had granted independence to their country of residence, but who were debarred by the Commonwealth Immigration Act of 1968 from entering Britain, had made out their case for a *prima facie* violation of the Convention. Before 1970 only a few individual cases had been accepted by the Court, and on each occasion the government concerned took action to right the wrong, as it affected the individual concerned, before the case was heard.

This European precedent that an international authority can safeguard the human rights of the individual may help to promote the eventual creation of a United Nations' Court of Human Rights, to which the citizens of all countries could appeal.

The European Community (Headquarters: Brussels)

The founding of the Community: Undeterred by the failure to make the Council of Europe into a supranational body, Jean Monnet decided that a new approach was necessary. Rather than set up an imposing federal structure and give it tasks to do, it would be better to employ a sector approach, forming supranational bodies, with a limited membership for specific tasks. So he sent a plan for what was to become the first European 'Community' to Robert Schuman, the French Foreign Minister. The latter was excited. After securing the approval of the French Cabinet and of Dr Adenauer, and the blessing of the American Government, he issued the famous 'Schuman Declaration' on 9 May 1950. He proposed:

> Placing the whole of Franco-German coal and steel output under a common High Authority, in an organization open to the participation of the other countries of Europe. The pooling of coal and steel production will immediately provide for the establishment of common bases for economic development as a first step in the federation of Europe, and will change the destinies of those regions which have long been devoted to the manufacture of munitions of war, of which they have been the most constant victims ... This transformation will make possible other joint actions which have been impossible until now ... The solidarity thus achieved will make it plain that any war between France and Germany becomes not only unthinkable, but materially impossible.

Italy, Belgium, the Netherlands and Luxembourg agreed to cooperate, but Britain, whose participation was also sought, refused to accept the principle of the delegation of powers to a supranational High Authority.

The Treaty of Paris, signed in April 1951 by the six governments, set up Europe's first supranational body, the European Coal and Steel Community, with Monnet as the first

President of its High Authority and its headquarters at Luxembourg.

Monnet launched Europe not only into a new type of organization, but into a new method of negotiation. A Dutch diplomat who was at Paris described this method as follows.

'Some of the delegates, formed in the tug-of-war of economic negotiations of the "Schachtian" decade (1933–9), at first believed that they were being simply tricked when, during meetings, they saw the little group of Frenchmen around Monnet disagreeing among themselves just as much as with other delegations. How could one negotiate one's nation's special interest in orderly fashion against another's, if the inviting delegation seemed to have no clear view of the national interests it wanted to defend? But Monnet's method was so contagious, the attempt to find solutions for common problems instead of defending simply one's own national interests was so liberating and exhilarating, that none of the chief delegates resisted this new approach for very long. Monnet thus succeeded in creating out of these hard-boiled negotiators a group of ardent Europeans, many of whom later came to Luxembourg and Brussels to make the Community work.'[1]

An important aspect of the 'Monnet technique' was to secure the participation of all interests and groups. He soon established friendly relations with the French and German Socialist parties and trade unions, and eventually even the Italian Communists felt impelled to support the formation of the Communities.

When the imaginative project for a European Defence Community, initiated by Monnet in 1952, was rejected by the French Parliament in 1954, most of the federalists were in despair. But the Six soon conceived two new Communities. The European Economic Community (EEC), loosely called the 'Common Market', and Euratom were established under the Treaties of Rome of 1957, which came into force on 1 January 1958. Britain was invited to join, as she had been invited to join the European Defence Community, and again she refused.

The aim of Euratom – the logical extension of the Coal and

Steel Community – is to integrate the new, complex and expensive industry of peaceful atomic energy production. The concept of the European Economic Community is much wider. Its first aim was to abolish tariffs and other restrictions on trade, and on the movement of capital and labour between the Six, (they were already being abolished for coal and steel by ECSC), and to establish around the frontiers of the Six a common set of tariffs *vis-à-vis* the rest of the world. This would create a single or common market of some 188,000,000 people (in 1971), comparable to that prevailing within the United States. The Treaty's intention was that the customs union, to be achieved by 1970, would lead to a broader economic integration, which in turn would lead to political federation. Membership was open to all democratic European states. In 1967 it was agreed that the three Communities should be merged into one, under the name of the 'European Community'. (We will, therefore use the word 'Community' even when referring to one of the three bodies.)

The structure of the Community: The international organizations are based on the principle of the *association* of separate sovereign states; the semi-supranational European Community is based on the principle of *integration*. The international organizations are institutionally static; their constitutions do not anticipate any further evolution from what they now are. The Community is dynamic; it aims at economic and political evolution.

The executive power of the Community is vested partly in a Council of Ministers representing the national governments, and partly in a unique 'Commission' of thirteen members, normally distinguished experts or civil servants, appointed for four years by the member governments. Once appointed, they are responsible only to the Community. The Commission works *with,* and not *under,* the Council of Ministers. It initiates policy proposals, on which the Council of Ministers takes final decisions, and it is responsible for all decisions of day-to-day administration. Its regulations become part of the domestic regulations of the member countries and the national law courts are expected to enforce them. To a limited extent, therefore, the Commission has supranational powers; the member states have delegated some of their sovereignty to it. The partnership between the Commission and the Council of Ministers ensures that the Commission's 'Community' approach is harmonized with the national policies which the Ministers represent.

The third partner in the Community is a parliamentary body, the 'European Parliament'. Like the Consultative Assembly of the Council of Europe (with which it is easily confused, since it meets in the same Chamber in Strasbourg), this Parliament consists of 142 deputies nominated by the Parliaments of the member countries. (Its members were increased from 142 to 198 when the Six became the Nine – see below). In contrast to the Consultative Assembly, it has real, though limited, powers. It can dismiss the Commission *en bloc*; the Commission must consult it about plans and policies, and it can question the Commission. The members of the European Parliament sit in party groups, thus forming embryonic 'European' parties. They include a group of Italian Communist deputies.

Finally, a European Court of Justice interprets the three treaties which established the Community, and hears cases involving individuals, firms, governments, the Commission and the Council of Ministers. Since the Community is putting into practice new kinds of policies, many of its decisions are concerned with matters over which no national court has jurisdiction. A body of European law is being created.

During his rule in France from 1958 to 1969 General de Gaulle prevented the Community from expanding its functions and its membership, and from evolving towards fuller supranationalism.

De Gaulle's European policy was inspired by two incompatible attitudes. The first was his dislike of supranationalism, his determination that united Europe should be *l'Europe des états*, which precluded supranationalism in the political and military fields. The second was his dislike of the United States, his desire that *l'Europe des états* should disentangle itself from the American involvement and become an independent 'third force' in world affairs. The contradiction lay in the fact that only a supranational

Europe would be powerful enough to dispense with American military support.

Institutionally, the Community should be developing in three directions. First, under the Treaty of Rome majority voting on all major matters in the Council of Ministers should have been introduced on 1 January 1966 – but in 1970 unanimity was still being required. Second, the European Parliament should have real powers to legislate and to control the Community's large budget, which is derived from the agricultural levies (see below), the import duties on all non-agricultural goods, and from one per cent of a value-added purchase tax which all the Community members are introducing. After de Gaulle's retirement in 1969 the European Parliament was given some control over this budget. Third, the Treaty of Rome provides that the European Parliament should be directly elected. A scheme for this was put forward in 1960 but was pigeon-holed. (In 1971 the Parliament's President was threatening to sue the Council of Ministers in the Community's Court of Justice for failing to implement this provision of the Treaty.) By 1970, the Community was therefore something of an institutional hybrid. The executive Commission was out on a limb, not fully responsible either to the Council of Ministers, as in an international organization, or to the European Parliament, as in a real federation.

General de Gaulle also blocked the enlargement of the Community's membership. In 1961, the British Government suddenly applied to join it, and Norway, Denmark and Ireland followed suit. Britain's main motive was economic: entry into this going concern seemed the only sensible solution to its chronic economic difficulties; and the division of Western Europe into two rival trading blocs – for the European Free Trade Association (EFTA) had been formed in 1960 (see below) – was felt to be wrong. The 'special relationship' with the United States and the Commonwealth mystique were waning. It was realized that, with certain exceptions (see chapter 13), the Commonwealth states would not be seriously hurt economically by Britain's entry into the Community. More serious was the problem of British agriculture, which will be discussed below. The basic fact that 'going into Europe' would probably mean an ultimate commitment to joining a political federation, was played down by successive British Governments after 1961.

On 14 January 1963 General de Gaulle vetoed British entry. He had agreed to the negotiations because he thought that Britain, which already had its nuclear arsenal, would join him in a nuclear partnership which might lead to European nuclear independence of the United States. (Britain had been greatly helped by American nuclear technology, but in the McMahon Act of 1951 Congress had precluded Britain from passing this technology on to France or any other ally). Then, at the end of 1962, the British Prime Minister, Harold Macmillan, arranged with President Kennedy that the United States should supply Britain with Polaris (nuclear submarine) missiles; Britain, in return, would merge its own nuclear weapons in a NATO, not a European, multilateral force under American command (the second part of this agreement was still-born). De Gaulle took this as a final sign that Britain was at heart non-European, – in fact, an American satellite. The other five members of the Community, who had strongly supported British entry, were deeply disappointed.

In May 1967, again with the full support of the other five, Britain renewed its application to join and again, at the end of 1967, de Gaulle vetoed it, but President Pompidou, who succeeded de Gaulle in 1969, withdrew the French veto on British membership. Negotiations, reopened for the third time in July 1970, were successfully concluded in 1971. On 28 October 1971 the British Parliament voted in favour of 'going into Europe'. The applications of Denmark, Norway and Ireland for membership were also accepted, but the application of Norway was withdrawn after a negative popular vote. After ratification by the other three applicant countries, on 1 January 1973 the Six became the Nine with a total population of 250,000,000. The three countries will be allowed a transition period of five years in which to integrate all relevant aspects of their economies with those of the Six.

This event is likely to be momentous for Britain and for

Europe. After making the necessary, and perhaps difficult, adjustments during the transition period, Britain may well gain a permanent solution to its balance of payments problem, through the transfer of the sterling balances into a new European or world reserve system. And, at the time when the Community is seeking to push forward into fuller supranationalism, Britain has the vital contribution to make of its unique politicial, constitutional and legal experience. A leading French politician wrote in July 1970 that: 'France feels that the democratic tradition of Britain will reinforce the common concepts of human dignity within the Community and will increase our chances for freedom'.[2]

The achievements of the European Community: On 1 July 1968, eighteen months ahead of schedule, the 'Common Market' was achieved: all customs duties on the movement of industrial goods, coal, iron ore and steel between the member states were finally abolished. Simultaneously the common external tariff was established: each member now charges the same duties on goods coming from non-member countries (France and Italy had to reduce their tariffs, the other four to increase theirs). The common tariffs were then reduced fifty per cent by the 'Kennedy Round' (see chapter 8), and further cuts subsequently took place. This tariff-slashing has borne fruit: between 1958 and 1967 trade between the Six more than trebled, while world trade doubled. The Community of 188,000,000 people has become the world's largest trading unit; its imports and exports from other countries each rose about two and a half times to about fifty-five billion dollars, while the United States' imports were nearly doubled to twenty-six billion dollars, and its exports rose sixty-six per cent to fifty-one billion dollars.[3] In world trade negotiations the Community now acts on behalf of its members. By 1970 seventy countries had ambassadors accredited to it and it had concluded association or preferential trade agreements with seven states (apart from the African states with which it has a special relationship – see chapter 13) and was planning a trade agreement with Japan.

The next step was to remove other obstacles to fair industrial competition. Differences of cost might arise out of taxation systems. Goods were being held up at intra-Community frontier posts because of the different rates of value-added taxes (a form of purchase tax paid at the various stages in the production of the goods) which had been adopted in all Community countries. The Community is therefore working for agreement between members on uniform taxation rates. Another obstacle is constituted by trade practices such as price-fixing, limitation of production and market-sharing agreements, which are forbidden by the Treaty of Rome. The Community has the right to examine and, if it deems fit, to disallow such agreements. By June 1971 it had investigated 625 complaints, and in all these cases it made rulings with which the companies concerned complied.[4]

In the sphere of agriculture the Community is not merely concerned with trade, but with controlling prices and restructuring the national production systems. The farmers of the Six are a powerful political group; they constitute fourteen per cent of the combined labour force of their countries, but because they are generally inefficient, they produce only five and a half per cent (in value) of total production while working longer hours and earning lower incomes than industrial workers. Most of them are still 'peasants', farming small self-owned holdings of an average size of seventeen and a half acres by primitive methods. The Community is the world's largest importer of tropical foodstuffs, but it is practically self-sufficient in non-tropical foodstuffs, and a substantial exporter of agricultural produce. In these circumstances it has been the traditional policy of the governments of the Six to protect their farmers from the competition of cheap imports.

The ground was cleared by establishing agricultural free trade between the Six by 1 July 1968. Meanwhile it was agreed that the Community should fix common price levels throughout the six countries for all major agricultural products, and should protect farmers from foreign competition by a system of variable levies on imports of food, based on the difference between the cheap prices of the latter and the high prices which the Community farmers are allowed to set for their produce. These levies are paid into a Community Agricultural Fund, which buys up unsold surpluses at guaranteed prices; refunds governments for export subsidies to producers, to enable them to compete with world market prices, and has begun to finance the modernization of farms. In 1968–9 the Fund spent over $2,400,000,000. By 1970 the weaknesses of this policy were apparent: it was producing a combination of large surpluses and high prices while bolstering up the inefficient farmers. In 1971, therefore, a drastic agricultural reform was approved. The basic aim of the reform is to improve methods of production,·so that the standard of living of the Community's farmers can be brought up to the level of that of the industrial workers without having to control markets and prices at the expense of the consumer. The migration of farmers from the land into industry will be encouraged – 5,000,000 abandoned their farms in the sixties and it is hoped to reduce the agricultural labour force from ten million to five million by 1980. The Community will give elderly farmers pensions and younger ones financial help and retraining; those remaining on the land will be helped to increase the size of their holdings and to modernize them and overall area of farm land will be reduced. The scheme will be financed partly by the governments of the Six, and partly by the Community, which has budgeted £1,500,000,000 for 1971–5.[5] One result will be that the Community's main food importers, West Germany, and Britain after 1973, will be helping to finance the reform of French agriculture, since France produces more than it consumes and is in fact the breadbasket of the Six.

Here we may take note of Britain's special agricultural problem. Britain's farms are larger and more efficient than those of the Six, and only three per cent of its labour force is employed on the land, but it has to import about forty per cent of its foodstuffs. Its policy has, therefore, been to keep food prices low by importing cheap, duty-free food, and to pay farmers subsidies, financed out of taxation, based on the difference between the price which yielded them a reasonable return and the price at which the food was sold (in 1968–9 the subsidies amounted to £125,000,000). The imposition of Community levies on its food imports may increase the British cost of living by three or four per cent over a period of five years.

The Community is required to give special attention to certain industrial sectors: coal, steel, energy – in particular atomic energy – and transport. Between 1951 and its merger with the other two Communities in 1967, the Coal and Steel Community removed tariffs, discriminatory transport rates and other measures which tended to distort trade in coal, iron ore, scrap and steel products. It prevented countries from protecting their coal production from the competition of oil. It provided financial help to facilitate the closing down of uneconomic mines and to compensate and retrain the miners.

The Community is working out an overall energy programme, for the demand for power is doubling every decade. In 1960 coal accounted for seventy-five per cent of the energy production of the Six; in 1968, for thirty per cent, and oil (ninety-seven per cent of which was imported into Community countries) for sixty per cent. New sources of energy are being opened up: natural gas from the Netherlands, south-west France, the North Sea and the Sahara; and nuclear power. In 1965 one per cent of the electricity of the Six was produced in atomic reactors; by 1980 one quarter, and by AD 2000 two-thirds, is expected to come from nuclear power.[6] The responsibility for the production of nuclear power is in the hands of the individual governments; but Euratom, which has already sponsored an extensive research programme, is likely to play a larger role in the future.

The Community has created a transport common market. Community road licenses for goods traffic between member countries have partly replaced national licences. Community freight charges have been fixed, and working conditions for Community drivers prescribed.

The Community is responsible for helping the development of the backward areas of its members. Its European Investment Bank has made loans for projects in southern Italy, and in two associated states, Greece and Turkey. Its help to African countries is discussed in chapter 13.

The Community has established a common labour market.

Since July 1968 its 90,000,000 wage-earners have been free to take jobs in member states; there they enjoy the same rights in respect to employment pay, working conditions and social security as the local citizens. 'This could foreshadow in the social field the goal of a common European citizenship'.[7] By 1970 about 2,000,000 workers had moved from one Community country to another, the largest group consisting of Italians working in West Germany. On an overall basis the Six had achieved full employment. The numbers of unemployed fell from 2,500,000 in 1958 to 1,600,000 in 1968.[8] The Community advises member governments on the training of migrant workers, and the provision of housing and social services for them, and finances training and re-employment programmes out of its European Social Fund.

The Community is promoting the application of the principle of equal pay for equal work by men and women, laid down in the Treaty of Rome. Since 1964 the right to equal pay has been guaranteed in the courts of most member countries. Directives have been issued dealing with the conditions under which professional persons such as doctors, architects, engineers, pharmacists and accountants of one Community country may practise in another.

Movements of capital between Community countries have been largely freed, and there is close collaboration between Community finance ministers and monetary authorities.

In 1970, the governments and citizens of the Six were still controlling most aspects of their own social and economic affairs. But through the Community a beginning had been made in integrating economic and social policies, on a piecemeal basis. The success of this integration was indicated by the fact that between 1958 and 1968 the real purchasing power of the average wage-earner increased by sixty-nine per cent in the Netherlands, sixty-six per cent in West Germany, fifty-five per cent in Italy, and forty-six per cent in Belgium.[9]

The way ahead: The Community's achievements between 1958 and 1970 were concerned essentially with removing restrictions on the movement of goods, men and money among the Six. By 1970 it was felt that the time had come for positive steps towards the construction of a common economy. At a 'Summit' conference held at the Hague in December 1969, the premiers of the Six affirmed that the Community should develop towards an economic and monetary union. During 1970 specific plans were put forward to achieve this goal, in three stages, by 1986. In the first stage, from 1971 to 1974, the Six would commit themselves to a common monetary policy *vis-à-vis* other states, to keeping the exchange rates between their own currencies stable, and to general economic consultation on budgetary policies, taxation and economic planning. At the next stage, steps would have to ensure that the member countries would keep their economic and financial programmes and policies sufficiently in line to prevent divergencies which could affect their current parities. By 1986, a common currency, a common Reserve Fund or Community banking system, and common taxation systems and social policies would be established. The Council of Ministers and the Commission would then have to turn into some sort of European Government, responsible to a European Parliament directly elected by 'Europeans'.

The European Free Trade Association (EFTA) (Headquarters: Geneva)

After Britain had refused to join the European Community in 1958, it decided to organize an alternative trade organization with the loose confederal structure and limited functions which it preferred. In 1960, it persuaded the anti-federalist, peripheral countries – Austria, Denmark, Norway, Sweden, Switzerland, and Portugal – to join in establishing EFTA, an international body, whose task was to remove tariffs and other trade restrictions on industrial goods among its members, while each retained its own tariff system towards the outside world: Finland was closely associated with it, and Iceland joined in 1970. EFTA was a small body with a staff of some seventy officials, in comparison with the five thousand who served the Community. In July 1961 the members of EFTA agreed that none would join the European Community without the consent of the others.

By 1970 the EFTA countries had created an industrial free

trade area of about 100,000,000 people – of whom half were British. Tariffs and other restrictions on free trade in industrial goods and on some foodstuffs were eliminated by the end of 1966, three years ahead of schedule (a longer period was granted to Portugal). Between 1959 and 1967 the exports of EFTA countries to each other rose by about 132 per cent, and their exports to all other countries by about fifty-eight per cent.[10] Although the EFTA countries accounted for only about three per cent of the world's population, in 1967 they provided four-teen per cent of the world's trade. As a group they imported and exported more per head of the population than either the European Community or the United States.

In 1970 Austria, Sweden and Switzerland, the neutral, non-NATO members of EFTA, felt unable to join their four partners in applying for membership of the Community, fearing it would compromise their political neutrality. Instead, they and the other members of EFTA not joining the Community. concluded sepa-rate agreements with it, establishing free trade in industrial goods, each country being free to negotiate tariffs with third parties. The EFTA arrangements among members not joining the Com-munity are largely maintained; so, after a transitional five-year period, a free trade zone will have been established covering rich countries with about 260 million people. EFTA remains, to co-ordinate those of its members which are not in the Community.

Other Western European organizations

The Nordic Council, composed of Denmark, Finland, Iceland, Norway and Sweden, was established in 1953. It consists of sixty-nine delegates elected by the Parliaments of the member countries; it holds informal discussions on economic, social and cultural matters; it has established a common labour market, with co-ordinated social security arrangements, and co-operation in legal, cultural and educational matters. A plan to develop the Council into Nordek, a Nordic Common Market, was torpedoed in 1970 by Soviet hostility to Finland's participation; they feared that it might be a device to attach Finland to the European Community, using the other Nordic countries as a bridge.

A number of international bodies have been founded to serve specialized technical needs. They include the European Centre for Nuclear Research (CERN), set up in Geneva in 1954, the European Nuclear Energy Agency, the European Organization for Space Research (ESRO), and the European Launcher Development Organization (ELDO). It has been suggested in the Consultative Assembly of the Council of Europe that a single European Organization should be set up to centralize space activities.

Conclusion

Dotted around north-west Europe are eight Councils of Ministers which meet periodically; eight Councils of Ministers' Deputies, with their staffs, which meet continuously; a large number of committees of experts on a very wide range of subjects; eight international secretariats comprising a total of some 8,000 officials; five indirectly elected European parliaments, and two European Courts of Justice. For over twenty years there has been a constant stream of national politicians, diplomats, civil servants, experts and parliamentarians flying between their capitals and these centres, sitting together hour after hour, headphones clapped to their ears, listening to the swift-tongued simultaneous interpreters pouring out torrents of words about tariffs, quotas, dumping, defence, infrastructures, grain prices, energy policy, equivalence of educational and professional qualifications, the maintenance of European parks, labour migration, assistance to Africa and so on. Working with them are the international officials, many of whom are now young men starting their adult careers as 'Europeans'.

As a counterpart to all the official organizations, a host of non-official European organizations has sprung up, ranging from the European Association of Teachers, founded in 1958, to the European Bed Union.

In all the organizations, whether international or supranational, the Western European countries are in practice working out joint policies. To do this they are telling each other about their national situations and problems. In OEEC–OECD the 'confrontation technique' has been developed, whereby a panel of experts from member states examines the economy of another member and gives it advice. In NATO an 'annual review' is carried out in which each country provides confidential information about its military, economic and financial programmes, in order that NATO may help it to relate military expenditure to economic development. This kind of communication between nations, of sharing information and exchanging advice at every level, was unthought of before 1939. Multilateral diplomacy is supplementing and even replacing bilateral diplomacy.

At present, the overall structure of the West European institutions is untidy and unbalanced. There are too many bodies with overlapping functions. They are top-heavy at the executive level. The sixteen Councils of Ministers and Ministers' Deputies are clumsy bodies, obliged to refer back continuously to twenty-two governments. The general impression is that the new Europe is at a transitional stage. Meanwhile, the European Community is, we would hope, pointing the way towards the Europe of the future, not a confederation nor a federation in the classical sense, but a new form of association in which static concepts of a strict division of powers between governments are replaced by dynamic concepts of *process* and *integration* in freedom – the harmonization of differences from below, not their obliteration from above – occurring at all levels, from the smallest local government group to, ultimately, perhaps, the world state.

REFERENCES

1. Kohnstamm, Max, 'The European Tide', in *A New Europe?*, ed. Graubard, Stephen, Houghton Mifflin Co., Boston, 1964, pp. 151–2.
2. *European Community*, July 1970, p. 19.
3. *United Nations Statistical Yearbook*, 1968.
4. *European Community*, June 1971, p. 22.
5. *European Community*, June 1971, pp. 12–15.
6. *Euratom*, European Community Information Service pamphlet, undated.
7. Ribas, Jacques Jean, 'Social policy: What the EEC has Achieved', in *European Community*, June 1971, p. 18.
8. *Ibid.*, p. 19.
9. *Ibid.*, p. 19.
10. *EFTA Bulletin*, Volume X, No. 1, January-February 1969.

10. Towards the unification of Eastern Europe

International Organizations in Eastern Europe

In the immediate post-war years some of the new Communist governments of Eastern Europe were anxious to revive the idea of a Balkan federation, which had been in the air since 1919: Yugoslavia and Bulgaria, for many years enemies over the Macedonian question,[1] planned an alliance and Rumania and Bulgaria a customs union and the co-ordination of economic plans. The creation of an independent Eastern European federation did not suit Stalin. He wished the East European states to be linked only through their common subservience to Moscow. This subservience was expressed through a series of bilateral military and trade agreements, supplemented by the Council for Mutual Economic Assistance (Comecon), set up in 1949 on an informal basis, and the Eastern European Mutual Assistance Treaty (Warsaw Pact), signed in 1955 (see chapter 3). The original membership of both organizations included the Soviet Union and all the East European Communist states except Yugoslavia. In 1962 Mongolia joined Comecon, and in 1964 Yugoslavia became an associate member of it. In 1961 Albania resigned from both bodies (see chapter 14). Since supranationalism in the context of these organizations could only be a means of cementing Soviet domination, the East European states insisted that they should be fundamentally *international* in structure. Both constitutions affirm the principle of the sovereign independence of their members. Each has a consultative commission of permanent representatives and a secretariat in Moscow, and Comecon is serviced by twenty functional committees, with headquarters in different capitals, each charged with surveying one sector of the economy of all its members. The Warsaw Pact's constitution provides, like that of NATO, for a unified command, but this was never established; unlike NATO it does not have forces allocated to it.

The Warsaw Pact is a military alliance under which each member agrees to assist any other which is attacked in *Europe*. It is therefore specifically directed at NATO. Under the terms of the Pact, thirty-one Soviet divisions were stationed in East Europe in 1970, in East Germany, Hungary, Poland and Czechoslovakia.[2] The Pact has in fact been invoked to assert Soviet military control over its partners. We saw in chapter 7 how Hungary's attempt to withdraw from it in 1956 precipitated the Soviet military invasion of that country, and how the Soviet Union used the Warsaw Pact again to suppress the Czech revolution of 1968. This revolution led to the promulgation of the 'Brezhnev Doctrine' in November 1968. Speaking at the Congress of the Polish Communist Party, the Soviet leader declared that:

> When the internal and external forces hostile to socialism seek to turn back the development of any socialist country to restore the capitalist order, when a threat emerges to the cause of socialism in that country, a threat to the security of the Socialist Commonwealth as a whole, this is no longer a matter only for the people of the country in question, but it is also a common problem, which is a matter of concern for all socialist countries.[3]

The Brezhnev Doctrine thus flouts the principle of sovereign independence affirmed in the constitution of the Warsaw Pact. It was given legal embodiment in a Soviet-Czech Treaty of Friendship signed in May 1970. This Treaty also widens the scope of mutual assistance to cover an armed attack by 'no matter what state or group of states' – which could mean that Czechoslovakia would have to send troops to help the Soviet Union if it were involved in a war with China. By the end of 1970, the other Warsaw Pact countries had resisted any extension of their Treaty commitment beyond 'Europe'.[4] Rumania had gone further and announced in March 1969 that it would permit no Warsaw Pact forces, including those of the Soviet Union, to enter its territory without its permission.[5]

Comecon has been somewhat more successful than the Warsaw Pact as a means of uniting the Soviet Empire. It sprang to life in 1959 to face the challenge of the Western European Community, which the Kremlin damned as a mechanism for bolstering up capitalism. There were, however, many difficulties. First, the Soviet Union is at present largely self-sufficing, exporting only two per cent of its output, in contrast to Hungary, for example, which has to export thirty per cent of its output to earn needed imports. The Soviet Union does not, therefore, need to trade with its allies. Second, the determination of the East European states not to be subject to the economic domination of the Soviet Union made them concentrate on economic self sufficiency, when a regionally diversified economy might be in their long-term interests. In 1962, Khrushchev put forward a plan for the integration of the Eastern European economies with those of the Soviet Union, based on the 'international socialist division of labour', and involving a supranational planning body. The Rumanians torpedoed this plan by refusing to participate in it, and announcing an extremely ambitious programme for the development of a self-contained machine-building and iron and steel industry within their own country. The Russians then dropped the whole scheme. Third, under Communist planning systems, imports are presently restricted to goods asked for by a state planning agency and inter-Comecon trade is conducted on the basis of bilateral government-to-government agreements. This rigid system more or less impels countries which are trying to develop a socialist market economy to try to trade with countries where market forces have play, that is, the countries of the Western world. Finally, the Communist countries as a group cannot meet from their own resources their major need for the sophisticated technical equipment which the Western world is producing.

Nevertheless, Comecon has some constructive achievements to its credit. The 'Friendship Oil Pipeline', the longest pipeline in the world, pumps oil from Russia to Poland, East Germany, Czechoslovakia and Hungary, and is being linked up with Rumania and Bulgaria. The 'United Power System' connects the power grids of all the Eastern European states with the Soviet Ukraine, and will ultimately link up with the generating facilities of Siberia. Multilateral plans have been projected up to 1980.[6]

Polycentrism

Despite the iron grip of the Soviet military presence, the East European states did not, after 1956, remain entirely subservient to the Soviet Union. The 'thaw' in Russia after Stalin's death led to the proclamation by Khrushchev, in 1956, of the doctrine of 'different roads to socialism'. This was followed by the Soviet Union's reconciliation with Yugoslavia, and five years later, in 1961, the eruption of its mighty quarrel with China and Albania. The Eastern European countries took advantage of this situation to play off one Communist super-power against another, to gain for themselves a greater elbow-room. The Rumanians, for instance, were given aid by the Chinese and collaborated with the Yugoslavs in building, on the Danube, the largest hydro-electric power station in Europe. In 1970, even the touchy Albanians, after twenty years of 'malevolent isolation', were seeking the support of their old enemies the Yugoslavs in the face of the threat of Soviet might – the Soviet fleet prowling around the Mediterranean.[7] The Italian Communist leader Togliatti called this state of affairs 'polycentrism'. When he died in Russia in 1964, a highly respected elder statesman of the Communist world, he left a political testament warning against a general 'Party Line' controlled from one centre. His warning was heeded. A conference of eighty-one Communist parties of the world, held in Moscow in 1960 and attended by the Chinese but not the Yugoslavs, affirmed that the Soviet Union was 'the universally recognized vanguard of the world Communist movement'. At a similar conference of seventy-five Communist parties held in Moscow in June 1969 and attended by the Yugoslavs but not the Chinese or their friends (the Albanians, the North Koreans and the North Vietnamese), the Russians were forced to accept the statement that, 'there is no leading centre to the International Communist Movement'. The implications of this statement are hardly compatible with those of the Brezhnev Doctrine.

'. . . the Communist world is in a profound crisis – of regime, of ideology, and of structure. Underlying this crisis there is a thirst for knowledge . . . for objective information . . . for truth. Here is the West's opportunity . . .' wrote a Commission of 'Europeans' set up in Brussels in 1964. But until the Soviet rulers are prepared to allow free rein to the 'thirst for truth' within their own frontiers, liberalization within and between the Eastern European countries can only be limited. Polycentrism represents an omen of change, rather than an actual change, in the structure of the Communist Empire.

REFERENCES

1. Macedonia is a province containing a mixed population of 1,500,000 Yugoslavs and Bulgars, which was awarded to Yugoslavia in 1919. There is a province of the same name in Greece.
2. Mackintosh, Malcolm, 'Soviet Strategic Policy', in *The World Today*, Chatham House, London, July 1970, p. 274.
3. *The Guardian*, London, 14 November 1968.
4. *The Observer Foreign News Service*, No. 27730, London, 8 May 1970.
5. *Strategic Survey 1969*, The Institute for Strategic Studies, London, 1970, p. 12.
6. Ionescu, Ghita, *The Break-Up of the Soviet Empire in Eastern Europe*, Penguin, London, 1965, pp. 124–5.
7. *The Observer Foreign News Service*, No. 22706, London, 4 May 1970.

11. Europe – East and West

By 1970 the two Europes were slowly and tentatively being drawn together by various forces: the mutual desire to trade; the mutual desire for security, involving some solution to the 'German problem' and some disarmament; and the mutual desire of many ordinary people to travel.

East-West Trade

Until 1968 the value of East-west Trade was slight. In that year over sixty per cent of the trade of the Comecon countries (including the Soviet Union) took place within the Comecon area, which accounted for only a fifth of the world's GNP. Only twenty-three per cent of the exports of the Comecon countries went to the European members of the OECD and only four per cent of the exports of the OECD countries went to the Comecon states.[1]

Since 1968 the Comecon countries have shown a greater eagerness to trade with Western Europe, for the reasons indicated in chapter 7. Firms like Krupps and Mercedes-Daimler-Benz of West Germany, Fiat of Italy and Simon Engineering of Britain are co-operating with Comecon governments in designing and operating engineering plants, in particular polythene plants, factories for the manufacture of passenger and commercial vehicles, and the development of rail freight container systems. In 1969 an international investment corporation of over forty

Western and Yugoslav banks was set up in London to finance such investment in Yugoslavia.[2] In 1970 plans were on foot for Daimler-Benz to lead a Western consortium in building the world's largest lorry factory on the banks of the Kama, a tributary of the Volga. A West German trade delegation visited Yugoslavia for the first time since 1933 and the Czechs, who increased their trade with West Germany by fifty per cent between 1968–9, signed a five-year trade agreement with that country. In 1970 West Germany was leading the new Western European commercial thrust into the Communist bloc but the French were not far behind. In October 1970 President Pompidou visited the Soviet Union, and a British reporter commented:

> The new stage of the Franco-Russian relationship established by the President, together with the Treaty with Bonn (see below) means above all a technological revolution for the Soviet Union. The credits which will flow from Europe for large-scale enterprises in mining and industry, and the new and up-to-date technology which countries like Britain, France and Germany will impart to the Soviet Union in the process, will help the Soviet Union to keep up with the Americans in this important field.[3]

(The United States was inhibited from entering this vast, hungry consumer-goods market by legislative controls on exports to Communist countries, although by 1970 these controls had been considerably pruned. Nevertheless, political pressure forced Henry Ford to turn down the lorry production contract which was subsequently awarded to the German consortium). In order to repay Western credits, the Soviet Union, like the other Eastern European states, may have to start producing industrial goods which can compete in Western markets. Soviet scientists, engineers and managers may have to join the Hungarians, East Germans and other Comecon colleagues in travelling in the West. Trade might be a major means of impelling the 'hermit state' to open up.[4] Institutionally, Yugoslavia is the link country in this field. It is an associate member of Comecon and has a special status with the OECD. It sends representatives to some of the Council of Europe's conferences; and in May 1970 it signed a trade agreement with the European Community.

The United Nations' Economic Commission for Europe (ECE)

The United Nations' Economic Commission for Europe, set up in 1947, was, in 1970, the only regional body of a general character in which representatives from both Eastern and Western Europe met regularly to discuss economic problems. The United States is also a member; West Germany was admitted in 1956 and Switzerland participates in the Commission's work. Every year, on the basis of impartial surveys, the Commission reviews Europe's main economic issues, particularly those concerning relations with the rest of the world and the problems of planning.

The ECE has contributed to post-war reconstruction and the removal of obstacles to international trade. Its main achievements, however, have been in technical fields. For instance, when there was a shortage of coal in Europe, its balance sheet of the production and needs of different countries provided a basis for fair distribution. It has promoted a European network of roads and inland waterways, the removal of obstacles to facilitate the through traffic of passengers and goods, the development of intercontinental container traffic, and the interchange of electric power between European countries. Because of the ECE's activities, motorists pass customs barriers with minimum formalities, and surplus power is switched from one country to meet the needs of another. Surveys and statistics have been published on housing, agriculture, coal, steel, natural gas, timber, the rational use of water resources and water pollution.

In the ECE, therefore, the representatives of all the European countries and the United States, conduct broad exchanges of views on matters which are factually verified, and co-operate closely at working levels on a wide range of practical problems.

The Division and the Unification of Germany in the East-West Context.

By 1955 West Germany was integrated economically and militarily into Western Europe, in NATO, OEEC, the European Community and other organizations, and East Germany into Eastern Europe through the Warsaw Pact and Comecon.

To bring West Germany fully into Western Europe, and to link it with the United States was Chancellor Adenauer's fundamental aim. This policy did two vital things for the country: it stabilized its new democratic institutions – the West Germans became healthily sensitive to any criticism from their Western partners of the slightest sign of the recrudescence of Nazism; and it gave its citizens a new ideal – that of 'creating Europe' in 'community' with its partners. But from 1949 onwards the West German Government, supported by its allies, affirmed that the reunification of Germany on the basis of 'free elections', that is, multi-party elections of the Western democratic type, was also a fundamental aim; and because of this it could not recognise the legal existence of East Germany. This state was treated as a diplomatic nonentity. Only Communist states entered into diplomatic relations with it and West Germany refused, accordingly, to enter into any diplomatic relations with those states. And after 1955 the West German *Bundeswehr* of 466,000 men glared across the Iron Curtain at the East German Peoples' Army of 129,000 men.[5]

In August 1961 the last chink in the Iron Curtain was closed when the Russians built the Berlin Wall between East and West Berlin. Before then free passage between East and West Berlin was possible, and some three million people left East Germany through this chink between 1949 and 1961. Originally built of concrete blocks and barbed wire, by 1970 the wall consisted of a neat wire-mesh fence, a cement-lined moat three metres deep and four and a half wide, and a cleared 'death strip', patrolled from a chain of observation towers. 'One of the most terrible sights in East Berlin is to see people congregating near the Brandenburg Gate, looking across into West Berlin. If they move a step westwards, they may be shot dead.'[6] And the Wall is merely an ex-

H

tension of the electrically wired, mined and watch-towered death zone – the architecture of the concentration camp – which stretches along the 830 km frontier between the two Germanies. Between 1961 and 1968 some 27,000 people managed to cross this fearsome frontier; 200 were shot trying to traverse the Wall.[7] The Wall has, however, helped to stabilize the situation by giving East Germany a greater sense of identity. No longer able to protest their fate with their feet, the East Germans have been forced to build a constructive future for themselves within their own frontiers.

From 1954 onwards, the Russians and their allies repeatedly made proposals for relaxing the tensions between the two blocs (see below): they suggested the denuclearization of central Europe, troop reductions in the area, a non-aggression pact between NATO and the Warsaw Treaty Organization, even the dismantling of both organizations. But the conditions underlying all these proposals were that West Germany should withdraw from NATO; that the legal existence of East Germany should be recognized and the permanence of the Oder-Neisse frontier between East Germany and Poland accepted. These conditions were not acceptable to the Western powers. So the Russians tried to force their hand by threatening, in 1958, in 1961 and in 1969, to allow East Germany to take over West Berlin, which would involve a separate peace treaty between East Germany and the Soviet Union.

Until 1969 the only Western European statesman to make any serious attempt to break through the Iron Curtain stalemate was General de Gaulle. He courted Russia and the Eastern European countries; he proclaimed the unity of Europe 'from the Atlantic to the Urals'; he withdrew France from NATO in 1966. But 'his error was to have thought in terms of France's glory rather than to have used his prestige to speak for Europe as a whole. Acting for France alone, he could not accomplish more than flourishes that occasionally seemed spectacular but in the end left few lasting traces.'[8] Meanwhile, in 1967, Rumania, the diplomatic rebel of the Communist bloc, flouted its Warsaw Pact allies by establishing diplomatic relations with West Germany.

When Willi Brandt became Chancellor of West Germany in September 1969, he set himself to break through the fifteen-year stalemate. He determined that the time had come for West Germany to make a constructive relationship with its former enemies in the East, as it had with those in the West. And the two Germanies, he said, could not behave as foreign countries to each other. So he launched his *Ostpolitik*, based on West German recognition of the permanence of the Oder-Neisse frontier and the *de facto* existence of East Germany. The result was West Germany's signature of a non-aggression pact with the Soviet Union in August 1970 and of a treaty with Poland in December 1970. Similar West German treaties with Czechoslovakia and East Germany were also on the horizon at the end of 1970. (Two 'summit' meetings had taken place between Willi Brandt and East German Premier Willi Stoph.) But at the end of 1970 the ratification of the Soviet treaty, the lynchpin of the *Ostpolitik*, depended on Soviet agreement to stabilize the situation in West Berlin, by confirming the rights of access to West Berlin of the West Germans and the Western forces stationed there, as laid down in the Potsdam and other agreements. (In 1971 such an agreement was negotiated, and Willi Brandt was awarded the Nobel Peace Prize).

This web of treaties has culminated in the admission of East and West Germany as separate states into the United Nations in 1973. In 1919 a bitterly resentful and humiliated Germany was forced to make territorial concessions. In 1970 a self-confident West Germany was taking the initiative in finally renouncing the 'lost territories' as a fundamental act of reconciliation. And in so doing the *Ostpolitik* opened the door to a new approach to a military détente in Europe.

Relationships between NATO and the Warsaw Pact.

The nuclear race, discussed in chapter 14, transformed the situation of the two opposing military blocs in Europe. At the time of NATO's foundation in 1949 its strategic concept was simple: its limited conventional forces were to act as a 'shield' while the United States unsheathed its 'sword', the atom bomb. Now, could Western Europe, wedged in between the two nuclear

223

super-powers, expect the United States to expose itself to a direct Soviet missile attack in order, for example, to save West Berlin from a Communist take-over? The 'credibility' of the United States' commitment to Europe no longer seemed quite so strong. After his election in 1968 President Richard Nixon had begun cautiously to pursue the 'Nixon Doctrine': to try to scale down the mighty American military presence around the world by pursuading the local countries to take more responsibility for their own defence.

Between 1945 and 1970 there were over fifty armed conflicts in the world. With the exception of the Soviet invasions of Hungary and Czechoslovakia, all took place outside Europe and all were fought with conventional weapons. But if war broke out inside Europe between the forces of NATO and those of the Warsaw Pact, would it be possible to avoid the use of nuclear weapons? NATO was confronted in the sixties with a painful strategic dilemma: either to increase its conventional forces to the level of those of the Communist powers, or to develop the capacity for a nuclear response. The European members of NATO were reluctant to spend the large sums of money needed and further to conscript their young men for expanded conventional forces (France had been bled white by the Algerian War, and Britain had abolished conscription in 1962). The United States was chafing at the fact that its European allies were only spending five per cent of their GNP on defence while it was spending over ten per cent; and in 1969 Canada brought most of its men home from Europe.

A new NATO strategy was therefore evolved in 1967, the strategy of 'flexible response'.

The basis of this concept is that credible deterrence of military actions of all kinds is necessary, and that this can be secured only through a wide range of forces equipped with a well-balanced mixture of conventional and tactical and strategic nuclear weapons. The purpose of this balance of forces is to permit a flexible range of responses combining two main principles. The first principle is to meet any aggression with direct deterrence at approximately the same level, and the second is to deter through the possibility of escalation. . . . The keystone of the new strategy is that an aggressor must be convinced of NATO's readiness to use nuclear weapons if necessary . . .[9]

Long before this doctrine was announced Britain and France had developed their own nuclear deterrents. Britain exploded an atomic bomb in 1952 and a hydrogen bomb in 1957. After 1963, with American help, it spent about £1,800,000,000 on a small force of four British-built Polaris submarines each armed with sixteen American missiles, and seventy-five medium-range bombers also armed with nuclear weapons. In 1958 General de Gaulle inaugurated France's *force de frappe*, without American help. By 1970 it had cost £5,000,000,000 and consisted of some forty medium-range Mirage IV bombers, nine missiles with nine more to come, and one missile-carrying submarine, with three more to come whose missiles have a shorter range than Polaris.[10] In August 1968 France, which did not sign the Test Ban Treaty of 1963, exploded a hydrogen bomb in the South Pacific.

Meanwhile the Americans were arming NATO with some 7,200 tactical nuclear weapons. Most of these were on West German soil. The American Secretary of Defence, Robert McNamara, once remarked that the United States had the equivalent of '5,000 Hiroshimas' stored in West Germany. The troops of seven countries were being trained to use these weapons, but they remained under American control.

Estimates of the comparable strengths of the NATO and Warsaw Pact forces vary. The assessment of the American Ambassador to NATO in 1969 was that 'NATO has two-thirds as many men, half as much equipment, perhaps a third as many tanks, and two-thirds as many strike attack aircraft (that is, aircraft designed to attack ground targets) as the Warsaw Pact had.[11] Another authoritative estimate was that in 1970 1,100,000 NATO troops confronted 1,300,000 Warsaw Pact troops, of which 660,000 were Russian. (In contrast to the NATO troops, all those of the Warsaw Pact have standardized Soviet or Soviet designed equipment). NATO disposed of 7,600 tanks and 3,000 tactical aircraft, and the Warsaw Pact of 19,000 tanks and 5,000 tactical aircraft.[12] What did this signify? The Ambassador also pointed out that, 'a European confrontation is always potentially a nuclear confrontation. Such an environment is without precedent – no defence partnership in history has had to reckon with escalation into oblivion.'[13]

By the end of 1970 the Western European attitude to the United States' military presence in Europe was ambivalent. On the one hand there was fear of the dangers to which an American withdrawal would expose them – a fear which prompted them to agree to pay one billion dollars towards the cost of the United States' 300,000 troops. On the other hand, there was a growing feeling that 'Europe' should be militarily independent of the United States. 'In spite of the anxiety that this (the prospect of substantial American troop withdrawals) has aroused, there *need* be nothing disastrous about it. New technological developments are making it perfectly possible to envisage a more adequate conventional defence of Western Europe than exists today, and with considerably fewer troops' wrote an expert.[14] The first step towards European military independence would presumably involve some form of nuclear sharing between Britain and France – of which there was no sign by 1970. Moreover, a European nuclear defence force could hardly be formed without the inclusion of West Germany – armed, perhaps, with most of the 7,200 tactical nuclear weapons as a parting American bequest. Yet such inclusion would involve abandoning the Paris Treaty of 1955, under which West Germany undertook neither to make nor possess nuclear weapons; and violating the non-Proliferation Treaty of 1968, which West Germany had ratified by the end of 1970. And it would almost certainly arouse the strongest reaction from the Russians. The arguments against making a united Western Europe into a third military super-power would therefore seem to be strong.

There would seem to be two possible ways of achieving a military detente between Eastern and Western Europe. The first is to establish a denuclearized, demilitarized area in the heartland of central Europe – in 1970 the most heavily armed area in the world. This was proposed in 1957 by the Polish Foreign Minister Adam Rapacki. He suggested that the area should include East and West Germany, Poland and Czechoslovakia. The second is for the two blocs – in effect, the two super-powers – to agree to a mutual reduction of arms in Europe. The Soviet Union proposed on various occasions that an East-West Security Conference should be held; but the Western powers were sceptical of its intentions. In 1970 it renewed the proposal – partly perhaps in order to secure its rear in Europe so that it could deal with China. By the end of 1970 there was a growing feeling that in the context of the nuclear arms race, the military stalemate which had lasted in Europe since the formation of NATO and of the Warsaw Pact was no longer a stabilizing force.

This feeling, combined with Willi Brandt's *Ostpolitik*, and the growing desire to be militarily independent of the United States, made the prospects of a military detente in Europe more favourable, at the end of 1970, than at any time since 1948.

REFERENCES

1. OECD figures.
2. *The Economist*, London, 25th July 1970.
3. *The Observer Foreign News Service*, No. 29204, London, 20 October 1970.
4. *The Economist*, London, 3 October 1970.
5. *Institute of Strategic Studies*, London, 1970.
6. *The Times*, London, 15 August 1968.
7. *Ibid.*, 13 August, 1968.
8. *The Observer Foreign News Service*, No. 27276, London, 17 December 1969.
9. *NATO: Facts and Figures*, NATO Information Service, Brussels, 1969, p. 66.
10. *The Manchester Guardian Weekly*, 30 October 1971, p. 7.
11. Cleveland, Harlan, *NATO: The Transatlantic Bargain*, Harper and Row, New York, 1970, p. 84.
12. The Institute of Strategic Studies, London, *The Military Balance, 1970–71*, pp. 91–4.
13. Cleveland, *op. cit.*, p. 35.
14. Windsor, Philip, 'Current Tensions in NATO', in *The World Today*, July 1970, Chatham House, London, p. 293.

12. Social developments in Europe

The Primacy of Social Objectives

A major social revolution has taken place in Europe in the twentieth century. Before 1914 the *laissez-faire* attitude, which was discussed in chapter 8, prevailed in social as well as in economic affairs. Social action aimed merely at providing basic assistance to those deemed too weak to defend their own interests; this excluded men of working age, who had, in general, won the legal right to form trade unions and to strike.

Between the wars a social conscience developed, partly through the pressure of the trade unions, the ILO and the Socialist and Communist political parties. Many countries took steps to mitigate serious hardship which, nevertheless, was still regarded, except in the Soviet Union, as an inevitable aspect of the *laissez-faire* system.

The stresses of the Second World War let loose a new spirit in the world. In January 1941, in a message to Congress, President Roosevelt proclaimed the 'four Freedoms', one of which was 'freedom from want'. In the Atlantic Charter of 1941, the British and American governments affirmed that they sought to secure for all 'improved labour standards, economic advancement and social security'.

In 1944 the International Labour Conference affirmed that national and international policy should aim at enabling all human beings to pursue their material well-being and spiritual development in conditions of freedom and dignity, of economic security and equal opportunity.[1] It added that, 'all national and international policies and measures, in particular those of an economic and financial character, should be judged in this light and accepted only in so far as they may be held to promote and not to hinder the achievement of this fundamental objective'. This declaration, which completely reversed the traditional approach to social problems, was accepted by all European states except East Germany and Albania.

Social objectives were affirmed in the Charter of the United Nations and in the constitutions of the United Nations' specialized agencies. They were embodied in Declarations and Covenants of Human Rights at world-wide and European levels – a European Social Charter was adopted by the Council of Europe in 1961.

The Churches added their voice. In 1937, the Protestant Churches stated that, 'as long as industry is not organized to serve the community, but primarily for the financial benefit of certain members thereof, it cannot be considered as fulfilling its social purpose.'[2] Pope John XXIII made it clear that 'economic progress must be accompanied by corresponding social progress so that all classes of citizens can participate in the increase of production'.[3] In 1968, the World Council of Churches urged Christians to 'participate in the struggle of millions of people for greater social justice and for world development'. It pointed out that, 'the political and economic structure groans under the burden of grave injustice, but we do not despair because we know that we are not in the grip of blind fate'.[4]

These social objectives became part of the way of life in post-war Europe, and governments based their policies on them. The welfare state was born.

Standards of Living

Because of the havoc wrought by the First World War, galloping inflation in certain countries and the depression, the overall rise in standards of living between the wars was slight. Economic recovery was achieved much more quickly after the Second

World War, and by 1948 most countries had regained or slightly improved upon their pre-war level. After 1948 living standards rose dramatically as a result of higher wage levels and the development of social security (see table 3).

TABLE 3

Country	Increase in average real wages 1948 or 1953 to 1967 [5]	Per capita gross national product US $ 1968 [6]
	1948 = 100	
Austria	172	1,320
Belgium	182	1,810
Cyprus	NA	780
Denmark	192	2,070
Finland	157	1,720
France	181	2,130
West Germany	213	1,970
Greece	NA	740
Italy	176	1,230
Iceland	NA	1,690
Ireland	NA	980
Malta	NA	570
Netherlands	193	1,620
Norway	165	2,000
Portugal	NA	460
Spain	NA	730
Sweden	209	2,620
Switzerland	162	2,490
United Kingdom	153	1,790
	1953 = 100	
Albania	NA	400
Bulgaria	229	770
Czechoslovakia	154	1,240
East Germany	233	1,430
Hungary	182	980
Poland	198	880
Rumania	NA	780
Yugoslavia	225	510
USSR	213	1,110

Increase in Wages

'All workers have a right to a fair remuneration, sufficient for a decent standard of living for themselves and their families'.[7]

By 1970 practically every country in Europe had developed some machinery for determining minimum wages. Some, such as Britain, West Germany, Italy, Switzerland and the Scandinavian countries, relied mainly on collective bargaining; others, such as France and the Eastern European countries, relied largely on regulations having force of law. The aims were to establish a minimum for those at the bottom of the scale and to ensure that wages rose as fast as the economy of the country permitted. By 1970 there were, however, still wide divergencies in real income between the different parts of Europe, as will be seen from the GNP figures in table 3. To see the European situation in perspective, we may note that the comparable figure for the United States was just under $4,000, and for many African and Asian countries under $100.

Social Security

Before 1939, social security in the Western European countries was provided, by piecemeal insurance schemes covering particular contingencies such as sickness, accidents at work, unemployment and old age. The schemes normally applied to limited categories of workers and provided benefits for only limited periods. There were therefore many people who had no coverage and who had to rely on 'assistance' – called in Britain 'the dole' – which was granted not as a social right, but as a form of governmental charity for the destitute. Only in the Soviet Union was the concept of the 'umbrella' welfare state conceived: the provision by the State of social security services as a *right* to all citizens in all contingencies. (See chapter 6).

After 1945, most Western European democracies adopted the concept of the 'umbrella' welfare state. It involved a new approach. Instead of pegging benefits to insurance, needs were to be assessed in the light of the minimum standards which it was felt that a person, as a person, ought to have, and then the

231

state would see that these needs were met. The International Labour Conference affirmed in 1944 that social security schemes 'should relieve want and prevent destitution by restoring, up to a resonable level, income which is lost through inability to work (including old age), or to obtain remunerative work or because of the death of the breadwinner.'[8]

In Britain, the funds required to finance the greatly expanded social services were raised in two ways: by contributions from all active members of the population, whether they were wage or salary earners and by increased taxation (in the 1950s most West European workers became subject to income tax). In other countries, the switch over from the principle of insurance was more gradual. Where separate insurance policies remained, 'assistance' was provided when the insurance was exhausted, or to fill the gaps which insurance did not cover. But everywhere the principle of 'bringing the magic of averages to the rescue of the millions'[9] was generally accepted. Thus the new approach, by establishing a comprehensive system to which *all* contributed and from which *all* were entitled to receive, aimed not only at eliminating want but at removing social barriers. Post-war social security in Western Europe therefore normally covered pensions, unemployment and sickness benefits, assistance in raising a family, such as pre- and post-natal care, school meals, family allowances and health services.

After 1945 the Soviet umbrella welfare state was transferred from paper to practice. Soviet citizens gained free health services – and a higher proportion of doctors per patient than in any other European country – and non-contributory sick pay and pensions for all men over sixty and women over fifty-five. (Unemployment does not, of course, in theory exist in Communist countries). The Communist states of Eastern Europe followed the Soviet model.

By 1970 there was, however, still much to be done before social security was firmly established for all. In some countries groups of workers remained outside all the schemes. Pensions and other benefits, and the care provided by health services, were often inadequate. There was a need to simplify formalities and to give the administration of social security 'a human face'. And sometimes the availability of these benefits fostered improvidence. Nevertheless, the welfare state, a European invention, will probably rank as one of the great creative achievements of the human race in the twentieth century.

Housing

In twentieth-century Europe the principle has been generally accepted that the community is responsible for providing adequate housing for all its members. This has been a tremendous challenge: the growth of population, the rise in standards of housing which affluence has brought, the nineteenth-century legacy of decrepit slums, the destruction wrought in two world wars, and the shift of population from the country to the towns, combined to produce a drastic housing shortage in both Western and Eastern Europe. In 1970 between a third and a half of European housing was over fifty years old and much of it lacked modern amenities.

Before 1914, little was done by the public authorities to provide houses. Between the wars, governments provided help by such means as tax remissions and rent control. In Britain 1,000,000 'council houses' were built by the County Councils, financed by government subsidies and let at subsidized rents, and 3,000,000 private-enterprise houses were built with government subsidies. The large, barrack-like blocks of working-class flats in Vienna were a typical example of a large-scale government housing scheme of this period.

After 1945, the provision of housing at moderate rents to those who could not afford to pay market prices came to be regarded as a basic social service. In 1961 governments accepted the principle that:

It should be an objective of national policy to promote, within the framework of general housing policy, the construction of housing and related community facilities with a view to ensuring that adequate and decent housing accommodation and a suitable living environment are made available to all workers

233

and their families. A degree of priority should be accorded to those whose needs are most urgent. The aim should be that such housing should not cost the worker more than a reasonable proportion of income.[10]

In Britain, nearly ninety per cent of the 1,000,000 houses built between 1948 and 1952 were publicly built, though the proportion dropped later. In Italy, a payroll tax financed a national building institute. France used government-assisted housing co-operatives to build moderate rent houses. Rent control was extensively applied in many countries, but it tended to discourage private building and led owners to neglect maintenance. By 1960, nearly ninety per cent of the new houses in France, Ireland, the Netherlands and Sweden had been built with some sort of government contribution. In Britain, Denmark, West Germany and the Netherlands most of the governmental help was for rental houses. Only in Greece, Portugal and Switzerland was governmental help insignificant.[11]

Before the war a very grave housing shortage had already developed in the Soviet Union; and during the war 25,000,000 Russians were made homeless. After 1957, the Soviet Union pioneered the technology of mass produced housing units of 'pre-cast, pre-stressed, reinforced concrete elements that can be pre-assembled in the factory and erected on any site in minimum time with minimum labour'. The style of these buildings was becoming daily more sophisticated; the costs were a third of those of the United States where, as elsewhere in Europe, much housebuilding was still done by hand. This housing breakthrough constituted a kind of 'architectural Sputnik'. In 1967 3,000,000 new housing units a year were being built in Russia.[12]

The Results of Rising Wages, Social Security and Government Housing

The granting of wage increases and the development of social services was made possible by two factors: first, the vast increase in the sheer production of goods brought about by technology;

and second, the redistribution of wealth which took place in every European country. Essentially, the great extremes of poverty and wealth which determined the social structure of Europe for centuries became a thing of the past. The aristocracy were either eliminated by war and revolution, as in Eastern Europe, or persuaded, as in Western Europe, to surrender most of their incomes or property through such devices as income tax and death duties – nineteenth-century inventions. Throughout Europe many of the great mansions and castles whose owners had lorded it over the serfs and peasants became museums, amusement parks, schools or trade union rest homes. Europe has experienced a fundamental social revolution in the twentieth century.

In 1970 the results of the dramatic rise in living standards were visible in every European country, East and West. For the first time in the history of the continent, almost all its inhabitants were adequately fed and clothed. Millions were living in new houses or flats of a standard and aesthetic design unthought of before the war. Public utilities – piped water, modern sewage, gas, electricity and telephone services – had vastly expanded.

Cars are a significant indication of living standards: in 1922, there were only 854,000 passenger cars in the whole of Europe – in the fourteen leading countries, one car for every 370 inhabitants. By 1970, in Western Europe on an average every other household had a car : one Swede or Frenchman in four, one West German, Belgian, Briton or Swiss in five; one Austrian, Italian or Dutchman in six; factories were providing parking lots for their workers. On the other hand, there was still only one car for 16 people in Spain, one for 50 in Greece, and one for 250 in Turkey.

Better living conditions combined with the developments of medical science to transform the health of the Europeans. Between 1900 and 1970 the death rate was halved, and life expectancy at birth prolonged by twenty years. Many hitherto fatal diseases, such as malaria, typhus, typhoid, tuberculosis, smallpox, diptheria and scarlet fever, were brought under control. Europe was becoming an 'affluent society'.

Labour and Management

A major change occurred in the attitudes of governments and peoples towards trade unions, and in the role of the unions in determining conditions of work and of life. (In a few countries, notably Greece and Portugal, dictatorial regimes repressed free trade unions.)

The workers' organizations had to struggle to gain recognition. A widely ratified convention adopted by the International Labour Conference in 1948 provided that 'workers and employers, without distinction whatsoever, shall have the right to establish, and subject only to the rules of the organization concerned, to join, organizations of their own choosing without previous authorization'.[13] Further, in capitalist countries, employers and workers came to recognize the advantages of negotiated arrangements, and, in 1949, it was internationally agreed that measures should be taken in each country 'to encourage and promote the full development and utilization of machinery for voluntary negotiations'.[14] The ways in which employers' and workers' organizations influence conditions of work and life by their joint action varied greatly from one country to another and were constantly changing. Only some general patterns can be set out here.

First, in nearly all European countries they negotiate collective agreements. In some countries such matters as hours of work, holidays with pay, and minimum wage scales, were laid down by law. Agreements between unions and employers may then be concerned with other matters, taking these standards for granted; or with improving on the legal minima. In other countries, such as Britain, West Germany, those of Scandinavia, and, to a lesser extent France and Italy, nearly all matters are dealt with by collective bargaining. In the Soviet Union, wage classification, hours of work and many other conditions are fixed by regulation. The trade unions are mainly concerned with the drawing up and fulfilment of the production plans, and above all with the use to which the 'surplus', or the margin between sales proceeds and production outlays, should be put. Often this surplus is allocated to workers' social and welfare activities. The unions also administer a large part of the social insurance funds financed by the State. In most countries collective agreements were adopted for all the workers in a given industry on a national basis, though sometimes there are 'company agreements', limited to the workers of that firm.

Second, most countries have established some form of machinery for consulting the workers: shop stewards, trade union or workers' delegates are given the right to take up grievances with the management and to discuss matters not covered by the collective bargaining. Works councils, usually with advisory powers only, are required by law in Austria, Belgium, France, Finland, West Germany, the Netherlands and Spain. They have also been set up as the result of national agreements in Denmark, Norway, Sweden and Italy, and exist in Britain. In the Soviet Union factory committees exercise condiderable powers, including that of sharing in the enforcement of factory regulations. In many countries and industries the employers and workers meet not only to bargain but to discuss common problems.

Third, employers' and workers' organizations are normally consulted by governments in the framing of legislation on all matters which affect them, and they are involved with governments in national economic planning (see chapter 8).

Fourth, several countries have set up advisory economic and social councils, a substantial proportion of whose workers are appointed by the employers' and workers' organizations.

Fifth, at the international level, employers and workers' organizations participate by right in the meetings of the ILO, where their joint voting powers are at least equal to those of governments. They also appoint about one-third of the members of the advisory Economic and Social Committee of the Commission of the EEC, and send observers to the discussions of the other European organizations which deal with economic matters.

By 1970, therefore, the employers' and workers' organizations had become partners in government.

The Problem of Control over Industrial Power

Even if the employers' and workers' organizations usually come to an agreement, their interests are often in basic conflict. Trials of strength occur, usually in the form of strikes or lock-outs, which may be damaging to the economy of the country concerned and hurt others not involved in the dispute. Further, when the parties do agree, they may do so on terms which are inconsistent with the major policies of the country concerned, such as the prevention of inflation or the protection of the balance of payments.

In the nineteenth century the power of the employer was unlimited: he could 'hire and fire' at will. In the twentieth-century this power has been progressively restrained, first by the legislators and then by the trade unions. As a result, 'just like the monarchies of the past, the modern undertaking is now gradually evolving from absolutism to a "constitutional" system under which authority is exercised in accordance with a set of principles, criteria and rules that have all been discussed and agreed upon beforehand.'[15]

Much of the social history of the post-war period consists of attempts to reconcile a large measure of freedom in collective bargaining with the maintenance of stated objectives of national policy: control over the wage and price structure as a whole and control over national economic policy, including the fulfilment of production plans and the prevention of monetary crises, inflation and industrial disruption through disputes. By 1970 there had been some successes, but no statisfactory solution had been found. Some of the experiments tried are briefly described.

In the early 1950s the Netherlands was successful in keeping agreed wage increases within limits agreed by the Foundation of Labour, a body of representatives of employers and of workers which watched and reported on the general economic situation, but later, when the need for reconstruction effort was over, inflationary pressures undermined the system. In Sweden, by 1970, a system was established whereby the top level organizations of employers and of workers agreed on the maximum increases in wages compatible with the maintenance of reasonable economic growth and the prevention of inflation, and left it to the unions to allocate this increase among themselves. This meant that if any claims by one union for more-than-average increases were met, some other group had to get less. The system worked well for some years, but in 1967 and 1968 agreement became increasingly difficult to achieve and some strikes ensued. In Switzerland, employers' and workers' organizations in major industries conclude 'industrial peace agreements', which provide for gradual improvements in wages and conditions over a period of three years or so without recourse to strikes or lock-outs. Both parties place money in bond with a bank as a surety for the observance of the agreement. As a result the Swiss had virtually no strikes. Measures taken in Britain included exhortation, attempts at voluntary control by the top level employers' and workers' organizations, examination of proposed agreements by the government or by a Prices and Incomes Board and wage freezes. By 1970 none had been effective.

The issue was also arising within the EEC. The unions of the six countries were opposing any attempts to embody incomes control in the Community's economic development plans.

In the Communist countries wage and price levels are embodied in the general economic plan. Even so, the funds available for distribution by the unions for welfare purposes may vary considerably from one undertaking to another, particularly as individual undertakings are given more initiative in methods of production, pricing and marketing. Where there is greater decentralization, as in Yugoslavia, the problem of wage control has also arisen.

Conditions of Work

By 1970 modern technology and higher standards of welfare had transformed conditions of work throughout Europe, although to a lesser degree in the south.

Farming, which for 2,000 years was a way of life and of sustenance, was becoming a specialized and scientific industry. The change from horse to tractor took place within a generation;

239

in 1960 there were 5,000,000 tractors in use in Western Europe, fifteen times as many as in 1939. Farmers were aiming at equality of income with industrial workers, and to achieve this they were acquiring larger holdings – except in Britain, Denmark and the Netherlands, where holdings were already of an economic size. In the future far fewer farmers will produce by modern methods all the food that can be sold.

Industrial life had also greatly changed. In the smaller workshops and in handicrafts in which the substantial majority of all industrial workers were still employed, power-driven tools and mechanical equipment were now the rule. In many industries, such as that of wholesale clothing, electrical components and motor-car assembly, the repetitive performance of limited and boring operations was giving way to automated processes, where the worker becomes a machine-minder monitoring a succession of operations. The calculator and the computer were similarly taking over many dull and repetitive clerical jobs. Work places were cleaner, brighter, better ventilated and healthier than in the past, and adequate welfare facilities were often a legal requirement. Progress had, however, been uneven. Old and new methods of production existed side by side. The gleaming modern office and factory, with its large windows and green lawns, was often flanked by workshops in old and dreary buildings, by sweat shops in backyards, by offices in badly-lit backrooms or underground premises.

Increased productivity led to a great reduction in standard hours of work. Before 1914 a working week of fifty-six or sixty hours, or more, often prevailed. By 1970 a forty to forty-five hour week was general, although in Britain and France in particular a high proportion of overtime was worked. The five-day week, largely a post-1945 innovation, and holidays with pay, before 1939 granted mainly only to professional workers, were also generally established: two weeks holiday was the minimum. In Belgium, Denmark, Finland, Iceland, Luxembourg, some Swiss Cantons and the Soviet Union, three weeks were given; and in France, Sweden, Norway and Poland (for non-manual workers), four weeks.

The length of the working life had also been reduced by raising the minimum age for admission to employment, thus preventing child labour, and by lowering the age of retirement by providing pensions.

There was a growing awareness of the problem of finding the right balance between more production in order to achieve a higher standard of living, and more leisure in which to live creatively. And beyond this lies the problem of how to make productive work itself a creative activity for the expression of human personality.

Planning the Environment

Before 1945, in Western Europe, houses and factories were built, areas developed and public utilities provided as independent operations to meet particular needs. After the war, an entirely new concept emerged: that the community was responsible for *planning* all services and amenities in the interests of all.

First, a person should be able to live in a *balanced* environment in which he has access to the healing forces of nature as well as to the cultural amenities of the city. This is particulary important as Europe becomes increasingly urbanized. In 1970 two-fifths of the town dwellers in Europe outside the Soviet Union, and one-third in the Soviet Union, lived in cities of over 500,000 people. 'Conurbations' were rapidly developing in such areas as northeast France, the Dutch ports area and the German Ruhr. Second, this environment should be in itself healthy and free from dirt, air pollution and discordant noise. Third, buildings should be designed according to the highest aesthetic standards and should be 'landscaped' – nature should be brought into every town and every building.

The implications of this concept are fundamental. First, the individual must surrender much of his freedom to mould his immediate environment as he likes. In most countries, by 1970, the public authorities had taken wide powers to control town and country planning, which meant that a person had to obtain 'planning permission' before he could put up any building.

241

Second, the individual should be as fully involved as possible in the planning process. A search was going on to find the right size of planning region in terms of area and population. For some purposes, the British county or the French 'département' was too small; and the state too large. Thus, the need for planning was producing a new kind of internal federalism. For other purposes, the planning regions might need to traverse national frontiers.

The need for planning was also stimulating a public interest in new forms of architecture. Using materials unknown to medieval man – copper, concrete, plastics, aluminium, stainless steel, sheet glass – modern architects were constructing buildings which, at worst, were severely functional, and at best, had a kind of ethereal beauty. These buildings had somehow to be blended with the marvellous old villages, towns and mansions which still spangled the West European countryside, while eliminating the hideous heritage of the first industrial revolution. Between 1945 and 1970 much research was devoted to this subject at the national and international level. The Council of Europe assumed responsibility for co-ordinating this work in Western Europe. Long-term plans were drawn up in almost all European countries. After the war the British County Councils carried out the first comprehensive survey of the country's land utilization since the Domesday book of 1087. The Dutch plan of 1966 was probably the most comprehensive in Western Europe; it covered every aspect of national life and provided a blue-print for life in the Netherlands for several generations. As a result of these plans, large parts of many cities were being modernized; 'green belts' were being established round them and new ideas for dealing with traffic were being developed.

Britain, the most urbanized country in Europe, was the West European pioneer of new towns; twenty-seven new towns were built with Government aid after the war. The Soviet Union also built more than 900 new towns between 1917 and 1965, 400 of them in entirely new territories. Towns planned in northern Siberia included 'dome-enclosed communities with covered *gallerias* and gardens that defy Siberian storms, drifting snows and howling winds' ... or ... 'a remote abstraction of cool white slabs lined up in military formation in white snow. The buildings are on piles, and basements are ventilated to avoid the curious hazards of melting permafrost and having the structure sink suddenly and surrealistically into the ground'.[16] A Soviet speciality was the new town of scholars, such as Akademgorodok in Siberia, 'built to bring scientists together in a planned research community'. The concept of a 'European' environment was thus emerging. The Consultative Assembly of the Council of Europe affirmed that governments should 'direct regional planning policy and studies towards the society of tomorrow, and the framework of human life in the year 2000 ...'[17] The Council of Europe dubbed 1970 'European Conservation Year', and launched a major publicity drive to awaken Europeans to the problems of pollution, conservation and birth control.

Migrant Workers

After 1945 the great mass movement of unskilled workers out of Europe was over; migrants from overseas were, instead, coming into the continent. Britain, in particular, took in some 900,000 Indians, Pakistanis and West Indians from Commonwealth countries, although entry was restricted in 1968. France absorbed a large number of unskilled Algerians without much difficulty, but the million French *colons* who returned to France after the Algerian War did not find it so easy to adapt themselves.

Hundreds of thousands of workers from the poorer countries of Southern and Eastern Europe migrated to Western and Northern Europe, where they were treated in the same way as the local workers, and their social security was cared for. The problems of providing material amenities and of psychological adjustments were often great, but the positive effect on the migrant workers was incalculable. It was a cheering sight to see a barely literate Neapolitan worker in a Swiss hotel caring for her new-born baby as fastidiously as if it were a Swiss bourgeois child. The phenomenon of the migrant worker was a small but significant factor in 'creating Europe'.

Education

The countries of twentieth-century Europe inherited education systems which still bore the marks of the medieval concept that people should be trained to perform the function attached to their 'station' by God. The peasant's child should be *trained* to till the soil, the girl to mind the home, the craftsman to create his 'masterpiece', the cleric to be a scholar and the aristocrat to rule. Thus, before the nineteenth century most peasants and many craftsmen were illiterate, and most schools and universities were Church foundations.

The ideas of the Rights of Man and the development of science introduced a fundamental change. Every boy and girl was now held to have a *right* to education, which it was the duty of the state to provide. As regards content, there were mixed motives. Rousseau and other seminal educational thinkers proclaimed that education should be 'child-centred'; that its purpose should be to *draw out* of the child its inherent talents and creative powers. The advent of the industrial revolution, however, reinforced the concept of training, but with a different and more sombre emphasis.

The factory 'hand' was to be trained to perform a mechanical operation efficiently, which necessitated a basic knowledge of the 'three R's' – reading, writing and arithmetic. The granting of the vote to workers also gave a great impetus to mass education. And 'career open to talent' meant that clever children must be educated to pass the stiff examinations for entry into the universities, the civil services and other higher professions.

By 1939, therefore, free elementary education, in state or Church schools, was generally available for all children from the age of six or seven (five in Britain) till thirteen or fourteen (the countries of Southern and Eastern Europe had not fully achieved this). Secondary schooling, in state or Church schools, was available for those who could afford to pay (it was free in the Soviet Union) and for a small number of poor children from the elementary schools who managed to win scholarships. At the third stage, that of higher education, the pyramid narrowed very sharply and the ladder of ascent through scholarships became very slender. The great majority of secondary schools were single-sex schools and far fewer girls than boys went to universities.

In most countries the state education system was highly centralized, and in some, such as France and Italy, the state controlled the universities as well as the schools, so that all teachers, from the university professor to the kindergarden mistress, were civil servants. In France, the courses to be taught, the text books to be used, and even the time-tables were laid down by the Ministry of Education, whose inspectors maintained a high uniform standard of *instruction publique*. At the other end of the spectrum was the decentralized British system, in which Parliament had vested the responsibility for the state schools in the hands of the elected County Councils.

By 1939 the concept of child-centred education had made only a slight impact, except in the Soviet Union, where Lenin's regime had introduced it in the early twenties with such unrealistic idealism that schooling had ground to a standstill.

Between 1945 and 1970 there were major developments. The underlying change was the growing recognition of the principle of child-centred education. This was expressed, for example, in the British Education Act of 1944, which asserted that every child should have an education, no longer merely in the 'three R's', but according to 'its age, aptitude and ability'. Education systems were therefore generally re-organized to give every child a free and compulsory two-stage education, primary and secondary. This involved the progressive raising of the school-leaving age, which by 1970 was fifteen or sixteen in most European countries.

In Communist countries most children receive their nine or ten years of schooling at the same school. But in Western Europe the structure is more complex, for mass secondary education had to be grafted on to a system designed to educate an elite to university level. There were two kinds of solution to this problem. One, adopted generally in England, France and West Germany, was to siphon off the twenty per cent or so of the ablest children

245

into the old academic secondary schools, and to send the remaining seventy or eighty per cent to a new type of less academic secondary school. This system discriminated against many children from humble backgrounds and denied many potentially able students a proper opportunity for developing their talents. The second kind of solution, therefore, was to develop a three-stage system : primary, intermediate and secondary schooling, such as already existed in the United States. By 1970 the Scandinavian countries had pioneered in this system; Britain, France, Italy and West Germany were beginning to develop it, and it had been established in the Communist countries, although the moves there were often made within the same school. Thus all European countries were moving towards the goal of giving every child the opportunity to get the kind of education required to develop his aptitude and abilities, to tailor the system to the child rather than the child to the system.

After 1945 the concept of child-centred education also increasingly influenced education methods. In Western Europe activity methods of learning, sport, clubs, societies, foreign travel and the use of audio-visual aids and teaching machines were rapidly expanding. The Communists laid great emphasis on 'polytechnic education', relating education to practical life and work. All Soviet children between sixteen and eighteen had to spend some of their school time in the factory or on the farm. In Communist countries education was co-educational at all levels. In Western Europe co-education was slowly spreading at the secondary level, and the proportion of girls who went to the university was far higher than before the war.

Higher education also responded to the social revolution in quantitative terms. The ancient seats of quiet scholastic reflection were being asked to provide something like the mass higher education of the New World. (In the United States, by 1970, education to eighteen had become almost universal, and over forty-five per cent of the young people went on to further education in some 2,000 institutions). By 1970 the Soviet Union was giving thirty per cent of its young people five years of free higher education in forty universities and over 700 other institutions.

In Britain and France the comparable figure was fifteen per cent, and in West Germany nine per cent. In contrast to the United States, where the first-degree university curriculum was almost as wide as that of the high school, the European universities retained the tradition of rigorous specialization, the Soviet Union being the only country to provide this kind of higher education on a mass scale: with four times the population of Britain, it was producing twenty times as many highly specialized engineers.

The growing emphasis on the study of science and technology in European higher education was an aspect of the second industrial revolution. In the seven years 1957–64, the world's expenditure on scientific research was the same as in the 181 years between 1776 and 1957; and the rate was accelerating all the time. The large numbers of skilled workers required to man the new machines had to be trained, not merely in one particular skill, but to adapt themselves, throughout their lives, to new skills and new ideas. The Communist concept of 'polytechnic education' was based on an awareness of these needs, but in Western Europe the basic mode of technical training was still the medieval system of apprenticeship, in which semi-literate youths who left school at fourteen or fifteen were trained 'on the job'. Nineteenth-century methods were being used to train the workers of the twenty-first century. Prompted, however, by such bodies as the Council of Europe, the OECD and the ILO, facilities for sophisticated full-time technical training were being rapidly expanded. West Germany established a technical university and Britain expanded a number of colleges of advanced technology into full universities with a technological bias. In general, however, the implications of education as a continuous life-process had yet to be fully thought out.

This brings us to the question of *quality*. The result of modern man's rejection of revelation as a source of knowledge, of his application of the scientific method to his environment, has been the enormous expansion of human experience in the dimension of *quantity*. The educated person is deluged with a plethora of *facts*. The problem of organizing them may be solved by the development of computers and data-retrieval machines. But the problem of giving them meaning and value has become a supreme challenge of our time. No machine can undertake it, since meaning and value inhere only in persons; and persons, as such, can be understood only by the faculty which the poets call imagination – a faculty which, in the scientific climate of the twentieth century, has generally been regarded with extreme suspicion in the academic world. Academics have tended to become data-processing machines, refusing to be involved in matters of conscience – Bertrand Russell and Jean-Paul Sartre were among the outstanding exceptions.

This situation had its impact on the structure of the universities. Their teachers were normally appointed for research; they often had little contact with the students; and the organization of the university was authoritarian. In 1968 students throughout Europe and North America suddenly errupted in a passionate attack on the university establishment. Their immediate demands were concerned with 'student power' – the demand for 'participation' in the governing body of the university. But this seemed to be an expression of a deeper and more inarticulate protest against the depersonalization of contemporary society and the prostitution of the universities to this depersonalization. Since depersonalization leads logically to the ultimate absurdity of nuclear annihilation, the students' protest was surely a crucial challenge : to educate young people to be meaningful persons and not absurd machines. We suggested earlier in this chapter that Europe was becoming an affluent society. The young people were saying : is affluence enough?

REFERENCES

1. *Declaration of Philadelphia*, subsequently incorporated in the Constitution of the International Labour Organization.
2. *Faith and Order Conference*, Oxford, 1937.
3. Encyclical, *Mater et Magistra* 1961, para. 37.
4. World Council of Churches, Fourth General Assembly, *Report on World Economic and Social Developments*, paras. 3–4.

5. International Labour Office, 'Fifty Years of Social History: A Statistical Outline', in *Yearbook of Labour Statistics 1968*. The figures are based on official sources but there are divergencies in definitions and methods of computation. Some independent research workers are inclined to place the increase in the East European countries at a somewhat lower level.

6. World Bank figures.

7. *European Social Charter*, Part I, para. 4.

8. International Labour Conference, *Income Security Recommendation*, 1944, No. 67.

9. Churchill, Winston, *The Second World War*, Houghton Mifflin Co., Boston, 1958, vol. 4, Appendix F, p. 862.

10. International Labour Conference, *Workers' Housing Recommendation*, 1961, No. 115.

11. Barach, Arnold B., *The New Europe and its Economic Future*, A Twentieth Century Fund Publication, New York, 1964, p. 48.

12. Salisbury, Harrison E., ed., *The Soviet Union: Fifty Years*, The New York Times Company, 1968, pp. 291–3.

13. International Labour Conference, *Freedom of Association and Right to Organise Convention*, 1949, No. 98.

14. International Labour Conference, *The Right to Organise and Collective Bargaining Convention*, 1949, No. 98.

15. De Givry, Jean, 'Developments in Labour-Management Relations in the Undertaking', *International Labour Review*, Vol. 99, No. 1, January 1969, p. 2.

16. Salisbury, *op. cit.*, pp. 317–8

17. Council of Europe, Consultative Assembly, *Recommendation No. 525* on the convening of a European Conference of Ministers responsible for Regional Planning, adopted on 10 May 1968.

13. Europe and the Third World

Colonialism

In 1939 almost the whole of Africa, of Asia south and east of China and Japan, and many Pacific and Caribbean islands, consisted of colonies or dependencies of the West European powers. Only South Africa, Liberia, Ethiopia, Egypt, Saudi Arabia, the Yemen, Iraq, Iran, Afghanistan, Tibet and Thailand were independent states. The United States ruled the Philippines and Japan ruled Korea and Taiwan.

Africa had been colonized mainly between 1880 and 1912 in an unscrupulous process of territorial grabbing which ignored the natural areas of tribal settlement and geographical coherence. West Africa, in particular, was a senseless jumble of British and French territories. In the Middle East a similar 'balkanization' – the creation of a number of small, weak states – had been carried out by the British and French in 1919 in an area which was naturally homogenous in race – Arab – and in religion – Muslim. One of the main motives for this grab, which involved the breaking of a British promise to grant independence to the Arabs, was the discovery of large reserves of petroleum in the Persian Gulf area.

One of President Woodrow Wilson's famous Fourteen Points, announced as the basis for the peace settlement after the First World War, was that colonial claims should be considered in the light of the interests of the territories concerned. As the victors divided up the colonies and dependencies of the vanquished among themselves, they therefore affirmed that they would rule them as a 'sacred trust of civilization', as 'Mandates' under the auspices of the League of Nations. Under this settlement Britain obtained Palestine. In 1917 the British government had already promised, in the famous Balfour Declaration, to give Jews from any country a 'National Home' – a conveniently vague phrase – in the land of their ancestors. The Arabs who had inhabited the territory for a thousand years were not consulted.

In general colonial rule was at best paternalistic, at worst harsh. None of the colonial powers regarded it as their responsibility to raise the standards of living of the 'natives' to the white man's level; but the frequently-made assertion that the colonies were 'exploited' is an exaggeration. In 1937 the colonies produced three per cent of all the world's commercially important raw materials, and no colonial power exercised a monopoly over the resources of its territories. The groundwork for the great development after 1945 was laid by ending internal strife, building roads and railways, starting health and education services, and developing some industries, mainly those concerned with the production of raw materials. The most fundamental failure of the colonial powers was probably that, in general, they made no real attempt to understand the psychological and social effects of the impact of modern Western civilization upon the traditional cultures which they were invading. For many Africans and Asians the sudden jump from their timeless, static, customary way of life, where everything was sacred and secure, into the dynamic, secular, competitive modern world, was hard enough. When this world was arrogant and unwelcoming, the enterprise could be agonizing.

The British Commonwealth of Nations

In 1945 there was one precedent for decolonization. Before 1914 Britain had granted self-government to the 'Dominions' of Canada, Australia, New Zealand and South Africa (in South Africa power had been transferred to the British and Boer white minority, ignoring the black majority). At an Imperial Conference of 1926 their full independence was recognized, but

251

TABLE 4

New states created since 1919 as a result of decolonization [1]

State	Year of Independence	Previously	Former Rule	Population[2] (1,000)	GNP[3] per head $
AFRICA					
Algeria	1962		French	14,330	300
Botswana	1966	Bechuanaland	British	611	110
Burundi	1962	Part of Ruandi-Urundi	Belgian Trust Territory	3,544	60
Cameroon	1960		Part French, part British Trust Territory	5,836	180
Central African Republic	1960	Part of F. Eq. A.[4]	French	1,552	140
Chad	1960	Part of F. Eq. A.[4]	French	3,640	80
Congo (Brazzaville)	1960	Part of F. Eq. A.[4]	French	899	300
Dahomey	1960	Part of F. W. A.[5]	French	2,708	90
Equatorial Guinea	1968	Rio Muni and Fernando Po	Spanish	291	210
Gabon	1960	Part of F. Eq. A.[4]	French	489	630
Gambia	1965		British	360	120
Ghana	1957	Gold Coast and Togo Trust Territory under British administration	British	8,640	310
Guinea	1958	Part of F. W. A.[6]	French	3,980	120
Ivory Coast	1960	Part of F. W. A.[6]	French	4,941	310
Kenya	1963		British	11,250	150
Lesotho	1966	Basutoland	British	923	90
Libya	1951		Italian, then British Military Administration	1,940	1,770
Malagasy Republic	1960	Madagascar	French	7,310	130

Country	Former name / notes	Colonial power	Year		
Mali	Part of F. W. A.(6)	French	1960	5,018	70
Mauritania	Part of F. W. A.(6)	French	1960	1,170	140
Mauritius		British	1968	836	240
Morocco		French	1956	15,495	230
Niger	Part of F. W. A.(5)	French	1960	4,020	90
Nigeria	Nigeria and parts of British Cameroons Trust Territory	British	1960	55,070	120
Rwanda	Part of Ruanda-Urundi	Belgian Trust Territory	1962	3,596	60
Senegal	Part of F. W. A.(5)	French	1960	3,870	230
Sierra Leone		British	1961	2,555	190
Somalia	Somaliland under Italian Trusteeship and British Somaliland	Part Italian and part British	1960	2,828	70
Sudan		British-Egyptian Condominium	1956	15,695	120
Swaziland		British	1968	423	180
Tanzania	Tanganyika and Zanzibar	British	1961	13,270	100
Togo		French Trust Territory	1960	1,956	140
Tunisia		French	1956	5,075	250
Uganda		British	1962	9,814	130
United Arab Republic	Egypt	Ottoman Empire, then British Protectorate	1962	33,329	210
Upper Volta	Part of F. W. A.(5)	French	1960	5,384	601
Zaire	Congo Dem. Rep.	Belgian	1960	18,800	90
Zambia	Northern Rhodesia	British	1964	4,136	400
AMERICA					
Barbados		British	1966	256	570
Guyana	British Guiana	British	1966	745	370
Jamaica		British	1962	1,888	670
Trinidad and Tobago		British	1962	1,027	860

TABLE 4 – contd.

State	Year of Independence	Previously	Former Ruler	Population(2) (1,000)	GNP(3) per head
ASIA					
Burma	1948	Part of Indian Empire	British	27,584	80
Ceylon (Sri Lanka)	1948		British	12,514	110
Cyprus	1960		British	640	750
India	1947	Separate Member of the League of Nations since 1919	British	538,129	110
Indonesia	1949	Dutch East Indies	Dutch	115,567	80
Iraq	1932	Mesopotamia	Ottoman Empire, then British Mandate	9,678	320
Israel	1948	Part of Palestine	Ottoman Empire, then British Mandate	2,910	1,960
Jordan	1946	Transjordan and part of Palestine	Ottoman Empire, then British Mandate	2,313	250
Khmer, Rep. of	1953	Part of French Indochina	French	7,485	80
Korea, North	1948	Part of Korea	Japanese, then Russian Military Administration	13,890	330(6)
Korea, Rep. of	1948	Part of Korea	Japanese, then American Military Administration	31,793	250
Kuwait	1961		British Protectorate	760	3,760
Laos	1949	Part of French Indochina	French	2,962	120
Lebanon	1944		Ottoman Empire, then French Mandate	2,726	590
Malaysia	1957	Malaya and North Borneo	British	10,945	380
Maldive Islands	1965		British	108	100

					[6]
Mongolia		Chinese	1924	1,280	920
Pakistan	Part of India	British	1947	130,166	100
Philippines		United States	1946	36,850	210
Singapore	For a time part of Malaysia	British	1965	2,075	920
Syria		Ottoman Empire, then French Mandate	1944	6,098	290
Vietnam, North	Part of French Indochina	French	1949	21,150	100
Vietnam, Rep. of	Part of French Indochina	French	1949	18,332	200
Yemen, South	Aden and 17 Amirates and Sultanates	British and British Protected	1967	1,255	120
EUROPE					
Iceland		Danish	1944	210	2,720
Ireland	Part of United Kingdom	British	1922	2,970	1,072
Malta		British	1964	330	587
OCEANIA					
Nauru		Trust Territory of the United Kingdom, Australia and New Zealand	1968	7	?
Samoa, Western		New Zealand Trust Territory	1962	143	140
Fiji		British	1970	520	430

(1) Several of the territories mentioned had acquired varying degrees of self-rule before the date of independence mentioned in this table.

(2) 1970. World Bank figures.

(3) Gross national produce per head in U.S. dollars, 1970. World Bank figures.

(4) French Equatorial Africa.

(5) French West Africa.

(6) International Bank for Reconstruction and Development, estimate.

Source: United Nations Statistical Yearbook, 1968.

in order to retain their 'special relationship' with each other and with Britain, all five nations were declared to be 'autonomous communities with the British Empire, equal in status, in no way subordinate one to another ... though united by a common allegiance to the Crown and freely associated as members of the British Commonwealth of Nations'. A 'Commonwealth' – a Tudor term implying common 'weal' or welfare – of nations united in freedom without constitutional ties was something new in the world.

Decolonization

The experience of the Second World War made decolonization inevitable. First, it became morally difficult for countries which had fought to establish the Rights of Man to deny these rights to their colonies – some of which had given them invaluable aid in the war. Second, the colonial powers now realized that they were morally responsible, not merely for the administration of these territories, but for developing them – a task which they could not undertake without the help of the United States, which regarded 'colonialism' as wicked. Third, the colonies themselves, particularly those in Asia, had been jolted out of their inferiority-complex by the spectacle of Western defeat at the hands of a non-white power. The war gave a great impetus to nationalist colonial movements, some of them forged in resistance to the Japanese.

Table 4 lists all the colonial territories which were granted independence between 1945 and 1970.

The pace and mode of decolonization varied. British colonial rule had been based on the understanding that in due course, when British institutions had been firmly established, self-government would be granted. The results of the war impelled the British to implement this understanding sooner than they had intended. The main difficulty lay in getting hostile religious and racial groups to collaborate in the rule of their country. A 100,000,000 out of 150,000,000 Muslims in India insisted in establishing the separate state of Pakistan – and 600,000 lives were lost in the process of separation. The refusal of the Arabs and the Jews in Palestine to form any kind of state together resulted in the first Arab-Israeli War when the British withdrew in 1948. The refusal of the 60,000 British settlers in Kenya to accept African majority rule produced the Mau-Mau revolt of 1952–60. The refusal of the Greeks and Turks in Cyprus to collaborate led to the revolt of the Greek Cypriots against British rule from 1955–9. And the suppression of both the latter revolts involved the use of harsh methods, such as the enforced evacuation of villages and the imprisonment of suspects without trial. In general, however, the grant of independence to about 800,000,000 people by Britain between 1945 and 1970 took place in an atmosphere of peace and amity.

France and the Netherlands decolonized with less good grace, partly because defeat in war had deeply shaken their pride, and partly because they had based their colonial policies on the concept of permanent rule. The French had treated their colonials as French citizens – though second-class citizens – entitled to be represented in the National Assembly in Paris: the Dutch had simply ruled paternalistically. After two 'police actions' against the nationalists in Indonesia, they granted that country independence in 1949, and relinquished their rule of West New Guinea in 1962 only under pressure from the Security Council of the United Nations. The French fought two long and unsuccessful wars to retain Indo-China and Algeria. Their vast commitment of men and money in Algeria impelled them to secure the friendship of their black African colonies by granting them independence in 1960. In the same year Belgium suddenly gave independence to the Congo and in 1968 Spain relinquished Equatorial Guinea – an economic liability. By 1970 independence had been gained by over 1,000,000,000 people in Africa, Asia and the Caribbean. The territories which still remained under British, French and Dutch rule had a total population of only some 12,000,000; they were mainly small islands or enclaves which would not be viable as independent states. The largest is Hong Kong, the mainland part of which is bound by international treaty to return to Chinese sovereignty in 1997. Two territories, the French colony of Afars and Issas (formerly

French Somaliland), and the British colony of Gibraltar, voted in 1967 and 1968 respectively to remain under colonial rule rather than be absorbed into Somalia or Spain. The latter country kept control of Spanish West Africa with its valuable iron ore deposits.

By 1970 Portugal was the only European country which had refused, in principle, to decolonize. It still ruled the African territories of Angola, Mozambique and Guinea, with a total population of nearly 13,000,000, as well as four small territories in the Atlantic and the Pacific. These colonies were treated, after 1951, as metropolitan provinces of Portugal. In the sixties the African colonies were in a state of incipient revolt, flaring into open rebellion in Angola in 1961. The regular injunctions to decolonize made by the General Assembly of the United Nations seemed only to stiffen Portugal's determination to hold on to these colonies, in which it had, in 1970, some 150,000 troops. Plans were afoot to invest in them some £500,000,000, mostly supplied by South Africa, and to settle in them some 1,500,000 Portuguese. If these policies matured the territories might become satellites of South Africa, a development which would exacerbate the racial and political tension in the southern part of the continent.[1]

Between 1923 and 1965 Rhodesia (called Southern Rhodesia until 1964) enjoyed a unique constitutional status. In 1923 Britain had granted the British settlers internal self-government, retaining the right, which was never exercised, to veto legislation affecting African interests. The 220,000 settlers allocated half the cultivable land to themselves, and enacted, in 1961, a constitution which in practice denied the vote to all the 4,000,000 Africans except the small majority who were relatively affluent and educated. In 1965 the white-settler government, led by Mr Ian Smith, demanded full independence. Constitutionally this could only be granted by the British Parliament; and the British Labour Government insisted that it should be conditional upon the establishment of universal suffrage – which would necessarily mean African rule – within a reasonably short time. The Rhodesian Government rejected this condition and in November

1965 declared independence unilaterally – an act of rebellion. The British government did not consider it feasible to suppress the rebellion by military action. Instead, they took economic action to reduce British trade with the country; and when this proved ineffective, they asked the United Nations' Security Council, in December 1966, to impose mandatory sanctions on Rhodesian exports, together with an embargo on the supply of arms and oil to the country. This, the first international attempt to discipline a country by economic sanctions since the unsuccessful imposition of such sanctions on Italy by the League of Nations in 1936, was something of a test case for the United Nations. Article Two of its Charter, which precludes its interference in the domestic affairs of member states and their dependencies, inhibits it from doing more than utter moral exhortations when its members violate the Universal Declaration of Human Rights at home. By voluntarily taking the Rhodesian case to the United Nations Britain gave that body a unique opportunity to establish the principle of international action to enforce human rights; but the success of the sanctions depended on the co-operation of the Portuguese and South African Governments and these two states, themselves pursuing racial and colonial policies which were persistently condemned by the United Nations, refused to observe the sanctions, and connived at their breach by other states. In 1969 countries which had promised to observe the sanctions were sending £44,000,000 worth of goods to Rhodesia[2], and arms were flowing in from South Africa. By 1970 the failure of the European ex-colonial powers to bring Rhodesia to heel, to persuade Portugal to decolonize, or South Africa to observe the basic human rights, had greatly weakened their moral influence in Africa.

The Extension of the Cold War into the Third World

Until the mid-fifties world politics was dominated by the Cold War between the United States and its allies and the Soviet Union and its satellites and its main field lay in Europe. The rise of Communist China and the Korean War were disturbing episodes on the side-lines of affairs.

Decolonization transformed this situation. Just when the Cold War had reached a stalemate in Europe, the two protagonists were faced with a vast new arena, containing half the world's population, in which to manoeuvre and compete. They were also faced with a new kind of war, the non-ideological war against hunger, illiteracy and disease, in which the world is divided essentially into two different camps, those of the rich and the poor. The Soviet Union and the East European states are linked with Western Europe, Japan and the United States in the rich man's camp, while Communist China is in the poor man's camp.

The eighty or so new states are faced with almost insuperable problems. Many are having difficulty in sustaining their very existence as political entities. India, Indonesia, Pakistan, Nigeria and the Congo, for example, have at times hovered on the brink of disintegration. Others, such as the smaller states of West Africa, are economically unviable. The most urgent need of these states is 'to develop', to lift their societies into the modern world. And development is overshadowed by the population explosion. By the year 2,000 world population, which rose from 1,700,000,000 in 1913 to 3,600,000,000 in 1970, is expected to reach 6 or 7,000,000,000, seventy per cent of whom will be living in the poor countries, including China. Unless drastic measures are taken in the seventies and eighties, hundreds of millions of the inhabitants of these countries will consist of unemployed young people, many of them mentally retarded and psychologically disturbed by malnutrition in infancy.

In most of the new states there are two basic prerequisites for development: internal social reforms, which may involve dispossessing a feudal class; and trade with and aid from the rich countries. Almost without exception the new states want to be 'non-aligned', to get all the help they can from the rich nations, Communist and non-Communist, while preserving their national independence and their freedom to carry out social revolution, if they need it, in their own way. The non-aligned countries – that is, the poor countries minus China, Cuba, North Korea, North Vietnam and Outer Mongolia – constitute the 'Third World'.

Pre-war Marxism-Leninism taught that the colonies were the victims of the most vicious phase of exploitation by the dying and desperate capitalist powers. Their inhabitants were believed to be yearning for the Communist world state in which, under the leadership of the Soviet Union, they would be liberated from this exploitation. When the capitalist countries handed over power to new states which were determined to be non-aligned, the Communists had to rethink their policy. At the Moscow conference of eighty-one Communist parties, including that of China, held in 1960, it was agreed that the aim should be to promote revolution *inside* the countries of the Third World, while accusing the Western powers of 'neo-colonialism', that is, of maintaining an economic, military and cultural control behind the façade of independence. Fairly serious Communist revolts had already occurred in the forties and fifties in India, Burma, the Philippines, Indonesia and Malaya; all were suppressed – the Indian and Malayan by British forces before independence. By the sixties it was clear that the groups and parties within the new states which were working for social change were as determined as any feudal reactionaries to maintain national independence. Staunch left-wing socialists like Presidents Nasser of Egypt and Ben Bella of Algeria accepted massive Soviet aid, and were decorated by Khrushchev as Heroes of the Soviet Union – while they kept their local Communists in prison. The Soviet Union reacted by playing down the policy of 'subversion', and advising the local Communist parties to support their local nationalist movements. The Chinese proceeded to accuse the Russians of 'revisionism' and to take independent action to stir up subversion and guerrilla warfare, evoking race prejudice in their cause. 'We blacks', they told the Africans, 'must stick together against the whites', including the Russians. In Asia they denounced the Russians as 'imperialists'. The Western powers, for their part, in general respected the desire of the Third World to be politically non-aligned, although in certain instances they worked to overthrow regimes which they disliked.

Between 1955 and 1970 the Cold War erupted into the Third World at a number of particular points.

The Arab-Israeli War of 1956

Colonel Nasser, who came to power in Egypt in 1952, sought to rearm his country after its ignominious defeat in the first Arab-Israeli War of 1948. The British and Americans refused to sell him arms while he remained non-aligned in the Cold War, so he bought arms from Czechoslovakia. Furious, the British and Americans, and at their instigation the World Bank, suddenly withdrew offers of $270,000,000 aid for a vital new irrigation dam at Aswan – which the Russians subsequently built. Equally furious, Nasser suddenly took over the Suez Canal from the Anglo-French Company which owned and operated it. The British Prime Minister, Sir Anthony Eden, was haunted by memories of the appeasement of Hitler and Mussolini in the thirties. Although the Canal was on Egyptian soil and was due to be handed over by the Company to the Egyptian Government in 1968 anyway, he chose to regard Nasser's action as a form of international aggression. When, therefore, the Israelis suddenly launched an attack on Egypt on 29 October 1956, the British and French, who had been for some time in collusion with the Israelis, landed paratroopers on the Canal, hoping to bring about Nasser's downfall. At the instigation of the United States, the United Nations' Security Council ordered Britain, France and Israel to withdraw from Egypt, but Britain and France vetoed the motion. The General Assembly, however, endorsed it by an overwhelming majority, and the Soviet Government privately threatened to oust the invaders with nuclear weapons. So on 6 November the British and French agreed to withdraw, and the United Nations sent a 'peacekeeping force' of 5,000 men, drawn from ten lesser states, to act as a buffer between Egypt and Israel – a significant international innovation. This episode diverted world attention from the Soviet Union's simultaneous act of imperialism in suppressing the Hungarian revolt.

The 'Suez crisis' brought to an abrupt end the era of British and French political influence in the eastern Mediterranean which had lasted for 150 years. Their 'presence' was soon replaced by that of the United States and the Soviet Union.

American naval forces, which had been in the Mediterranean since the war, were expanded, and a smaller Soviet fleet turned up in 1964 – thus at last fulfilling one of the consistent aims of Russian foreign policy since the days of Peter the Great. The Americans and the French proceeded to arm Israel, and the Russians Egypt, for the next round, the third Arab-Israeli war, which took place in June 1967 after Nasser had asked the United Nations to withdraw the peace-keeping force.

The Congo Crisis: 1960-4

When Belgium suddenly granted independence to the Congo (renamed Zaire in 1971) in 1960 the country erupted into anarchy. The Congolese Government asked the United Nations' Security Council to send a peace-keeping force, which was composed, again, of troops supplied by the lesser powers. The Soviet Union, exploiting the rivalry which existed between the pro-Soviet Premier Lumumba and the pro-West President Kasavubu, sent in its own military aid, together with Communist agents. Lumumba was murdered, and the United Nations' General Assembly passed a resolution demanding that all military aid to the Congo should be channelled through the United Nations. When the peace-keeping force was withdrawn in 1964 the country had settled down. The intervention of the United Nations, and the despatch of its peace-keeping force, again prevented certain of the great powers from exploiting a Third World conflict to promote their Cold War interests. Dag Hammarskjöld, the Swedish Secretary-General of the United Nations, to whose personal diplomacy the success of the United Nations' intervention in the Suez and the Congo crises was largely due, lost his life in an aircrash in the Congo in 1962.

The Cuban Crisis: 1962

The Cuban crisis sparked off the only direct military confrontation which occurred between the United States and the Soviet Union between 1945 and 1970. In 1958 Fidel Castro, a young revolutionary, ousted Cuba's old and horrible dictator and established a socialist régime. He proceeded to confiscate

263

one billion dollars worth of the property of American companies, regarded as the assets of neo-colonialism. The Americans retaliated by refusing to buy Cuban sugar, stopping American exports to Cuba, breaking off diplomatic relations and supporting an emigré invasion force which made an unsuccessful landing at the Bay of Pigs in April 1961. Castro then accepted substantial aid from the Communist states, and proceeded to integrate Cuba's economy into that of the Communist bloc – the only developing country voluntarily to join this camp, apart from the special case of North Vietnam. In 1960, three-quarters of Cuba's trade was with non-Communist states; by 1962, the proportion had been reversed.

Khrushchev could not resist the temptation to take military advantage of this situation. In July 1962 he secured Cuban agreement to the installation on the island of Russian missiles of 1,600/3,200 km range. On 14 October an American U2 spy plane detected the build-up of the installations. President Kennedy thereupon ordered a naval blockade of the island and contemplated its invasion. For a few days the world hung on the brink of thermo-nuclear war. Then Khrushchev agreed to withdraw the missiles if the Americans would withdraw their blockade. The nuclear confrontation had a sobering effect on the Cold War protagonists. They looked over the brink of disaster, and drew back, horrified. In 1963 a 'hot' telephone line was installed between the White House and Moscow, so that in any future confrontation the human voice could act as a bridge.

The Vietnam War: 1963-73

In 1963 the United States began sending troops to prevent Communist North Vietnam from supporting the Communist Vietcong rebels in South Vietnam and over-running that non-Communist country. This war, which was still going on at the end of 1970, falls outside the scope of this book. Suffice it to say that some regard it as an unwarranted intervention by a Western Power in the affairs of the Third World, and others as a morally justifiable act of peace-keeping. It is perhaps significant that, in contrast to their action in the Korean War, the United States'

West European allies sent no troops to support it in Vietnam. The British government gave moral support, the French expressed moral disapproval.

The International Arms Trade

The Cold War rivalry in the Third World is fomented by the international arms trade. Between 1945 and 1970 over fifty wars were fought in the Third World, almost entirely with weapons supplied by the governments of rich countries.

> The annual volume of this trade to all destinations between 1962–68 has been estimated at nearly $6 billion, of which over $2 billion were exported to the Third World. In contrast to the situation before 1939, these sales have been made by governments; less than 5 per cent of the trade is in private hands. Although 90 per cent of the arms were supplied by the United States, the Soviet Union, Britain and France, every arms producing country in East and West Europe plunged into the market. The West Germans resold obsolete equipment which they had obtained from America, and smaller countries found a ready market for high quality specialist weapons such as the Belgian FN rifle.[3]

In thus arming the countries of the Third World with supersonic aircraft, ground-to-surface missiles, tanks and other sophisticated weapons which their 'military-industrial complexes' were pouring out, the rich countries were motivated, partly by a desire to gain advantage in the Cold War, and partly by the simple urge to earn hard cash. Their poor and unsophisticated clients were equally eager to buy these weapons, which they could not afford and often could not use properly. India, for instance, one of the poorest of the poor countries, was in 1970 spending forty per cent of its budget on defence. It was purchasing arms from the Western powers and the Soviet Union, and its main enemy, Pakistan, was obtaining arms from the same sources, with the addition of Communist China. Between 1945 and 1970 no proposals were made, either by governments or by world public opinion, for the establishment of any international

265

controls over the world arms trade.[4] Most of the wars in the
Third World have brought untold suffering to many innocent
people; some have threatened to escalate into a Third World
War. The fact that they have supplied the weapons for these
wars makes the aid given by the rich countries to relieve their
suffering seem hypocritical, and weakens their moral position
when they try to mediate.

Constitutional Relationships between Europe and the Third World

When a British colony was granted independence, it was invited
to join the Commonwealth, which dropped the adjective 'British'
in 1949. Most of the new states wished to become republics, and
on this account Burma and Eire refused to join. In order, however, to secure the admission of India and Pakistan, it was
decided in 1949 that republics could be members, provided only
that they accepted the British Monarch as head of the Commonwealth. By 1970 all Britain's other colonies had joined except
the Sudan. The Commonwealth then had thirty-one members,
scattered over five continents.

The Commonwealth's only formal organization consists of a
Secretariat, set up in London in 1965. Since 1945, periodic informal conferences of Commonwealth Prime Ministers have
been held to establish a consensus on issues of world policy.

During the fifties the concept of the Commonwealth
cushioned, for many British people, the traumatic effect of their
country's rapid decolonization and subsidence into the status of
a second class power. They believed that they had not so much
lost an Empire as transformed it into a Commonwealth of
countries united by devotion to British institutions. But as the
majority of these countries soon abandoned the British parliamentary system (India was an outstanding exception), and ceased to
observe the principles of British justice, this image began to fade.
By the mid-sixties it was clear that the only solid bond of political
unity among the members of the club was adherence to the
principle of racial equality. In 1961 South Africa was forced to
resign on account of its racial policies; and Britain's faltering

266

handling of Rhodesia after the unilateral declaration of independence in 1965 shook Commonwealth unity.

After 1932 the Commonwealth countries gave each other certain tariff preferences as against imports from non-Commonwealth countries – most Commonwealth goods entered Britain duty-free. These preferences were eroded, after 1945, by the world-wide tariff reductions negotiated through GATT; and Commonwealth trade shifted steadily away from Britain. Now that Britain has joined the European Community it has to cancel these preferences and impose the Community's common tariffs on imports from the Commonwealth, but except in the case of sugar from the West Indies and Mauritius (which is also protected by guaranteed prices in the British market), and farm products from New Zealand, these are not expected to cause much hardship. The Community has agreed that, as a special measure, Britain can continue to import New Zealand butter and cheese free of duty for five years after entry. It has also promised to 'have at heart' the interests of the sugar-producing countries – the Community's sugar market is protected in the interests of the sugar-beet growers of France and West Germany.

The constitution of the French Fifth Republic established a French 'Community' similar to the Commonwealth. By 1970 it consisted of France and six ex-French African states: the Central African Republic, Chad, the Congo (Brazzaville), Gabon, the Malagasay Republic and Senegal.

A more concrete organization is the Association of eighteen African states with the nine countries of the European Community. The eighteen include all the ex-French colonies in West and Central Africa except Guinea, together with Somalia, the Malagasay Republic and Zaire. Through this Association, which is provided for in the Treaty of Rome, the Nine give the Eighteen development aid ($200,000,000 a year for the period 1971–5) and tariff preferences. The Association is administered by institutions of a far more specific nature than those of the Commonwealth: a policy-making Council of Ministers, a Parliamentary Conference and a Court of Arbitration, all composed of representatives of the twenty-seven member states of the

267

Association, and, where appropriate, of the Commission of the European Community. Under the terms for Britain's entry into the Community, the Commonwealth countries of Africa, the Caribbean and the Indian and Pacific Oceans have been offered full membership of the Association in 1974. By 1970 Nigeria, Uganda, Kenya and Tanzania had made limited Association agreements, entitling them to the Community's tariff preferences, but not to its economic aid. Agreements had also been signed with Morocco and Tunisia.

The Commonwealth and the Eurafrican Association are thus essentially the progeny of colonialism. 'The passport to African entry into the European Community must bear the mark "Certified as ex-Colonial territory of a Member"', wrote an African University lecturer.[5] They have developed as separate, closed trade and aid blocs. When they merge in 1974, however, the Generalized Tariff Preference Scheme, discussed below, may have broken them down as regional preference systems.

Economic Relationships between Europe and the Third World

Before 1939 few international or even national surveys had been undertaken of the economic and social problems of the colonial territories. Between 1945 and 1970 the United Nations and its Specialized Agencies, and many national governments, researched into every major aspect of the development needs of the Third World. By 1970 an overall picture was emerging, embodied in particular in such surveys as the Indicative World Food Plan of the FAO, the World Employment Programme of the ILO and UNESCO's Long-Term Outline Plan for 1971–6. If these plans are implemented, the widening gulf between the rich and the poor countries – the rich getting richer and the poor poorer – might be bridged by the end of the century, but a substantial transfer of resources from the rich to the poor countries is required.

In the first place, the developing countries must obtain from the rich countries the capital equipment necessary for their economic infrastructure: railways, ports, power stations, steel mills, machine tool factories, and so on. They want to earn the money to pay for these essential imports by trade. But in the fifties and sixties the terms of their trade with the rich countries were basically unsatisfactory. Ninety per cent of their export earnings derived from the sale of primary products, which were in declining demand in the rich countries, and most of the latters' imports from the Third World, whether of primary products or of manufactured goods, were subject to tariffs and other protective restrictions. In the sixties the rich countries greatly expanded their trade with each other (see chapters 8 and 9), but apart from 'commodity agreements' to stabilize the prices of a few primary products they did little to promote trade with the Third World. The latter's share of world trade fell from twenty-seven per cent in the early fifties to seventeen per cent in 1968.[6] In October 1970 the rich countries, after prolonged discussions with ninety-one poor countries in the United Nations Conference of Trade and Development (UNCTAD), finally agreed in principle to the Generalized Tariff Preference Scheme under which they would all give tariff preferences to imports of most manufactured goods from all the poor countries.

'Aid' is needed to bridge the gap, estimated at about twenty per cent, between the import needs of the developing countries and the amount of foreign exchange which they can earn through trade. The concept of 'aid to developing countries' – a concept new in history – was launched by President Truman in 1949 as a counterpart to the great programme of Marshall Aid for European reconstruction, when he asked Congress for the modest sum of $49,000,000. 'Aid' consists essentially of 'technical assistance' – advisers, scholarships, research projects – and of capital; and capital aid is officially regarded as including grants and loans by governments and international bodies, and, somewhat euphemistically, private investment. In 1970 aid was being provided in two main ways. About ten per cent was 'multilateral', channelled through the United Nations and its Specialized Agencies. The remaining ninety per cent was 'bilateral', given by an individual donor country to an individual recipient country. Bilateral aid was generally felt to be less satisfactory than multilateral aid. Its allocation was often dictated by political motives. The bulk of British bilateral aid was given to Commonwealth countries, and of French aid to France's former colonies, while the Americans concentrated much of their aid in certain countries which they wished to bolster up in the battle to 'contain' Communism. Five-sixths of the bilateral aid was 'tied' to purchases in the donor country, and an increasing amount was given in loans rather than grants. If this trend continued, by 1977 the developing countries would be paying back to the rich countries in debt charges at least as much as they would be receiving in aid.[6] Bilateral aid was, moreover, essentially unco-ordinated, and administered on- a trial and error basis, with results which often disillusioned the donors. In 1970 the OECD was providing a forum for consultation between all non-Communist donors; and the Eurafrican Association and the Colombo Plan (a Commonwealth project launched in 1950 to link the recipient Commonwealth states of South-east Asia to the Commonwealth donors) for the joint planning of aid pro-grammes between donors and recipients in particular regions. But only the United Nations offered a forum for multilateral planning between *all* recipients and *all* donors (with the excep-tion of East Germany until 1973 and of Communist China until 1971).

At this point we must note certain problems concerning private investment. The total of such investment by the rich countries in the poor countries was estimated at 30 billion dollars in 1966.[7] Without foreign capital and technology poor countries cannot develop their resources; but just as some European countries are asserting that American technology is reducing them to helotry (see chapter 14), so there is a growing feeling, in the developing countries, that this foreign investment is a form of technological colonialism. Underlying the fear that the companies and the governments which back them might use their economic power for politico-military ends, is a deeper anxiety. Nearly half the investment is in mining and petroleum – in extracting fossil fuels and minerals which cannot be replaced. At current rates, the rich countries are not only using up their own resources of fossil fuels and minerals, but through this form of 'aid' are sucking into their consumer-hungry maws the resources of the poor countries. It will take most of the latter several decades, at their present rate of growth – their steel production capacity is growing, from a very low level, at the rate of fifty per cent a decade – to reach the present level of industrial production of the rich countries. By then, unless the massive exploitation of undersea minerals and fuels is developed, resources of petroleum and of a number of vital minerals are likely to have been exhausted.[8]

In 1961 the General Assembly of the United Nations pronounced the sixties the 'Development Decade', and set two targets: an annual growth rate of five per cent of national income for the developing countries, and an aid contribution of one per cent of their GNP for the rich countries. (A GNP target is twenty-five per cent higher than a national income target, since it does not take into account the costs of capital replacement). By 1970 the poor countries as a whole had fulfilled their target but the rich countries had not fulfilled theirs. Between 1960 and 1970 the bilateral aid from the OECD countries increased from eight billion to sixteen billion dollars a year (the governmental component increased from $4,700,000,000 to $6,800,000,000); but since the GNPs of these countries were growing at the rate of three to four per cent a year, this increase in the quantity of their aid did not reflect the increase in their national wealth. Thus aid fell from 0.89 per cent of their combined GNP in 1960 to 0.75 in 1970.[9] The main defaulter was the United States, which nevertheless regularly produced half the total governmental aid. The fact that in 1970 such European countries as Belgium, France, the Netherlands and Britain were contributing their one per cent, could not make up the deficiency. Communist aid was on a far lower scale – $12,200,000,000 between 1954-1970.[10]

In October 1970 the General Assembly of the United Nations adopted a 'Development Strategy for the Second United Nations Development Decade'. The poor countries have been set an overall growth rate target of six per cent a year. This time population growth, at the rate of 2.5 per cent a year, has been taken into consideration, so that the target for *per capita* GNP growth is

271

3.5 per cent. The rich countries are again asked to give one per cent of their GNP by 1972, or at the latest by 1975, and to increase the component of governmental aid to 0.7 per cent of the one per cent. They are also asked to 'untie' bilateral aid, to 'soften' the terms of loans, to prevent debt crises arising in the poor countries' repayment of loans, and to give a higher proportion of their aid through multilateral channels.

During the sixties there was a growing realization that statistics of 'growth' are not an adequate criterion of 'development'. This realization is reflected in the new Strategy, which proposes *qualitative* objectives relating to education, health, nutrition, reform of land tenure, housing, and unemployment, and affirms that growth must be accompanied by social justice so that its benefits are shared by all.

The document has been interpreted by the poor countries, and accepted by the majority of the rich, as constituting 'a moral and political commitment', and, in the words of 'The Group of Seventy-Seven' poor countries, as 'the best possible reflection of the collective conscience of mankind in one of the most crucial areas of organizing human society'.

Nevertheless, at the end of 1970 the outlook was not bright. World expenditure on defence in 1969–70 amounted to $204,000,000,000 'the equivalent in dollar terms of a year's income produced by the 1,800,000,000 people in the poorer half of the world's population'. Nine-tenths of this expenditure was being made by the rich countries, including $80,000,000,000 by the United States Government, which despite the exhortations of the United Nations was reducing its $3,000,000,000 contribution to aid. There was little sign that the United States' European allies were putting pressure on it to alter its priorities, or that public opinion in the European countries had grasped the nature and importance of the moral commitment which their governments had made. Many experts were prophesying major disasters in the seventies and eighties unless a far more positive effort were made by the rich countries to help the poor countries to develop, in the broadest sense of the word.

No planet can survive half slave and half free; half engulfed in misery, half careering towards the supposed joys of almost unlimited consumption from unprecedented production with less work; and all in an atmosphere of greater ease and luxury than man has known since the declining days of Rome. Neither our ecology or our morality could survive such contrasts. And we have perhaps ten years to begin to correct the imbalance and to do it in time.

These words were spoken by Mr Lester Pearson, former Prime Minister of Canada, in 1970.[11]

REFERENCES

1. *The Guardian Weekly*, London, 14 November 1968. *The Observer Foreign News Service*, No. 26395, London, 15 April 1969.
2. *The Economist*, London, 11 October 1969, p. 78.
3. Thayer, George, *The War Business*, Simon and Schuster, New York, 1969, p. 180, p. 258 *et. seq.* and The Stockholm International Peace Research Institute: *The Arms Trade with the Third World*, Humanities Press, New York, 1971, pp. 3–11.
4. *Ibid.*
5. Krause, Lawrence B. (ed.), *The Common Market, Progress and Controversy*, Prentice-Hall, New Jersey, 1964.
6. Pearson, Lester B. (Chairman), *Partners in Development: Report of the Commission on International Development to the World Bank*, Pall Mall Press Ltd., London, 1969, p. 70.
7. Pearson, *op. cit.*, p. 100.
8. See *Scientific American*, September 1970, pp. 194–209 and 176–8.
9. OECD figures.
10. OECD figures.
11. Address to the Columbia Conference on International Development, February 1970, published in *The Widening Gap: Development in the Seventies*, ed., Barbara Ward *et al.* Columbia University Press, New York, 1971, p. 345.

14. 'Europe' between the Super-Powers

From the Renaissance until 1945, the nations of Western Europe were the dominant nations in the world. Power, wealth, culture and technology radiated from Western Europe. France and Britain, with populations of thirty-nine and forty-two million respectively in 1914, were individually great imperial world powers. In this diffusion of European power and culture overseas Russia was not involved. The areas of its expansion were the vast empty spaces of central Asia, and the countries of Eastern Europe. On the other side of Europe was the United States, whose teeming peoples were preoccupied, for 150 years, in distilling a distinctive American culture out of the ingredients of their European heritage, and in pursuing their 'manifest destiny' to occupy and tame their own continent.

Suddenly, after 1945, the whole picture was radically transformed. The United States and the Soviet Union found themselves forced by circumstances to emerge from their relative isolation into the centre of the world scene. They were super-powers, possessing a technical might such as the world had never seen before. Looming on the horizon was the mighty unpredictable force of Communist China. Meanwhile, the former 'great powers' of Western Europe were impelled, after giving up their colonies, to draw the focus of their attention back to their own continent; and there they found that as separate nation states, they were now second class powers.

The Relative Industrial Decline of 'Europe'
Excluding the Soviet Union

Before 1914 Western Europe was the workshop of the world. The United States was the only industrialized country outside Europe and its exports of manufactures were still on a fairly small scale.

In 1920 there were only about a 100,000,000 people engaged in manufacturing industries throughout the world, and of these about two-fifths (39,000,000) were in Europe. They represented a valuable capital of acquired skills. With the growth of industry in the United States and the Soviet Union, and later Japan and the Third World, Europe's proportion declined, by 1960, to one-third – 56 out of 181,000,000 workers in manufacturing industries. That the decline was not greater was due to the spread of industry from Germany, Britain and France to the other countries of Europe and to the shift of workers from traditional to newer industries.

Europe's industrial lead was largely dependent on coal and steel. In 1913, Europe produced just over half the total world production of coal (563 out of 1,255,000,000 tonnes). The other main producing area was the United States (517,000,000 tonnes). At that time coal was the main source of human energy, apart from human brawn. By 1967, just under two-fifths of the world's energy was derived from coal; petroleum and natural gas accounted for just under three-fifths and hydro-electric and nuclear power for about 2.3 per cent. This had radically altered Europe's position. In 1967, Europe produced only fifteen per cent of the world's energy, and the Soviet Union, which has large resources of coal, oil and natural gas, eighteen per cent. In Western Europe, coal still accounted for eighty per cent of energy production from natural sources. Natural gas, developed mainly in south-west France until the North Sea gas started to come into use in the late sixties, accounted for seven per cent, hydro-electricity and nuclear power for eight per cent, and European-produced crude petroleum only five per cent (these figures do not include the energy produced from imports, mainly petroleum).

275

The development of the engineering and transport industries was based on steel. In 1913, Europe produced over half the world's output of steel ingots and castings (43,000,000 out of 77,000,000 tonnes). In 1967, Europe and the Soviet Union produced thirty-three and twenty-one per cent respectively. For this production, Europe depended to a much greater extent than in 1913 on imported iron ore. Many of Europe's iron mines yield only low grade ore, more expensive to use than high grade ores imported by ship straight to the blast furnace site.[1]

By 1970, therefore, Europe had lost its industrial pre-eminence in terms of coal and steel, and as other sources of energy supersede coal, and as other materials, such as plastics, supersede steel, Europe is likely to decline further in relative industrial power.

The Technological Relationship between Western Europe, the United States and the Soviet Union

Until 1939 Europe was the pace-setter for technological development. Except for the mass export of foodstuffs, the United States had relatively little impact on European technology. On the whole the inventions were coming out of Europe and the techniques for the mass production of the European inventions were being evolved in America by men like Henry Ford.

In the second great technological revolution of the post-war period, however, the initiative and driving force have come from America, producing a 'technology gap' between Western Europe and the United States. This change is the result of several factors. First, the capital resources of the United States are now far greater than those of Europe. In 1967, for example, there were eighty American companies whose sales surpassed a billion dollars, as compared with eight of such companies in Britain, twelve in West Germany and three in France. There were 302 American companies, fifty-seven British, twenty-six West German and twenty-three French with sales surpassing $250,000,000.[2] As a result, the United States was able to spend over three times as much on research and development as Western Europe – 3.4 per cent of its GNP, as compared with

British expenditure of 2.3 per cent, French of 1.6 per cent and West German of 1.4 per cent.[3] Second, nearly half of the young people of the United States receive post-school education, as compared with ten or fifteen per cent of the youth of Western Europe; and its scientists and engineers have been supplemented by the 'brain-drain' of refugees and of inventive Europeans attracted by the wider opportunities of the New World. There were estimated to be 500,000 trained scientists working in research and development in the United States in 1965, twice the number working in Western Europe.[4] Third, American research is more 'goal-oriented' than that of West Europe. In the late sixties two-thirds of the funds were provided by the Federal Government, and half of this was directly related to defence. Even the research of private firms and universities is far more 'managed' than in West Europe.[5] Goal-oriented management produces practical results, but sometimes at the cost of some loss of intellectual freedom and scientific integrity.

The Russians aimed at catching up with and surpassing the United States in technological achievement. By the late sixties great progress had been made: they were also spending three per cent of their GNP on research and development and had trained some 500,000 scientists (a special town, Akademgorodok, has been built in Western Siberia with sixteen research institutes and an experimental factory, whose inhabitants are devoted entirely to research). The production of their major industries such as iron and steel, cement, machine tools and tractors, was approaching that of the United States, and in rocketry, military aircraft, space technology and nuclear energy, they were rivalling it. But Soviet development was unbalanced. In the production of computers, chemicals and almost all consumer goods Soviet technology was a long way behind the United States, and also West Europe, Czechoslovakia and East Germany.[6]

The West European states, caught between the two technological giants, were naturally worried. In January 1967 the British Prime Minister, Harold Wilson, told the Council of Europe that West Europe was entering a state of 'industrial helotry, under which we, in Europe, produce only the conventional apparatus of a modern economy, while becoming increasingly dependent on American business for the sophisticated apparatus which will call the tune in the seventies and eighties'. He proposed as a solution the formation of a 'Technological Community' in West Europe.[7] Technological rivalry between the two technological giants and the semi-giant might, however, produce a tragic misdirection of energies. Their collaboration to restore the ecology of the planet which their technology has disturbed, and to apply their technology to the development of the Third World, may prove essential to the welfare of the human race. A straw in the wind, in 1970, was the friendly co-operation which was taking place between Soviet, American and British scientists over the technological problems of making nuclear power from the hydrogen in the sea – a break-through in this field could transform the energy situation of the planet.

The Nuclear Arms Race

By the mid-fifties, the age of nuclear weapons had dawned. The biggest bombs dropped in the Second World War contained ten tonnes of TNT equivalent. The two atom bombs dropped on Japan in 1945 each contained the equivalent of 20,000 tonnes of TNT. By 1970, the United States and the Soviet Union had developed nuclear warheads ranging from tactical weapons of a quarter of a kilotonne (1,000 tonnes TNT equivalent) to a Soviet device of over fifty megatonnes (1,000,000 tonnes of TNT equivalent). It was estimated in 1970 that the total stockpile of both countries amounted to the equivalent of twenty tonnes of TNT for every inhabitant of the world – and thirty grammes exploded close to a person can be lethal.

The arms race was started, less by the development of the bombs themselves, than by new developments in the means of delivering them. Until 1957, the United States felt master of the situation. It could strike at the Soviet Union with nuclear warheads launched by medium or intermediate range missiles (MRBMs or IRBMs) fired from ships or from bases on allied soil in Europe or Asia, or from its B52 bombers, with a range of 9,600 km. By 1955, the Soviet Union was making bombers of equivalent range, but not, it was thought, in sufficient numbers to inflict massive destruction on the United States. Then, on 4 October 1957, the Soviet Union launched SPUTNIK (the Russian initials for a man-made earth satellite) from a carrier rocket, and a month later a larger satellite with a dog inside. The United States now realized that the Soviet Union could make intercontinental ballistic missiles (ICBMs) capable of hitting accurately any target in America. For the first time the United States was vulnerable to a surprise attack from a supposedly implacable enemy and since it had not yet developed ICBMs, it was not in a position to hit back in kind. The Soviet Union seemed to be ahead in the missile race. President Eisenhower's experts told him that by the end of 1959 the Soviet Union would be able to hurl at the United States 100 ICBMs with hydrogen warheads. The nightmarishness of this supposed 'missile gap' was enhanced by uncertainty. The whereabouts of the American air bases were public knowledge, and the first American ICBMs, the Atlas and the Titan missiles, were as vulnerable as long range bombers to a surprise attack because they were fuelled with liquid oxygen which could only be loaded just before despatch. The Soviet Union, on the other hand, hugged its secrets to itself within its vast spaces, and the United States was forced to rely exclusively on intelligence, mainly gathered by U2 spy planes photographing missile sites and air bases from twelve miles in the sky. By 1960 American intelligence showed that there was in fact no 'missile gap'. The United States had about fifty strategic missile warheads and the Soviet Union thirty-five.[8] The behaviour of the Soviet Union, however, was calculated to arouse American fears.

After years of handling the United States with fearful caution, the Soviet leaders could not resist using their new-found power to play brinkmanship, and the United States was rendered correspondingly nervous by its new vulnerability. For several years a series of crises occurred in which the Cold War threatened to erupt into a hot Third World War. Each time, Khrushchev drew back from the brink, but each time a residue of heightened tension remained. Out of this situation developed the most dangerous arms race in human history.[9]

Robert McNamara, who was American Secretary of Defense from 1961 to 1968, explained why the United States embarked on this race:

Since we could not be certain that . . . they (the USSR) would not undertake a massive build-up, we had to ensure against such an eventuality by undertaking a major build-up of our own Minutemen and Polaris forces . . . But the blunt fact remains that if we had had more accurate information about planned Soviet strategic forces, we simply would not have needed to build as large a nuclear arsenal as we have today. . . . What is essential to understand is that . . . actions – or even realistically potential actions – on either side . . . necessarily trigger reactions on the other side. It is precisely this action-reaction phenomenon that fuels an arms race.[10]

By 1970, the race had reached nightmarish proportions. It was estimated in July 1970 that the Soviet Union had approximately 5,622 and the United States 7,502 individual nuclear warheads, of which 6,000 American warheads were fitted to delivery systems capable of striking at targets in Soviet territory, and 2,000 Soviet warheads were fitted to delivery systems which could strike targets in America. Both sides were able, through satellites and other means, to detect the sites of each other's land based missiles, and, to a large extent, of their missile-armed bomber bases. Means of detecting missiles based on Polaris submarines, in the construction of which the Soviet Union was rapidly catching up with the United States, had not yet been developed. Both sides were establishing Anti-Ballistic Missile (ABM) systems, designed to protect cities of strategic importance by firing missiles to intercept oncoming missiles in the upper atmosphere or in space. In 1967 the Russians were estimated to have established sixty-seven such 'launchers' around Moscow. The Americans were behind in ABMs, but were producing multiple warheads, each warhead containing ten or twenty megatonnes, designed to saturate the defence.[11]

Meanwhile, McNamara had evolved the strategic doctrine of 'assured destruction capability by maintaining a highly reliable ability to inflict unacceptable damage upon any aggressor, even after absorbing a surprise first strike.' He explained to a Congressional Committee in February 1965 that 'assured destruction' would mean killing a quarter to a third of the enemy's population – 60–70,000,000 Russians – and destroying two-thirds of its industrial capacity. The Russians would simultaneously kill a maximum of 149,000,000 or a minimum of 41,000,000 Americans. By 1970, however, it was beginning to look as if a first strike by either side would completely annihilate the other. For both nations, at this time, were developing terminal guidance systems of such accuracy that a first-strike attack might make retaliation impossible. The term 'deterrent' was ceasing to have any objective meaning, and was beginning to be recognized as implying a subjective psychological attitude – perhaps an attitude of illusion? In 1966 a Canadian general wrote that:

The military should realize that the greatest threat to the survival of democracy is no longer the Russians or the Chinese or any other country professing anti-democratic ideologies, but rather war itself. It is nuclear war against which the military must protect their fellow-citizens.[12]

In April 1970 a United States Senate Resolution opened by saying that: '... the competition to develop and deploy strategic nuclear weapons has reached a new and dangerous phase which threatens to ... weaken the stability of nuclear deterrence as a barrier to war ...'[13] Apart from its suicidal implications, the arms race was economically crippling. Between 1961 and 1968 the American defence budget rose from $48–79,000,000,000 and that of the Soviet Union $20–39,000,000,00 – that is, they both nearly doubled (during the period the French defence budget was nearly trebled; only the British did not rise steeply).[14]

Before we discuss the attempts to secure international disarmament and arms control, we must consider the Soviet Union's political relations with the United States and China during the years 1955–70.

Soviet-American Relations: 1955-1964

We saw in chapter 6 that Khrushchev's attitude to men and to politics was very different from that of Stalin: humane rather that paranoid; pragmatic rather than dogmatic. Khrushchev knew that nuclear war would be suicidal. In July 1955, he participated, with President Eisenhower of the United States, and the Prime Ministers of Britain and France, at the first 'Summit' conference, held in Geneva to discuss collective agreements about European security after the decision had been taken to re-arm Germany. Then, at the 20th Congress of the Soviet Communist Party in 1956, Khrushchev enunciated the doctrine of 'peaceful co-existence'. World Communism was still regarded as inevitable, but Marxists needed no longer to believe that war was the inevitable means of achieving it. Thus, the doctrinal basis was laid for a rapprochement with the United States.

The attitude of the American government was also relaxing. In 1959, President Eisenhower invited Khrushchev to visit America. For Khrushchev the visit provided an opportunity both to demonstrate the equality of the United States with the Soviet Union and to affirm his conviction that the peace of the world depended on their collaboration. On his arrival he told the American National Press Club that he had come to end the Cold War. The American public greeted him coldly, regarding him as a sinister man of blood; but his genuine interest and enthusiasm, and the second Mrs Khrushchev's broad, beaming, peasant smile, thawed the atmosphere. The two leaders agreed to hold another Summit conference in 1960, and Khrushchev went home and announced that the Soviet armed forces would be reduced by 1,200,000 men.

Then, just as the four heads of state were gathering at Paris for the second Summit in May 1960, an American U2 spy plane, taking photographs of the Soviet Union at a very high altitude, was shot down by a Soviet missile. Khrushchev demanded an apology from Eisenhower, which he did not receive. He then broke up the conference in a rage. A further Summit meeting between Khrushchev and President Kennedy held in Vienna in

June 1961 produced no practical results. It was followed, in August 1961, by the building of the Berlin Wall – the symbol of the Soviet acceptance of a stalemate over the Berlin problem. In 1962 the Cuban missile crisis occurred, which in turn was a major factor in Khrushchev's deposition by the Soviet 'hawks' in 1964. After a brief and partial thaw, Soviet-American relations had hardened again by that year.

The Russo-Chinese Conflict

In 1950, Communist Russia and China were thrown by the American policy of 'containment' into alliance; but under the surface of their comradeship lay fundamental tensions. First, there were the basic differences of race and language, of history and culture. Second, there was the difference of situation. The Chinese, far more undeveloped in 1949 than were the Russians in 1917, were throughout the fifties in the early, fanatical stage of Communism, equivalent to the Leninist phase in the Soviet Union. They were full of crusading zeal for spreading Communism around the world, if necessary with bombs. Meanwhile, they were tightening their belts at home and experimenting in new forms of Communist organization. For centuries the Chinese had regarded the outside world as barbaric: Mao had never been abroad, except to Moscow, and so the dogmatic intolerance of the Communist was heightened by ignorance and arrogance. The Russians, on the other hand, stood with the United States in the centre of the international stage in the United Nations. They were becoming, since Stalin's death, more and more aware of the realities of world affairs and were adjusting Marxism-Leninism accordingly; in fact, abandoning revolutionary fervour and accepting the *status quo*. They were concentrating their resources on building up an affluent society in their own country, not on promoting world revolution. In China's eyes, the Russians were guilty of the heresy of 'revisionism'; in Russia's eyes, the Chinese were guilty of the heresy of 'dogmatism'. Third, there was a power conflict. China was challenging the Soviet Union for leadership of the world Communist movement. And finally, there was a traditional territorial rivalry. The

7,200 kilometres of common frontier is not a natural physical or ethnic boundary, and against it press the land-hungry masses of the most populous country in the world. For a hundred years, while China was weak, Russia had been penetrating into that wild, indeterminate area which traditionally had paid tribute to China – the territories of Sinkiang, Manchuria and Mongolia. Outer Mongolia had proclaimed its independence of China in 1915 and in 1924 had become a Communist state, the Mongolian Peoples' Republic, closely linked to the Soviet Union. In 1945, after declaring war on Japan, the Russians looted from Manchuria the industrial equipment established by the Japanese there before restoring the province to China.

The rift began in the mid-fifties, with Khrushchev's wooing of the arch revisionist Tito, his denunciation of Stalin, and his proclamation of the doctrines of 'peaceful co-existence' and 'different roads to socialism'. Russia's support of India in a border dispute with China, which erupted into war in 1962, its refusal to give China aid to make nuclear weapons, and Khrushchev's friendly visit to the United States brought the tension to a head. In April 1960 the Chinese publicly accused the Yugoslavs of 'revisionism' – and for 'Yugoslavia' read the Soviet Union. Khrushchev hit back, at the conference of 81 Communist Parties held later that year in Moscow, by accusing the Chinese of war-mongering, and of 'fractionalism', that is, of splitting the Communist movement. The assembled Communist leaders, none of whom wanted a Chinese-started nuclear war, backed Khrushchev – except for Enver Hoxha, the leader of Albania, who stood up in the conference hall and described him as a traitor, a weakling and a revisionist, and denounced him for betraying Lenin and Stalin.

Fearing that Tito was trying to turn it into a sub-satellite, Albania had become the most Stalinist of the Soviet satellites. When, therefore, Khrushchev tried to heal the Soviet breach with Yugoslavia in 1955, Albania became a Chinese instead of a Russian satellite; and whenever the Russians violently attacked Albania, everyone knew that they meant China, just as whenever the Chinese attacked Yugoslavia, everyone knew that they meant

Russia. The rift was exacerbated by the sudden termination, in 1960, of the aid which the Soviet Union had been giving China since 1949, estimated at over a billion dollar's worth of factory equipment and the services of 10,000 experts. The Soviet Union broke off diplomatic relations with Albania in 1961, and Albania withdrew from the Warsaw Pact and Comecon. Chinese economic aid – including wheat purchased from Canada – replaced Soviet bloc aid to Albania. This strange alliance between a giant and a pigmy gave China, for the first time in history, a foothold in Europe.

The quarrel soon waxed more intense. At the Twenty-Second Congress of the Soviet Communist Party in October 1961 the Chinese branded a Russian redraft of Lenin's 1919 Party Programme as 'a revisionist programme for the restoration of capitalism'. When they discovered that Stalin's body had been taken out of the mausoleum which it had shared with that of Lenin, and that Albania had not been invited to the conference, they walked out. The Cuban episode of 1962 and the Test Ban Treaty of 1963 appeared to them as Soviet capitulation to the United States.

China joined the nuclear club in 1964 when it exploded an atom bomb. In 1967 it exploded a hydrogen bomb. By 1970 it had begun to build bombers and rockets with ranges of 2,400 kilometres. By 1980 it may have acquired the capability to launch long-range missiles on the heartland of the United States and the Soviet Union.[15] In making these weapons it had no assistance from the Soviet Union.

In June 1969, the Russians finally succeeded in holding a conference of seventy-five Communist parties of the world, which they had been planning since 1964. One of their main aims was to rally the world Communist movement round Moscow and to excommunicate Peking, but they were only partially successful. The fierce Soviet criticisms of the Chinese (who were not of course present) were supported by the other fraternal parties, most of whom were themselves having to cope with Maoist splinter groups.[16] To criticize Peking, however, is not necessarily to support Moscow. Instead, the fraternal parties

285

K

seized the opportunity to affirm 'polycentricism' (see chapter 7).

During 1969 there were a number of 'border incidents' on the Sino-Soviet Frontier, where 700,000 Soviet troops confronted 800,000 Chinese troops.[17] It seemed possible that the Russians were contemplating a preventive war, in order to knock out Chinese nuclear installations in the remote border province of Sinkiang, but the tension abated somewhat in 1970, and full diplomatic relations, broken off in 1966, were renewed.

Disarmament and Arms Control

From 1945 to 1970 there was almost continuous discussion about disarmament, mainly in a series of commissions set up by the United Nations. In 1946, when the United States alone possessed the atom bomb, it offered to renounce it if all other countries would agree not to acquire nuclear weapons and if an international control organization, free of the veto, were established. The Soviet Union, obsessed with the need for security after the devastations of war, was determined to build its own bomb, and denounced the plan. Subsequently, sweeping proposals were made by both the Americans and the Russians for abolishing all nuclear weapons, by stages, and for reducing conventional forces. The Soviet plan of 1959 even proposed the abolition of all war departments, general staffs, and military training over a period of four years, but all the schemes foundered on two main issues. The first was the question of inspection: the Russians refused to allow any ground inspection in their country. The second was the question of how a disarmed world was to be policed. If nations were to agree to disarm, there would have to be some international police force to which they could look for protection. Both the Americans and the Russians accepted the principle that such a force should be established under the United Nations. The Americans proposed that this force should be fully international, involving, in effect, some form of supranational authority or world government to control it, which would mean amending the United Nations' Charter and abolishing the right of veto. They also proposed that the international force should be armed, at least for a time, with nuclear weapons, to make it 'so strong that no state would challenge it'. The Russians insisted that it should consist only of national units, that it should have no nuclear weapons, and that they should retain their veto at the command level as well as in the Security Council.

Although there was no agreement to disarm, there was some agreement to control the future spread of arms. On 5 August 1963, after 353 meetings, a Test Ban Treaty was signed in Moscow by the United States, Soviet Union and Britain, banning nuclear tests in the air and water but not underground. By 1970 110 states had adhered to this treaty, but France and China had refused to do so. In 1963 the three powers negotiated a treaty, adopted by the General Assembly of the United Nations, to keep outer space free of weapons. Antarctica was declared a nuclear free zone in 1959, and Latin America, by its member states, in 1967. Then, in 1968, the Soviet Union and the United States, with British support, agreed on the terms of a Nuclear Non-Proliferation Treaty, which came into force on 5 March 1970 when 97 countries had signed it and 47, including the United States, the Soviet Union and Britain, had ratified. France and China refused to sign. Under this treaty the nuclear powers pledged themselves not to supply nuclear weapons to non-nuclear powers or to help them to make them; and the non-nuclear powers pledged themselves not to make or acquire nuclear weapons. An international inspection team was provided by Euratom (for the member states of the European Community) and the United Nations' International Atomic Energy Administration in Vienna.

In 1970 this treaty appeared to be of crucial importance. Seventeen countries possessed nuclear reactors of sufficient size to produce plutonium for atom bombs as a by-product of their peaceful uses, and eight more were expected to have achieved this capacity by 1975.[18] New inventions were also in sight which might drastically reduce the cost of bombs and so make a 'poor country's' bomb possible: the gas centrifuge process for producing enriched uranium for atom bombs, and hydrogen bombs which could be detonated by lasers instead of by atom bombs.

Many countries naturally felt too insecure to renounce the

possibility of nuclear self-defence without the assurance of external protection. The United States, the Soviet Union and Britain therefore undertook to come to the aid of any non-nuclear signatory which was the victim of or threatened by nuclear attack.

> The significance of this was that the world's two super-powers were giving together, for the first time, direct guarantees of protection for smaller countries – a pledge which might become in the long run the basis of an effective and general system of protective guarantees for smaller nations under the United Nations.[19]

The Non-Proliferation Treaty appeared to inaugurate a new phase of collaboration between the two super-powers. In 1969 the United Nations approved a draft American-Soviet treaty to ban the placing of atomic weapons on the ocean bed. In November 1969 the United States and the Soviet Union started 'Strategic Arms Limitation Talks' (SALT) on the possibility of a moratorium on the testing or deployment of anti-ballistic missiles (ABMs) and of multiple independently targetable re-entry vehicles (MIRVs). The talks continued throughout 1970 in an atmosphere of secrecy. It will be noted that no 'European' country was included. The Big Four of 1945 had become the Big Two of 1970.

The impetus for disarmament did not come solely from the politicians. The majority of the electors in the Western countries, who were both ignorant and afraid, supported and therefore paid for the arms race, but a small minority of intellectuals and students raised protests. These were partly directed at the arms race itself, and partly at the 'military-industrial complex' which lay behind it, expressed in such Orwellian terms as 'hardware', 'war-games', 'systems engineering', 'think-tanks' and 'cost-benefit analysis'. It seemed as if terrestrial annihilation might be brought about, not by tyrants like Hitler and Stalin, but by faceless experts behaving like machines.

In Britain the protest movement was expressed in the Committee for Nuclear Disarmament (CND), whose most famous leader was the philosopher Bertrand Russell. There was no comparable movement in any other European country. By 1968 the CND had fizzled out – perhaps out of a sense of European impotence in the face of American might. In the United States itself, the protest movement, in spite of ebbs and flows, seemed by 1970 to be slowly but surely widening its influence.

The United States, Western Europe and the Soviet Union

From its birth in 1917, the Soviet Union regarded itself as possessing a historic mission to lead mankind into the era of global Communism. The United States also started its history, over a century earlier, with a sense of mission to found a better kind of society than that of the wicked Old World which most of its citizens had rejected. Both the Communist vision, and the 'American Dream' foresaw this society as based on the Rights of Man – although differently interpreted. But whereas the Communists believed that they ought actively to promote world Communism, the Americans, until the Second World War, were content in general to bring the American Dream to birth in America.

After 1945, the United States entered into its first peace-time commitments in Western Europe: in NATO, and in the OECD. In contrast to the Soviet Union's behaviour towards its satellites, the United States did its best to treat its NATO and OECD allies as equal partners. This policy produced in 1960 President Kennedy's 'Grand Design' for an 'Atlantic Partnership'. It was the springtime of the European Communities; and Kennedy conceived that the United States and a united Western Europe might form the twin pillars of a mighty edifice through which the 'Free World' would 'contain' Communism and help the Third World.

Kennedy himself was deeply inspired by the American Dream of the new kind of society, the 'New Frontier' as he called it, which America could create – in America. From the declaration of the Truman Doctrine in 1947 until his presidency, the United

States' political and military involvement in Europe and the Far East had been dictated essentially by the *negative* motive of opposing Communism. Kennedy projected a *positive* image of the United States as leading the whole world towards his New Frontier. He universalized the American Dream.

The Grand Design quickly faded away. Western European unification was arrested by de Gaulle, and the United States' great leap forward into the age of megatonne nuclear capability produced feelings of resentment and impotence. The resentment was focused by de Gaulle, who tried to hurt the Americans by such pinpricks as withdrawing France from NATO, manipulating the franc against the dollar and making friendly gestures towards the Communist powers, while projecting France's counter-image into Canada and Latin America. The sense of impotence had already induced the British to hand over the defence of Australasia to the United States in 1951 (Australia and New Zealand then formed the military ANZUS Pact with the United States, excluding Britain); and it culminated in decisions of 1968 and 1970 to maintain only token forces East of Suez, in Singapore, and to become, for the first time since the Renaissance, an essentially European power. In the nineteenth-century, Britain had been the self-constituted world policeman, using its fleet to maintain the *Pax Britannica*. By the mid-sixties, not only were the Americans adopting this role, but they were inviting the Russians to share it with them! After Khrushchev's downfall in 1964, there was no change in Soviet-American relations within Europe; but outside Europe the proliferation of conflicts seemed to be impelling the super-powers towards an understanding based on their common interests in maintaining world peace and on their common possession of the means to stop other countries' wars.

The experience of the Vietnam War may finally destroy the negative American dream of a mission to save the world *from* Communism, and so open the way for fuller co-operation with the Soviet Union – which is likely itself sooner or later to shed its commitment to Marxist ideology – in a growing number of areas of common interest.

The Soviet scientist Academician Sakharov, to whom we referred in chapter 6, foresees a time when '. . . the Soviet nation and the USA, having overcome their alienation, solve the problem of saving the poorer half of the world.'

What of the United Nations? Will European powers, and the Third World, be content to be permanently dominated by the United States and the Soviet Union, and possibly by China? Assuredly not. But, as the power of the two super-states grew in the sixties, so the influence of the United Nations declined, despite its increase in membership. The very concept of the nation-state was becoming out of date. We are, as a leading Canadian has said, a 'global village'. Nationalism was becoming as irrelevant as ideology in the face of the common problems of how to secure peace and eliminate poverty. The United Nations is supremely relevant as a forum where all the peoples of the world can meet to discuss their common problems. But its structure – each member state, whether its population be 500,000 (Fiji) or 500 million (India), having one vote – is becoming increasingly irrelevant to its function. The future exercise of effective influence in world affairs by both 'Europe' and the developing countries will therefore surely depend, not on their turning into regional power blocs confronting the United States, the Soviet Union, and China, but on the emergence of a *global consciousness*, a sense of the *community* of all peoples. Only this could be the solid basis for a world government, which could direct a world police force to stop conflicts, and a world planned economy, and a world welfare state to solve the problems of poverty.

REFERENCES

1. United Nations Statistical Year Book, 1969.
2. Knoppers, A. T., 'American Interests in Europe', in Moonman, Eric, ed., *Science and Technology in Europe*, Penguin, London, 1968, p. 108.
3. *The OECD Observer*, No. 30, October 1967, p. 34.
4. Knoppers, *op. cit.*, p. 112.

5. Knoppers, *op. cit.*, p. 112.
6. Davies, R. W., and Berry, M. J., 'The Russian Scene', in Moonman, *op. cit.*, pp. 118–131.
7. Reed, Lawrence, *Europe in a Shrinking World: A Technological Perspective*, Oldbourne Book Co. Ltd., London, 1967, p. 181.
8. Smart, Ian, 'The Strategic Arms Limitation Talks', in *The World Today*, July 1970, Chatham House, London, p. 296.
9. For much of the above I am indebted to Halle, *op. cit.*, pp. 343–8.
10. McNamara, Roberts , *The Essence of Security*, Harper and Row, New York, 1968, pp. 58–9.
11. Institute of Strategic Studies, *The Military Balance, 1970–71*, London, 1970, p. 89.
12. Burns, Lt. General E. L. M., *Megamurder*, Clark, Irwin and Co., Toronto, 1966, p. 9.
13. Smart, *op. cit.*, p. 296.
14. Figures supplied by the Institute of Strategic Studies, London, 1969.
15. Institute of Strategic Studies, London, *Strategic Survey, 1970*, p. 33.
16. *Observer Foreign News Service*, No. 26639, London, 19 June, 1969.
17. Institute of Strategic Studies, *The Military Balance 1970–71*, London, 1970.
18. Clarke, Robin, *The Warfare State*.
19. Bailey, Gerald, *Problems of Peace*, Ginn and Co., London, 1970, p. 28.

15. Towards the Future

We suggested in the introduction that the keynote of modern civilization is the urge to put into practice the ideals of liberty, equality and fraternity in a material environment transformed by applied science. Between 1914 and 1945 the old order in Europe was shattered, and the negative forces which surged into the vacuum, expressing the Freudian death-wish in the face of the challenge to grow up, were overcome. Between 1945 and 1970 the 'Europeans' came fully into the modern world; they 'came of age', in the famous phrase of the German theologian Dietrich Bonhöffer, martyred by the Nazis. They set in hand the restructuring of their national societies and they began to create international and supranational institutions in their continent. By 1970 the second industrial revolution was creating a completely new level of affluence in *quantitative* terms and it was altering the *quality* of life for millions of people by providing machines instead of human muscles to operate machines. Peace, economic progress and the sharing of wealth through the institutions of the welfare state and the liberalization of trade was eliminating the poverty of centuries and creating bourgeois societies in both Eastern and Western Europe. 'Peasants' and 'proletarians' still existed, but they were no longer the 'exploited masses' of the pre-war era. Their standard of living was rising to pre-war middle class levels; opportunities for personal advancement were expanding all the time; and above all, through the schools and colleges, through the mass media and through travel, they were becoming educated, not only in the formal sense, but in a wider sense of 'education for citizenship', and this was reducing their susceptibility to mass hysteria and to hero and enemy cults. These increasingly classless societies were developing in the context of greater internal political stability than modern Europe had yet experienced. In Western Europe personal freedom and parliamentary democracy were generally well established. Fascism had died away, Communism had mellowed, and political parties were becoming less concerned with ideological or factional conflicts and more with the pursuit of practical and pragmatic policies. In Eastern Europe personal freedom was still limited and political power remained in the hands of the monolithic Communist parties; but these parties were becoming less doctrinaire, more pragmatic, and more willing to allow free discussion within their own ranks. As Western Europe was becoming more socialist, Eastern Europe was becoming more liberal, and it looked as if the two systems might soon make real points of contact, based on factors of common experience and of the beneficial exchange of different experiences.

Nevertheless, only a beginning had been made in establishing the conditions for men and women to live creatively. Within the frontiers of Europe, the main targets for the next thirty years could be clearly discerned.

Basic personal rights were not yet established in the Communist countries, in Spain, Portugal, or Greece; in Turkey they were insecure; and in the other countries they still needed to be safeguarded with vigilance. The Council of Europe's Convention, Commission and Court of Human Rights were new instruments which, if strengthened in structure and expanded in membership, could secure personal rights for all Europeans. The social rights were not yet fully secured. The welfare state was only partially developed. The principle that those in greatest need should have the first claim on resources would involve establishing minimum incomes, in the form of either minimum wages or of minimum social security benefits; and giving priority to the needs of the sick, the old and the infirm. Most Western European social security systems had evolved in a piecemeal way and had many gaps which needed to be filled.

In the non-Communist countries the organizations and techniques for controlling economic fluctuations, already partially developed, needed to be perfected, so that 'growth' could proceed unimpeded and depressions become a thing of the past. This would also involve an extension of the international and supranational controls already being developed within Western Europe and between Western Europe, North America and Japan; and in due course, collaboration between the Communist and non-Communist systems. Specific lines of progress concerned the establishment of international monetary policies, probably involving a European currency, and planning for the social results of technological change, such as the unemployment resulting from the introduction of automation in industry.

Town and country planning, already started, would need to be much more fully developed in a continent whose population (including that of the Soviet Union) was expected to increase from 737,000,000 in 1971 to 898,000,000 in AD 2000.[1] Control of pollution, only in its first stages, was becoming urgent, and so was the conservation of minerals, fossil fuels and water – a matter which needed to be tackled in a global context and through global organizations.

European political systems needed to be changed both in structure and in the way they worked in order to handle effectively the problems outlined above. We have seen in this book how the multi-party systems of the Western European countries, regarded by liberal political thought as an essential feature of 'democracy', confronted the one-party systems of the Communist countries. By 1970, however, there were signs that both one and multi-party systems might be becoming out of date: an era of what might be called the meta-party *process* might be dawning. In both Eastern and Western Europe politics were increasingly based on a broad consensus regarding the goals which we have listed. The major issues concerned means rather than ends. The old controversy about public versus private ownership was becoming less relevant. In the private-enterprise countries control and management of major industries was increasingly vested in huge companies, some partially or wholly controlled by the state; while in the Communist countries the managements of major industries were being allowed more and more initiative. Management rather than ownership was becoming the key factor, and the problems of management were much the same in all industrialized countries. The concept of 'management in the public interest' was being extended in both parts of Europe into almost all fields of activity, and was being carried out through the *participation* of all interests – managers, workers, administrators, technologists and consumers, in the *process*. 'Participation', 'pluralism' and 'functionalism' were becoming key words among political scientists. They implied that administration should be carried out through flexible bodies which were in process of continuous evolution, rather than through static, rigid institutions. The management of the many functional tasks of modern government should be carried out through functional bodies, each adapted in size and composition to its task. Each functional body should be related to an appropriate administrative and governmental body. For some functions the unit would be very small – for example, a catchment area for sewage, related to the local town or district council; this would involve far greater decentralization than existed within most of the nations of Europe in 1970. For other functions, such as the organization of nuclear energy or the production of steel, nations would need to federate into supranational units, in the ways which the European Community was pioneering. In every case, 'democracy' would mean *active* popular participation. This was particularly important in an age when many matters requiring government action were so complex and so technical that often the members of parliament, and still more the ordinary citizens, could not make informed decisions on them. Yet these decisions – for example, about the number and type of nuclear reactors or the building of supersonic passenger planes – might commit the governments and the electors who paid the taxes for years ahead. The widening gap between executives, legislatures and electors in the 'technocracies' of the late sixties was producing a tendency for even the most 'democratic' executives, in the liberal sense of the word, to become too autocratic, and to carry out their wills through 'administrative justice', to deal with many matters which affected the ordinary citizen, such as the use of land, outside the ordinary courts of law. It also meant that the electors, losing interest in a government 'machine' which they felt unable to control, tended to become alienated from politics, or blindly to entrust their affairs to charismatic leaders, such as General de Gaulle.

In 1970 it seemed as if Europe were approaching a climacteric in its internal development. The way forward in the directions which we have outlined could not be followed without further material sacrifices by the privileged; without the renunciation of many vested interests, political, economic and national; without major changes of psychological attitude; and without much faster education of the masses. In Western Europe, for instance, it was hanging in the balance whether the European Community would take the leap forward into full supranationalism provided for in the Treaty of Rome, or subside into a parochial internationalism. In Eastern Europe it was unlikely that 'socialism with a human face' could be introduced until the generation of elderly leaders whose minds had been moulded before 1945 had passed from the scene. And over both parts of Europe hung the nightmarish prospect of a society in which machines became the masters rather than the servants of men, or even in which men themselves turned into 'faceless', amoral machines.

Nothing was more certain, however, in 1970, than that Europe's future during the next three decades was inextricably bound up with that of the rest of the world. Two central problems confronted the inhabitants of the 'global village'. The first was the three-pronged problem of armaments: the continuing nuclear arms race between the United States and the Soviet Union; the emergence of China as a nuclear power and the possibility that the Soviet Union might launch a pre-emptive nuclear attack on it to stop it from developing inter-continental delivery systems; and the probability that a united Western Europe would aim at becoming a fourth major nuclear power. The reversal of the compulsive spiralling of the arsenals of nuclear and highly sophisticated conventional weapons seemed a first priority for the survival of the human race.

The second problem was that of bridging the widening gulf between the rich and the poor countries. It looked as if this would require a far greater transfer of resources from the rich to the poor countries than was taking place in 1970; a deliberate decision by the rich countries to refrain from augmenting their consumer affluence and military power by sucking up the expendible mineral and fossil fuel resources of the poor countries; and the creation of something like a world welfare state and a world planned economy – for which Europe could provide the models – and world trading and monetary systems. All this would require some form of world government, not perhaps a 'government' in the 1970 sense, but some sort of global focus of the federal *process* which we have discussed – and here also Europe could provide a model if the European Community fulfilled its promise. Disarmament may not be an essential prerequisite to a great leap forward in bridging the gulf between the rich and the poor countries; but obviously the freeing of the vast sums of money, the vast amount of materials and the great concentration of scientific brain-power which was locked up in military affairs in 1970 would be a tremendous asset in fighting the battle against poverty and backwardness in the Third World. Conversely, a decision by Western Europe to become a fourth nuclear power might seriously impede the continent's ability to help the poor countries.

In global affairs, therefore, as well as in European affairs, it seemed in 1970 as if a climacteric had been reached.

In the middle of the nineteenth-century the great Italian statesman Cavour remarked that 'If we applied in our private lives the same moral principles which we apply in our public lives, what scoundrels we should be'. In those days international politics were 'power politics', each 'power' thinking it 'right' to promote its own interests at the expense of the interests of the others. We have seen how, after 1919, the idea has gained ground that international politics should be based on law, not simply on power; and that international law in its turn should be based on the moral principles of the Rights of Man. We have witnessed the establishment of various international organizations, ranging from the United Nations and the Nuremberg Court to the Council of Europe, to develop and uphold the rule of law and of morality. But by 1970 all these developments had taken the human race only half way along the road. At the end of it lay the goal of a world government to enforce international law through a world police force to which national governments would hand over some small proportion of their arms when they had beaten the rest into ploughshares.

Between 1919 and 1970 the foreign policies of the major nations wobbled between the pursuit of national interests and the pursuit of international principles. In 1970 it looked as if the dangers of the missile race and of the gulf between the rich and the poor countries would make further wobbling impossible. The human race would have to leap forward into the era of world law and world government or subside into disaster. No wonder that a general feeling of anxiety and uncertainty pervaded the European and American psyches and the councils of nations.

It was natural that the younger generation should respond more sensitively than their elders to 'the winds of change'. Many of the most thoughtful students in both Eastern and Western Europe were rejecting the value-systems of their parents and refusing to contract in to the 'establishment'. In Western Europe the students were protesting against capitalism, bureaucracy, technocracy, centralization, and authoritarianism in school and college. In Eastern Europe they were protesting against the suppression of civil rights and the all-pervasive authoritarianism, and demanding 'socialism with a human face', or a return to the 'pure' communism of Lenin. But their goals were not clear-cut. In general, in 1970 the most forward-looking Europeans seemed to be groping for a new inspiration to stimulate the will to move forward into the new order. The secular religions of the ideologies were discredited; and to some people the root cause of their failure was the fact that they were grounded in philosophic materialism. Since they denied man's spiritual nature, they ended by stimulating his animal nature, by fomenting hate and fear. And Freudian psychology had done its work: it had forced twentieth-century man to face the irrational forces in his 'unconscious' mind. But because of its philosophic materialism it had no means of dealing with factors which could not be explained in terms of physical instinct or material circumstance, such as a diseased or inert will, or of stimulating the forces in man's 'superconscious' which inspire him to deeds of fraternity and creativity.

Between 1945 and 1970 some European thinkers were pointing the way towards a new approach to religion, a new kind of religion. The French Jesuit theologian-scientist Pierre Teilhard de Chardin was adding a spiritual dimension to Darwin's theory of evolution. In his most important book, *The Phenomenon of Man*, first published in 1955, he suggested that the creative push from below which impells organisms to evolve from simple to complex forms is complemented by a creative pull from above, from a supreme Consciousness in whose Mind these forms already exist: a modern version of Aristotle's teleological idea that all organisms are evolving towards their inherent goal, complemented by Plato's idea of archetypal forms as ideas in the Mind of God. By 1970 many thoughtful Christians and non-Christians were finding inspiration in the spiritual optimism and universality of de Chardin's thought. Another seminal thinker was the Swiss psychologist Carl Jung. Originally a disciple of Freud, Jung rejected Freud's materialism and sought to relate psychological phenomena to non-physical 'archetypal' forms and situations – a term which also evoked Platonic philosophical idealism – expressed in symbols drawn from the 'collective unconscious' of all mankind. Meanwhile within the Christian Churches a mighty ferment was under way – two of its many sources of inspiration were the German Protestant theologian Dietrich Bonhöffer, and Pope John XXIII. This ferment was taking several directions: towards a new theology which sought to return to the simple gospel of the reality of God's love working in the human heart, and which therefore tended to reduce the importance of dogmas, rules and punishments; towards a new ethic of social and political service in the world; and towards a new unity of all Christian sects in the expression of this love and the practice of this service. At the same time, outside the Christian churches, there was a rapidly growing interest in the transcendental and mystical religions of the Orient, in their techniques for deliberately developing the super-conscious mind through meditation and spiritual exercises.

All these ideas and movements were signs that in the last three decades of the twentieth-century religion might return into public life in a completely new way: as a vision of the cosmic order which the Rights of Man reflect. Let us conclude by quoting the advice given in 1969 to the young members of the 'New Left' in both Communist and non-Communist countries by the Yugoslav heretic Milovan Djilas:

> ... At the beginning of a new era in which mankind has been released from the confines of earth and fused with the cosmos, humans have become aware of their worth, which cannot be compensated for or erased by any ideology or any forms of authority or property. Only by understanding the true nature of the modern world and emphasising spiritual freedom can young revolutionaries achieve universal visions of a freer human condition.[2]

REFERENCES

1. Figure of the Population Reference Bureau, Inc., Washington, D.C., USA.
2. Djilas, Milovan, in *The International Herald Tribune*, 20 October 1969.

Appendices

1 Population of European Countries in 1948 and 1970

Population (in millions)

	1948[1]	1970[1]
Albania	1·1	2·2
Andorra	0·005	0·01
Austria	7·0	7·4
Belgium	8·6	9·6
Bulgaria	7·1	8·5
Cyprus	0·5	0·6
Czechoslovakia	12·3	14·5
Denmark	4·2	4·9
Finland	4·0	4·7
France	40·8	50·7
Germany, East	19·0	16·0
Germany, West	46·7	58·4
East Berlin		1·1
West Berlin	3·3	2·2
Greece	7·8	8·9
Holy See	0·001	0·001
Hungary	9·2	10·3
Iceland	0·1	0·2
Ireland	3·0	2·9
Italy	45·7	53·6
Liechtenstein	0·01	0·02
Luxembourg	0·3	0·3
Malta	0·3	0·3

Monaco	0·02	0·02
Netherlands	9·8	13·0
Norway	3·2	3·9
Poland	24·0	32·8
Portugal	8·4	9·6
Rumania	16·0	20·2
San Marino	0·01	0·02
Spain	27·8	33·6
Sweden	6·9	8·0
Switzerland	4·6	6·3
Turkey[2]	19·5	35·2
Union of Soviet Socialist Republics[2]	193·0	242·8
United Kingdom	50·1	55·7
Yugoslavia	15·7	20·5
Non-Metropolitan Territories		
Channel Islands	0·1	0·1
Faeroe Islands	0·03	0·04
Gibraltar	0·02	0·02
Isle of Man	0·05	0·05

Source: United Nations' Statistical Yearbooks and International Bank for Reconstruction and Development.

(1)   Or nearest available year.

(2)   In Europe and Asia.

2 The Military Alliances

NATO countries
Warsaw Pact countries

ATLANTIC OCEAN

NATO AND WARSAW PACT FORCES IN EUROPE IN 1970 (*see below*)

United States
(forces in Europe)
Army: 200,000 (Italy and W. Germany)
Navy: 6th fleet (in Mediterranean): 2nd fleet (in Atlantic)
Air Force: 460 tactical aircraft in Europe

Canada
Army: 35,000 (3,100 in Europe)
Navy: 17,000 (34 ships)
Air Force: 41,000 (280 combat aircraft)

Netherlands
Army: 80,000 (6 brigades NATO assigned)
Navy: 20,000 (136 ships)
Air Force: 23,500 (105 combat aircraft)

W. Germany
Army: 326,000 (33 brigades all NATO)
Navy: 36,000 (204 small ships)
Air Force: 104,000 (980 combat aircraft)

Belgium
Army: 70,000 (2 divisions)
Navy: 4,400 (31 ships)
Air Force: 20,500 (208 combat aircraft)

Luxembourg
Army: 550 (1 battalion)

France
Army: 328,000 (2 divisions in Germany)
Navy: 72,000 (196 ships)
Air Force: 106,000 (500 combat aircraft)

Portugal
Army: 150,000 (largely in Africa)
Navy: 18,000 (172 ships)
Air Force: 17,500 (150 combat aircraft)

Britain
Army: 190,000 (B.A.O.R. 53,500 in 3 divisions)
Navy: 87,000 (including Marines) (174 ships)
Air Force: 113,000 (720 combat aircraft)

Italy
Army: 295,000 (almost all NATO) (7 divisions) (11 brigades)
Navy: 45,000 (139 ships)
Air Force: 73,000 (425 combat aircraft)

Denmark
Army: 27,000 (4 brigades + support)
Navy: 7,000 (69 ships)
Air Force: 10,500 (112 combat aircraft)

Greece
Army: 118,000 (12 divisions)
Navy: 18,000 (65 ships)
Air Force: 23,000 (200 combat aircraft)

Norway
Army: 23,500 (5 regional commands)
Navy: 8,600 (86 ships)
Air Force: 9,000 (114 combat aircraft)

Turkey
Army: 390,000 (20 divisions all NATO)
Navy: 37,500 (143 ships)
Air Force: 50,000 (310 combat aircraft)

Soviet Union
Army: 2,000,000 men (157 divisions) (one quarter would require major reinforcement) (31 divisions in Eastern Europe)
Navy: 475,000 men (over 2,000 vessels including 370 submarines)
Air Force: 480,000 (10,000 combat aircraft—2,400 in N. and Central Europe)

E. Germany
Army: 92,000 (6 divisions)
Navy: 16,000 (179 small ships)
Air Force: 21,000 (275 combat aircraft)

Poland
Army: 195,000 (15 divisions all under strength)
Navy: 22,000 (149 ships)
Air Force: 25,000 (750 combat aircraft)

Czechoslovakia
Army: 150,000 (15 divisions in all under strength)
Air Force: 18,000 (620 combat aircraft)

Hungary
Army: 90,000 (6 divisions)
Air Force: 10,000 (150 combat aircraft)

Rumania
Army: 90,000 (6 divisions)
Navy: 8,000 (54 ships)
Air Force: 8,000 (250 combat aircraft)

Bulgaria
Army: 130,000 (13 divisions)
Navy: 7,000 (36 ships)
Air Force: 13,000 (290 combat aircraft)

3 The Economic Groupings in 1970

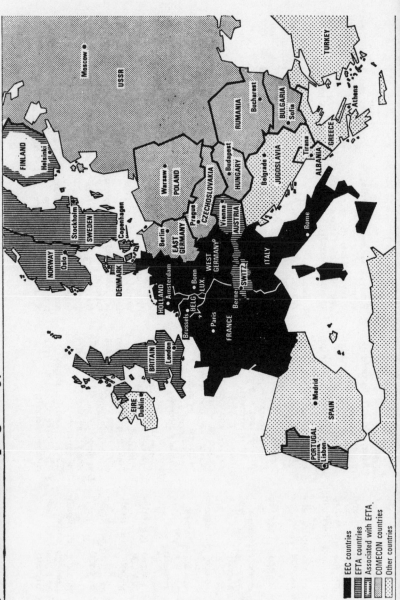

EEC countries

EFTA countries

Associated with EFTA.

COMECON countries

Other countries

MEMBERSHIP OF THE EUROPEAN ORGANISATIONS IN DECEMBER 1970 (i)

Country	U.N. E.C.E.	OECD	NATO	Council of E.	W.E.U.	Eur. Community	EFTA	COMECON	Warsaw Pact
Albania	*								
Australia		+							
Austria	*	*		*			*		
Belgium	*	*	*	*	*	*			
Bulgaria	*							*	*
Byelorussia	*								
Canada	*	*	*						
Cyprus	*			*					
Czechoslovakia	*							*	*
Denmark	*	*	*	*			*		
Finland	*	*					*		
France	*	*	*	*	*	*			
Germany (West)	*	*	*	*	*	*			
Germany (East)	*							*	*
Greece	*	*	*			A			
Hungary	*							*	*
Iceland	*	*	*	*			*		
Ireland	*	*		*					
Italy	*	*	*	*	*	*			
Japan		*							

Country	U.N. E.C.E.	OECD	NATO	Council of E.	W.E.U.	Eur. Community	EFTA	COMECON	Warsaw Pact
Luxembourg	*	*	*	*	*	*			
Malta	*			*					
Mongolia								*	
Netherlands	*	*	*	*	*	*			
New Zealand		‡‡ *							
Norway	*	*	*	*			*		
Poland	*							*	*
Portugal	*	*	*				*		
Rumania	*							*	*
Spain	*	*							
Sweden	*	*		*			*		
Switzerland	*	*		*			*		
Turkey	*	*	*	*		A			
Ukraine	*								
USSR	*							*	*
United Kingdom	*	*	*	*	*		*		
United States	*	*	*						
Yugoslavia	*	‡‡						A	

* Member.   A Associate Member.   ‡Australia, New Zealand and Yugoslavia have a special status in OECD.

(i) The section of this table dealing with Western European Organisations has been supplied by The European-Atlantic Movement (TEAM).

(ii) Australia joined OECD in 1971.

Index

Brussels Treaty Organisation, 47, 53, 54
Bulganin, 128, 149, 160
Bulgaria, 12, 13, 15, 29, 31–4, 40, 41, 102–3, 110, 146, 156, 213, 216, 230
Bundeswehr, 78–9, 221
Burma, 130, 266

Calculators, 240
Canada, 22, 47, 106, 156, 183, 193, 224, 235, 251, 273, 295, 290
Cars, per head, 235
Castro, Fidel, 263–4
C.E.N.T.O., 54
C.E.R.N., 211
Carnik, Oddrich, 160–61
Chardin, Teilhard de, 300
Chiang Kai-Shek, 4, 48–9, 50
China, (mainland), 12, 14, 29, 34–5, 40, 48, 50, 52, 54–5, 119, 130, 133, 137, 150, 151, 158, 214, 216–7, 227, 250, 259–61, 265, 270, 274, 281–7, 297
Ceatano, Marcelo, 101
Christian Democracy, 62–3
Christian Democrat Parties, 62, 75, 80, 81, 85, 88, 89
Christianity, 300–1
Churches and social policy, 229
Churchill, Winston, 13, 25–6, 38, 39, 50, 52, 63, 103, 190, 191, 232, 249
C.W.D., 288–9
Cobban, Alfred, 167, 187
Cold War, 34–5, 39–56, 81, 85, 131, 259–62, 264, 279
Collective Bargaining, 236
Colombo Plan, 270
Comecon, 150, 213–6, 218–9, 221, 285
Cominform, 42–3, 65, 83, 150, 157
Comintern, 60, 83, 97, 42
Commonwealth, 191, 202, 243, 251, 256, 266, 267–8, 270
Communism, 8, 40, 43–4, 48, 52, 61–2, 63–5, 66–7, 71, 72, 73, 84–6, 89–91, 103, 105, 111, 113 et seq., 123, 139–40, 141, 142–3, 150–52, 156, 157, 159–60, 162, 261, 289, 294
Communist countries wages and prices, 239
Communisation, 30–33, 43

Computers, 240, 247
Concentration camps, 16, 62, 76, 122, 145, 222
Conditions of work, 239–40, 241
Congo crisis, 263
Conservation year, (European), 243
Constantine II of Greece, 104
Council of Europe, 3, 90, 99, 100, 105, 111, 192, 194–8, 201, 211, 220, 229, 242, 243, 247, 294, 299
Couve de Murville, Maurice, 69, 72
Cuba, 55, 137, 260, 263, 283, 285
Currencies, see Monetary problems
Cyprus, 96, 105–7, 230, 257
Czechoslovakia, 12–14, 21, 23–4, 29, 31–3, 43, 55, 62, 140, 145–6, 148, 156, 159–62, 169, 214, 216, 219, 223, 226–7, 230, 262, 277

Daniel, Yuli, 136, 140
Data-processing machines, 247–8
Death rates, 235
Debré, Michel, 68, 69
Declaration of Philadelphia, 228–9, 248
Decolonization, 256–9, 260
Demiral, Suleyman, 111
DeNazification, 76–7
Denmark, 11, 14, 17, 61, 106, 185, 194, 197, 202–3, 204, 210, 230, 237, 240, 271
Depression, 1929–33, 163
Djilas, Milouan, 97, 126–7, 301
Disarmament, 286–8, 298
Divorce, 91
Dolci, Danilo, 87
Dubček, Alexander, 159–62
Dulles, John Foster, 48, 52, 53, 54

East African Asians, 197
Econometrics, 168
Economic Planning and Development, 164–87
Economic Growth, 184–6
Economics Indicators, 168
Eden, Sir Anthony, 53, 262
Education and training, 244–8
Egypt, 12, 28, 130, 153, 250, 261–3
Eisenhower, General Dwight, (later president), 13, 47, 48, 194, 279, 282
Electricity, public control, 169
Employment, 164–5, 182–3

Lenin, 113, 114–6, 119, 121–2, 123, 128, 132, 284, 285, 299
Liberal Party, 61
Liberalism, 7
Lidice, 15, 161
Limber, J. M., 186, 187
Lithuania, 12, 117
Litvinov, Pavel, 140–41
Longo, Luigi, 90, 97
Lubke, Heinrich, 16, 76
Lumumba, Patrice, 263
Luxembourg, 11, 14, 47, 194, 198, 199, 200, 230, 240

MacArthur, General, 51
McCarthy, Senator Joe, 48
Macmillan, Harold, 203
McNamara, Robert, 225, 280–81
Mafia, 87–8, 90
Makarios, Archbishop, 106
Malenkov, 127–8
Malraux, André, 65, 97
Malta, 96, 101–2
Management, problems of, 296–7
Manchuria, 284
Manuxiu, Iuliv, 32
Mao Tse-Tung, 48–9, 50, 151, 158
Marshall Aid, 22–3, 33, 42, 47, 53, 65, 79, 87, 98, 124, 146, 173, 189, 193, 269
Marx, Karl, 5–10, 57, 113, 114
Marxism, 9–10, 48, 60, 83, 91, 113, 114, 129, 132, 152, 155, 188, 261, 283, 290
Masaryk, Jan, 33
Medical science, 235
Menderes, Adnan, 109–10
Mendelsohn, Stefan, 174, 187
Metaxas, General, 102–3
Middle East, 250
Migrant workers, 178, 243
  in Britain, France, 243
  from Commonwealth, West Indies, 243
Mindszenty, Cardinal, 147, 153
Molotov, 83, 128, 151
Monetary policies, 173–7, 181–2
  Western European currencies, 175
  EEC, 177
  West German deutschmark, 178–80; French franc, US dollar, 174–5, 178–9;
  Sterling balances, 174–5, 204
Monnet, Jean, 64–5, 190, 198, 199

Mongolia, 18, 128, 213, 260, 284
Mussolini, 9, 62, 83, 98, 262

Nagy, Imre, 152–3
Nasser, Colonel, 261, 262–3
Nationalism, 7
Nationalisation,
  of coal, railways, Renault Motors, oil, steel, telecommunications, transport, 169–70
  in Austria, Belgium, Britain, Czechoslovakia, France, Germany, Italy, Netherlands, Poland, Scandinavia, USSR, Switzerland, 167–70
Nazis, and Nazism, 9, 14–17, 27, 28, 32, 52, 66, 76, 77, 93, 167, 221, 293
  SNDP, 81–2
Neisse, river, 25–6
Nenni, Pietro, 87
Netherlands, 11, 13, 47, 57, 92, 167, 169, 178, 185, 195, 197, 198, 203, 207, 208, 230, 234, 237, 238–9, 242, 257, 271
New Left, 142
New towns, 242–3
New Zealand, 54, 251, 267, 290
Nordic Council, 210–11
North Atlantic Treaty Organisation, (NATO), 46–7, 53–5, 71, 80, 90, 98, 99–100, 102, 104–6, 190–94, 203, 212, 214, 221–7, 289–90
Norway, 11, 14, 61, 167, 197, 202, 203, 209, 210, 237
Novotny, Antonin, 145, 155, 159–60
Nuclear Power, (peaceful), 207, 277–8
Nuclear Weapons, 13, 14, 34, 44, 47–8, 53–5, 99, 105, 129, 134, 203, 223–4, 225–7, 263 (possibility of war), 278–281, 282, 284, 285, 286–8, 298–9
Nuremburg Trials, 26–8, 299

Oder, river, 25, 80, 222–3
Oil,
  public control of industry, 169
  East European pipeline, 216
Organisation for European Economic Development, (OEEC), 23–4, 80, 87, 98, 100, 172, 177, 178, 191, 193–4, 211, 218, 221